NEW MEXICO & ARIZONA
STATE PARKS

A Complete Recreation Guide

DON AND BARBARA LAINE

THE
MOUNTAINEERS

Published by
The Mountaineers
1001 SW Klickitat Way, Suite 201
Seattle, WA 98134

Published simultaneously in Great Britain by Cordee, 3a DeMontfort Street, Leicester, England, LE1 7HD

Manufactured in the United States of America

Edited by Julie Hall
Maps by Barbara Laine
All photographs by Don Laine except as noted
Cover design by Watson Graphics
Book design and typography by The Mountaineers Books
Layout by Margarite Hargrave

Cover photographs: Clockwise from upper left: *Giant saguaro cactus at Catalina State Park, Arizona; Boating on Maloya Lake at Sugarite Canyon State Park, New Mexico; Oak Creek in Slide Rock State Park, Arizona; Petroglyphs at Lyman Lake State Park, Arizona.* All photographs by ©Don Laine

Library of Congress Cataloging-in-Publication Data

Laine, Don.
   New Mexico & Arizona state parks: a complete recreation guide/
   Don & Barbara Laine: [maps by Barbara Laine: photographs by Don
   Laine]. — 1st ed.
        p.   cm.
      ISBN 0-89886-559-X
      1. New Mexico—Guidebooks. 2. Parks—New Mexico—Guidebooks.
   3. Arizona—Guidebooks. 4. Parks—Arizona—Guidebooks. I. Laine,
   Barbara. II. Title. III. Title: New Mexico and Arizona State
   Parks.
   F794.3.L35 1998
   917.8904'53—DC21   97-43393
                                                                        CIP

 Printed on recycled paper

CONTENTS

Acknowledgments 5

Introduction 7

ACTIVITIES AND FACILITIES 8
Fees, Hours, and Regulations 9
Volunteering in State Parks 10
Outdoor Ethics 10
Climate, Health, and Safety 11
How to Use This Book 15
An Additional Note about Safety 15

NEW MEXICO PARKS 17

NORTHWESTERN NEW MEXICO 19
Bluewater Lake State Park 19
Coronado State Park 22
El Vado Lake State Park 24
Fenton Lake State Park 29
Heron Lake State Park 32
Hyde Memorial State Park 37
Navajo Lake State Park 41
Rio Grande Nature Center State Park 49

NORTHEASTERN NEW MEXICO 55
Cimarron Canyon State Park 55
Clayton Lake State Park 60
Conchas Lake State Park 64
Coyote Creek State Park 69
Morphy Lake State Park 72
Storrie Lake State Park 74
Sugarite Canyon State Park 78
Ute Lake State Park 83
Villanueva State Park 88

SOUTHEASTERN NEW MEXICO 93
Bottomless Lakes State Park 93
Brantley Lake State Park 99
Living Desert Zoo and Gardens State Park 104
Oasis State Park 107
Oliver Lee Memorial State Park 110
Santa Rosa Lake State Park 116
Sumner Lake State Park 120

SOUTHWESTERN NEW MEXICO 125
Caballo Lake State Park 125
City of Rocks State Park 130
Elephant Butte Lake State Park 133
Leasburg Dam State Park 139
Manzano Mountains State Park 143
Pancho Villa State Park 146
Percha Dam State Park 150
Rockhound State Park 153

ARIZONA PARKS 157

NORTHERN ARIZONA 159
Dead Horse Ranch State Park 159
Fool Hollow Lake Recreation Area 164
Fort Verde State Historic Park 167
Homolovi Ruins State Park 170
Jerome State Historic Park 174
Lyman Lake State Park 177
Red Rock State Park 181
Riordan Mansion State Historic Park 186
Slide Rock State Park 189
Tonto Natural Bridge State Park 192

SOUTHEASTERN ARIZONA 199
Boyce Thompson Arboretum State Park 199
Catalina State Park 204
Lost Dutchman State Park 210
McFarland State Historic Park 214
Patagonia Lake State Park 215
Picacho Peak State Park 220
Roper Lake State Park 225
Tombstone Courthouse State Historic Park 229
Tubac Presidio State Historic Park 231
Kartchner Caverns State Park (under development) 235
Oracle State Park (under development) 236

WESTERN ARIZONA 239
Alamo Lake State Park 239
Buckskin Mountain State Park 244
Cattail Cove State Park 248
Lake Havasu State Park 251
Yuma Crossing State Historic Park 257
Yuma Territorial Prison State Historic Park 259

APPENDIX 264
New Mexico Addresses and Telephone Numbers 264
Other New Mexico Information 265
Arizona Addresses and Telephone Numbers 265
Other Arizona Information 267

ACKNOWLEDGMENTS

One of the great pleasures in researching and writing this book was meeting and working with so many fine and dedicated people. They included, of course, our contacts in the park systems' state offices—Lauren Ward and Peter Greene in Santa Fe and Cheryl Steenerson and R. J. Cardin in Phoenix.

But the ones who really made this book possible—who make the parks in these two states such wonderful places to visit—are the park employees. Each park superintendent, manager, assistant manager, ranger, and volunteer we spoke with—and there were close to 100 of them—was helpful and knowledgeable. What impressed us more, though, is that they were genuinely proud of their parks and wanted to show them off. Many echoed the sentiments of one northern New Mexico park manager, who stood outside his office, looked around at the beautiful mountain scenery, breathed in the smell of pine trees, and marveled, "Can you believe they actually pay me to live here?" Our sincere thanks and admiration go to these deeply committed workers.

Among those park employees to whom we owe the greatest debt in New Mexico are Christine Dawson at Bottomless Lakes, Alan Fiala at Brantley Lake, Marshall Garcia at Cimarron Canyon, Charles Jordan at Clayton Lake, Joe Griego at Coyote Creek, Ben Duran at El Vado Lake, Phil Rogers and Louie Carrillo at Heron Lake, Larry Federici at Navajo Lake, Howard Thomas at Oliver Lee Memorial, Armando Martinez at Pancho Villa, Gilbert Duran and volunteer Harold Melton at Rockhound, Jaime Romero at Sugarite Canyon, and Frank Gutierrez at Villanueva.

Those in Arizona who deserve special thanks include Ray Dion at Boyce Thompson Arboretum, Danny Markus at Buckskin Mountain, Duane Hinshaw at Cattail Cove, Bob Clark at Fool Hollow Lake, Bob Munson at Fort Verde, Karen Berggren at Homolovi Ruins, Katie Montaño at McFarland, John Schreiber at Red Rock, John Marvin at Riordan Mansion, and Hollis Cook at Tombstone Courthouse.

We also wish to thank the staff at The Mountaineers Books—Margaret Foster, Thom Votteler, Cindy Newman Bohn, Jennifer Shontz, and Uma Kukathas—for their advice and constant support, and copy editor Julie Hall for her eagle-eyed attention to detail. Special thanks goes to The Mountaineers' art director Alice Merrill for her guidance and patience as we struggled with unfamiliar computer mapping software.

LEGEND

— ·· — · — ·· — ·· —	park boundary
▬▬▬▬▬▬▬▬	main road
————————	secondary road
— — — — — — —	trail
░░░░░░░░░░░░░	river
·· — · — ·· — ·· — ·	intermittent water flow
····················	mesa or bluff

25	interstate
89A	US highway
428	state highway
4921	forest road
	body of water—lake or river

◢	boat ramp	✗	mine
⚓	marina	▫	pay station
⛴	powerboat area	■	structure
⌒	no-wake area	playground	playground
⋈	bridge	▲	campground
⌇	fishing	⛱	picnic area
✖	swim beach	RV dump station	RV dump station
📷	scenic view	Ⓢ	showers
🔭	bird-watching area	Ⓣ	trailhead
♿	handicapped accessible	Ⓝ	nature trail
Ⓐ	amphitheater	⭕	mountain biking
P	parking lot	horseback riding	horseback riding

INTRODUCTION

Arizona and New Mexico are wonderful places to be outdoors, to explore and experience a rugged landscape of deserts, canyons, mountains, and forests. This is a land of variety and extremes, a harsh and sometimes unforgiving environment where rattlesnakes, tarantulas, bears, and mountain lions have lived for centuries. But it is also a land of beauty—sometimes stark, sometimes lush—where delicate wildflowers spread a blanket of purples, yellows, blues, and reds on rocky hillsides, and roaring rivers and trickling streams awaken the desert with life-giving moisture. In these two states you will find six of the United States' seven life zones—all except tropical. This is also the heart of the American West, land of vast cattle ranches and a rich history of gunslinging, Spanish conquistadores, and the Anasazis and other ancient human civilizations.

Among the almost five dozen state parks discussed in the following pages, choices abound for a wide variety of outdoor and indoor adventures. You might sail peacefully across Heron Lake, water-ski at nearby El Vado Lake, and then hike the trail that connects them. There is cross-country skiing in the mountains of Sugarite Canyon and Hyde Memorial State Parks, and you can explore the exotic desert zoo at Living Desert, all in New Mexico. Cross over the line into Arizona and relax in the natural hot springs at Roper Lake, gaze across panoramic vistas at Picacho Peak and Buckskin Mountain, hike among the giant saguaro at Lost Dutchman, step into the world of early American Indians at Homolovi, and relive the Old West at Tombstone Courthouse. These are just a handful of the opportunities that await the visitor at these relatively undiscovered gems.

The New Mexico State Park System was created in 1933 to provide jobs for unemployed workers during the Great Depression. Financed by federal relief funds, the Civilian Conservation Corps (CCC) constructed a network of roads, buildings, and trails that began New Mexico's Park System. Among the state's first parks were Bottomless Lakes and Hyde Memorial, and evidence of CCC-constructed stone buildings and trails remains today. Over the years, more parks were added, peaking in the 1960s and 1970s. Since then, the number of state parks has dropped, as some were turned over to towns or other government agencies, primarily to improve management efficiency. Officials today say they want to see the park system develop and improve, in quality if not in quantity.

Arizona's state park system is much younger than New Mexico's; in fact, it is the youngest in the forty-eight contiguous states and also one of the smallest. Actually, efforts to create the first state park in Arizona began in 1925, with a proposal for a park at Mormon Lake, near Flagstaff. However, the proposal was shot down by Flagstaff businesspeople who said it would hurt the timber industry, and by the governor at the time, who believed that because of the abundance of national parks and other public land in Arizona there was no justification for creating state parks there. Other attempts to create an Arizona state park system were also rejected, until a variety of interest groups, including recreationists, historic preservationists, the tourism industry, and cattle ranchers came to an agreement, and the Arizona State Parks Board was finally established in 1957. The first parks were historic sites, including Tubac Presidio, Tombstone Courthouse, Yuma Territorial Prison, and Fort Verde. The system has grown since then, adding not only recreation parks and additional historic sites, but also parks that concentrate on nature study.

As seems fitting for one of the newest state park systems in the nation, the Arizona State Park System is currently developing two new parks in the southern region of the state, Kartchner Caverns and Oracle State Park.

ACTIVITIES AND FACILITIES

The state parks of New Mexico and Arizona offer hiking, mountain biking, horseback riding, fishing, swimming, scuba diving, boating, cross-country skiing, rock climbing, rock hounding, wildlife viewing, and bird-watching, as well as environmental education, historic sites, and scenic beauty. Some parks also have concession-operated marinas, stores, and restaurants. Park programs include guided hikes and walks, nature and history talks, and slide and video shows. Visitor centers often have displays on local plants, animals, history, and recreational possibilities.

Quiet wooded area along the Rio Grande at Percha Dam State Park

Hikers will find that most state park trails are easy to moderate and relatively short—2 to 3 hours at most—although a few parks have longer and more demanding trails, and some provide access to adjacent national forest and wilderness trails. Desert trails, however, are often rocky, so sturdy hiking boots are recommended; and desert hikers are advised to carry plenty of drinking water. Many of the state park trails are also open to mountain bikers and horseback riders. The lake parks, most of which were created as a result of irrigation and flood control dams and reservoirs, provide a variety of boating and fishing opportunities.

A young desert iguana at Lake Havasu State Park

Parks in both states offer an abundance of wildlife viewing possibilities, with hundreds of species of birds—some quite rare—and other animals ranging from tiny lizards and pocket mice to bears and mountain lions. The best time to see mammals is usually early or late in the day; snakes and lizards are most likely to be seen in the middle of the day, when these cold-blooded creatures venture out to soak up the warmth of the sun. Birds will be seen at most any time.

Although facilities vary from park to park, all have strategically located toilets, parking areas, and pay stations with park information. What are called developed campsites usually have picnic tables, a grill or fire pit, and sometimes a shelter. They may or may not have RV hookups. Undeveloped sites may have only a picnic table or fire pit, and primitive sites usually are simply relatively flat areas where one can pitch a tent or park an RV. Restrooms are well-maintained and clean. Most park showers, especially in the newer bathhouses, have pre-set temperatures. Toilets range from rustic pits to heated and lighted facilities with flush toilets, electric outlets, and hot showers. Solar-powered and composting toilets are also used in some parks. All state parks provide disabled-accessible toilets and showers (if they have showers); a few parks with older facilities offer special equipment to make those facilities usable for persons with disabilities.

Both New Mexico and Arizona are making concerted efforts to upgrade their parks' facilities, and all the parks visited for this book either had improvement projects underway or in the planning stages. Many parks were adding RV campsites, capable of accommodating the new larger rigs. Some were also adding trails and visitor centers, and almost all were upgrading and adding to their disabled-accessible facilities.

FEES, HOURS, AND REGULATIONS

Day-use and camping fees are collected at recreation parks in both states, with charges slightly lower in New Mexico. Day-use fees are in the $3-to-$5 range, with camping fees from $6 to $15 per night, depending on amenities.

Little Florida Mountains are the backdrop to Rockhound State Park.

Fees are per private passenger vehicle. Generally, there are no extra charges for ranger-guided hikes, talks, and other activities offered at the recreation parks. Historical and some environmental education parks charge a per-person entry fee, which ranges from $1 to $3. Both states sell annual day-use permits good for most parks, and New Mexico also has available an annual camping pass. Keep in mind that prices are subject to change.

Day-use hours at recreation parks vary by park and sometimes by season, but usually are from 6:00 A.M. to 9:00 P.M. With only a few exceptions, parks are open seven days a week year-round. Day-use–only parks are usually closed on Christmas Day (December 25).

Although parks with camping are open for use 24 hours a day, some lock their gates overnight, starting anywhere from sundown to 10:00 P.M., and unlock them at 6:00 A.M. or 7:00 A.M. This occurs primarily at parks within a 20-to-30 minute drive of larger towns and cities to discourage locals from using parks for drinking parties. A few parks also post signs stating that gates are locked at night but seldom actually do so, and several others close gates but do not lock them. Campers planning to arrive at any park after dark should call beforehand to be sure a gate will be open, and also to find out the likelihood that campsites will be available.

Campsite reservations are not available at parks in either state (except for one campground in New Mexico's Elephant Butte Lake State Park), with camping strictly first-come, first-served. However, officials in both states said that due to increased popularity of the parks the possibility of accepting reservations is being considered. If reservation systems are put into effect, additional reservation fees of $5 to $10 most likely will be charged.

Park regulations are similar to those in other states and are mostly common courtesy and common sense. Quiet hours, usually from 10:00 P.M. to 6:00 A.M. or 7:00 A.M., prohibit loud music, the use of generators, or any other noise that disturbs other campers. Pets must be leashed at all times, and some parks request that owners clean up after their pets. Dogs are usually permitted on trails (if leashed) but, especially in Arizona, are not allowed on beaches. A few parks have additional pet restrictions. Glass containers are also usually prohibited on beaches.

Boaters must carry personal flotation devices, although whether they must be worn depends on the type of craft and the age of the boater. Both Arizona and New Mexico require that boats be registered and allow the use of boats properly registered in other states for up to 90 days. Laws of both states also prohibit operating boats while under the influence of alcohol or drugs. Brochures detailing each state's boating regulations are available from state park offices.

VOLUNTEERING IN STATE PARKS

Practically every state park in New Mexico and Arizona depends at least to some degree on volunteers. The most obvious volunteers are the campground hosts, who usually receive free campsites with RV hookups in exchange for being available to assist campers, and sometimes for other work, such as staffing visitor centers, presenting slide shows, or guiding walks. Volunteers also help maintain trails, tend botanical gardens, and create interpretive displays. While volunteers usually sign on for several months, and sometimes longer, park rangers often welcome occasional help. For instance, an avid bird-watcher spending a few days in a park might volunteer to give a talk or lead a walk. Those interested in volunteering can talk to park managers directly or contact the state offices listed in the appendix.

OUTDOOR ETHICS

The general rule of thumb for those spending time in the state parks of New Mexico and Arizona is the same as for those visiting public lands anywhere: Use planning, knowledge, and, most of all, common sense to have as little impact on the land as possible. The ideal situation would be that every visitor would see no evidence that anyone had been there before, but even here in the relatively empty Southwest that is a bit too much to expect.

State parks are by definition developed recreation areas, with designated campgrounds, trails, boat-launching sites, and an increasing amount of pavement. Our goal as visitors should be to minimize human impact by staying on trails, properly disposing of all trash, taking care not to disturb or harm animals and plants, and being especially careful to avoid polluting lakes, streams, and rivers. A number of New Mexico and Arizona state parks contain American Indian ruins and artifacts, as well as relics from the Wild West days of the 1800s. These pieces of history should be observed, appreciated, and photographed, but never disturbed.

Western dayflowers are among the many wildflowers at Coyote Creek State Park.

CLIMATE, HEALTH, AND SAFETY

One look at a national weather map, and it becomes clear: New Mexico and Arizona are lands of extremes. At the same time that winter snows close roads in the northern reaches of the two states, around Flagstaff and Santa Fe, southern areas near Phoenix or Las Cruces bask in the sun, with temperatures in the 80s. During summer, when desert temperatures soar to over 120 degrees F, the mountains remain pleasantly cool and can even be downright cold. The reason is elevation; together these states range from a low of 70 feet above sea level near Yuma, Arizona, to 13,161 feet at the top of Wheeler Peak, above Taos, New Mexico.

What this means for visitors is that those planning to explore different sections of one or both of these states will be carrying a great variety of clothing, so let's hear it for a duffle bag stuffed with Bermuda shorts, sandals, and a down parka! Preparation and planning are the keys to physical comfort, plus choosing the right season for the particular parks you plan to visit. Fall, winter, and spring are usually the best times in southern Arizona; spring and fall are recommended in southern New Mexico where it is not quite as warm; and the period from late spring through early fall is usually ideal at higher elevations in both states. Sudden, heavy rains are common, especially in August.

New Mexico has the highest skin cancer rate in the nation, and Arizona is not far behind, so those planning to be outdoors are strongly advised to use a good-quality sunscreen and wear broad-brimmed hats and ultraviolet-blocking sunglasses. If traveling in the mountains in winter, make sure your vehicle has snow tires or chains and carry extra blankets and emergency food and water, just in case.

Another potential problem in New Mexico and Arizona is elevation, because the higher you go, the less oxygen there is. Visitors from lower elevations who have heart or respiratory problems should consult their home physicians before planning trips to the mountains, perhaps anywhere above 5,000 feet. Those in generally good health need not take any special precautions, but can ease the transition to high elevations by changing altitude and increasing physical activity gradually.

Area health officials warn outdoor enthusiasts to take precautions against Hantavirus pulmonary syndrome, a rare but often fatal respiratory disease. First recognized in 1993, a large percentage of the country's 150-plus confirmed cases have been reported in the Four Corners states of Colorado, New Mexico, Arizona, and Utah, and just under half have resulted in death. The disease is usually spread by the urine and droppings of deer mice and other rodents, and, therefore, health officials recommend that campers avoid areas with signs of rodent droppings. Symptoms of Hantavirus are similar to flu—fever, muscle aches, nausea, vomiting, coughing, diarrhea—and can lead to breathing difficulties and shock.

Another local hazard is the rattlesnake, the most common poisonous reptile of the Southwest. Snakes are ectothermic, or cold blooded; in cold temperatures they often lie in the sun to get warm, and in warm temperatures they take refuge from the heat in cool shady places. Wise hikers always watch where they are stepping and check carefully before putting their hands or feet into spaces between rocks. Snakes enjoy the heat that rocks absorb, and take immediate offense when some human invades their space. On the other hand, snakes are not usually aggressive and will avoid people whenever possible.

One of the great joys of going into wild areas is the possibility of seeing wildlife, but the last thing you want is a confrontation. Mountain lions, which are nocturnal, rarely bother people, although there have been a few reported cases of attacks in recent years. Black bears, however, are another story. Although generally shy, bears have learned that there is food in campgrounds and other areas where humans are about, so many head to

Swimming in Lea Lake at Bottomless Lakes State Park (photo courtesy New Mexico State Parks Division)

Footprints of a mountain lion are displayed on the nature trail in Catalina State Park.

the parks when they get hungry, particularly in dry years when their usual food supplies are low. For this reason, campers or hikers in bear country need to check with park rangers about any current bear problems. If hiking at dawn or dusk, when bear encounters are more likely, make noise by talking or singing. Although this goes against the usual ethic of being quiet on the trail so as to not disturb other hikers, it will help prevent surprising a bear or, worse, finding yourself between a mother bear and her cub. Campers should store food away from tents and other sleeping areas and dispose of garbage properly. The best protection from scavenging bears is to hang your food bag (and even sweet-smelling items, such as toothpaste) in a tree, at least 4 feet from the trunk and 8 feet from the ground. Wildlife experts say that people going into particularly isolated areas where bears are known to be problematic should also avoid wearing perfume or other scents, and some say that people camping in bear country should even abstain from sexual activity.

Safety is an important concern in all outdoor activities. For even the shortest wilderness excursion, we recommend that you bring along the following Ten Essentials:

1. extra food and water;
2. extra clothing, in case of accidents or weather changes;
3. a first-aid kit;
4. matches in a waterproof container;
5. sunglasses and sunscreen, especially in snowy or desert climates;
6. a knife;

7. firestarter, such as chemical fuel;
8. a flashlight, with extra batteries;
9. a compass; and
10. a map of your immediate area.

You may also want to bring along water purification tablets or a water filter, raingear, and insect repellent. In addition, it is always a good idea to leave information about your trip (where you will be and for how long) with a reliable person, such as a park ranger or family member, so help can be sent if you do not make it home on time.

HOW TO USE THIS BOOK

The purpose of this book is to help visitors to the state parks of New Mexico and Arizona maximize their enjoyment while minimizing frustrations and disappointments. Parks are arranged geographically, in seven regions across two states, and often the majority of parks in a particular region will have similar climates and activities. You can choose to visit several parks in one region or just pick the one or two best-suited to your interests and then move on to the next region. There are also detailed maps showing the regions and park locations.

After reading the introduction (please do—it contains important information about costs, regulations, and safety, as well as an overview of the state park systems), you may find it helpful to glance over the sections on the various regions and then zero in on those you find of most interest.

Each park description begins with a list of vital statistics that provides a thumbnail sketch of what the park offers. The section that follows gives a bit of the park's background or history and elaborates on its facilities and activities—why you might want to spend time there. Because New Mexico and Arizona have extremes of elevation and climate, quite a bit of space is devoted to weather and what to expect during different seasons at a particular park. Those unfamiliar with the climate extremes found in the Southwest would be wise to look carefully at this part of the park description before planning a trip. Most park sections also include detailed maps.

Finally, the appendix provides a comprehensive list of addresses and phone numbers for additional information.

AN ADDITIONAL NOTE ABOUT SAFETY

No guidebook can alert you to every hazard or anticipate the limitations of every reader. Therefore, the descriptions of roads, trails, routes, and natural features in this book are not guarantees that a particular place or excursion will be safe for your party. When you follow any of the routes described in this book, you assume responsibility for your own safety. Under normal conditions, such excursions require the usual attention to traffic, road and trail conditions, weather, terrain, the capabilities of your party, and other factors. Keeping informed about current conditions and exercising common sense are the keys to a safe, enjoyable outing.

—*The Mountaineers*

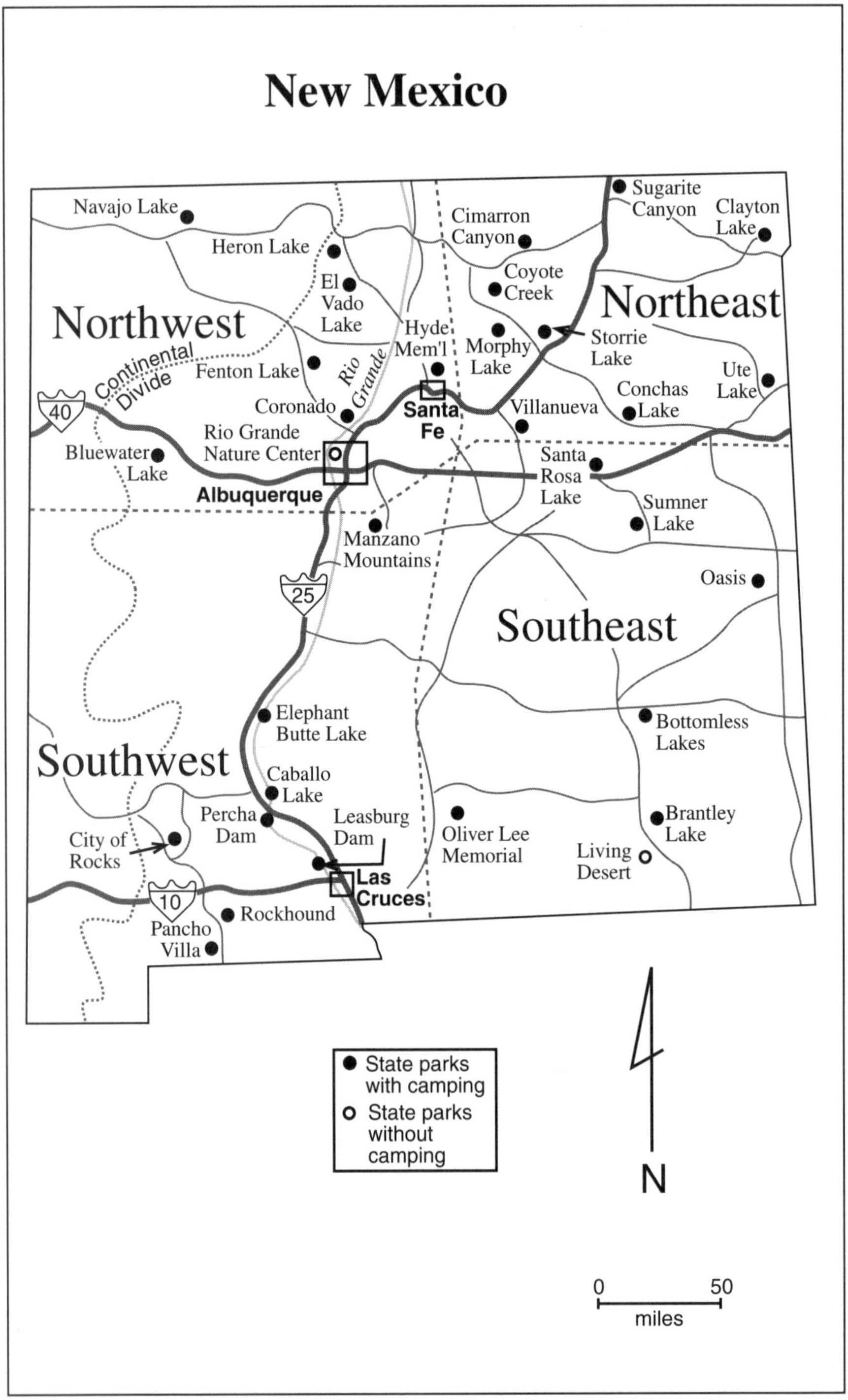

New Mexico

Navajo Lake ●

Heron Lake ●

Cimarron Canyon ●

Sugarite Canyon ●

Clayton Lake ●

Coyote Creek ●

El Vado Lake ●

Northwest

Northeast

Continental Divide

Fenton Lake ●

Hyde Mem'l ●

Morphy Lake ●

Storrie Lake ●

Ute Lake ●

Rio Grande

Conchas Lake ●

Coronado ●

Santa Fe □

Villanueva ●

Bluewater Lake ●

Rio Grande Nature Center ○

Albuquerque

Santa Rosa Lake ●

Sumner Lake ●

Manzano Mountains

Oasis ●

Southeast

Elephant Butte Lake ●

Southwest

Bottomless Lakes ●

Caballo Lake ●

Percha Dam ●

Leasburg Dam

Brantley Lake ●

City of Rocks →●

Oliver Lee Memorial ●

Living Desert ○

Las Cruces □

Rockhound ●

Pancho Villa ●

● State parks with camping

○ State parks without camping

N

0   50
miles

NEW MEXICO PARKS

An intriguing mix of rugged mountains, grassy plains, and barren desert, New Mexico marks the southern edge of the Rocky Mountains and the western limits of the Great Plains. The fifth largest U.S. state, New Mexico is literally in the clouds, with 85 percent of its land above 4,000 feet. Its lowest point is 2,841 feet, near Carlsbad Caverns National Park in the southeast, and its highest elevation is 13,161 feet, on Wheeler Peak in the northern mountains near Taos.

Elevation is the prime determining factor in weather and vegetation, with the mountains being considerably cooler, wetter, and more lush than the lowlands. The state's major river, the Rio Grande, cuts down through the middle of the state north to south, from its origins in southern Colorado through El Paso, Texas, into the Gulf of Mexico. The Continental Divide parallels the Rio Grande near the state's western border. Although New Mexico is never as hot as neighboring Arizona, which is lower in elevation, New Mexico does have its extremes, ranging from well over 100 degrees F in the southern deserts to minus 25 degrees F or lower in the northern mountains.

Long the domain of prehistoric Indians, who hunted mastodons and bison, the region became more dependent on agriculture after corn was introduced about A.D. 100. Spanish conquistadores arrived in the 1500s, and in 1610 the king of Spain named Santa Fe the capital of the province, predating the English settlement at Plymouth, Massachusetts by ten years. The Santa Fe Trail opened in the 1820s, turning Santa Fe into a bustling trade center. So many traders and settlers came over the trail that you can still see the ruts from their wagon wheels. The Treaty of Guadalupe Hidalgo in 1848 gave the United States jurisdiction over much of New Mexico, Arizona, and California; New Mexico was granted statehood on January 6, 1912.

For the purposes of this book, we have divided New Mexico into four regions: northwestern, northeastern, southeastern, and southwestern.

NORTH-WESTERN NEW MEXICO

▲ Home to the Anasazi civilization some one thousand years ago, the stark ⊥ mesas and buttes of northwestern New Mexico are now part of the Navajo Nation, America's largest Indian tribe. This region is a mix of mountains and plateaus, with life-giving rivers in some sections and dry, barren expanses in others. The state parks here take advantage of the lush parts of this region, where rivers have been dammed to produce lakes that offer a variety of boating and fishing opportunities, mostly in scenic mountain settings. Farmington is the largest city in the state's far northwestern corner. Also in this quadrant, although closer to the state's center, is Albuquerque, by far New Mexico's largest city, and the state's center of commerce and transportation. Here, a quiet state park along the Rio Grande provides a welcome respite from the city's busy pace. This quadrant also includes Santa Fe, the state's capital and a major art and cultural center, and, outside of Santa Fe, the state's highest-elevation state park.

BLUEWATER LAKE STATE PARK

Hours/Season: Overnight; year-round
Area: 3,000 land acres, 1,200 lake surface acres
Elevation: 7,400 feet
Facilities: Visitor center, picnic tables, playground, group shelters, 150 campsites (39 with electric hookups) and almost unlimited primitive sites along shoreline, restrooms with showers, public telephone, RV dump station, nature trail, boat ramps, phone: (505) 876-2391
Attractions: Fishing, ice fishing, hiking, swimming, boating, water-skiing, bird-watching

Opposite: *Dam and reservoir at Bluewater Lake State Park*

Nearby: Cibola National Forest
Access: 28 miles west of Grants via I-40 and NM 412

▲ Bluewater Lake is a large, open lake set among low hills covered with piñon and juniper trees. Bluewater Lake's main claim to fame is fishing, but the state park is also popular with boaters and campers and offers a bit of hiking. Situated in the Zuni Mountains just east of the Continental Divide, this high-elevation park has good ice fishing and also attracts occasional ice-skaters in winter.

The site of an inland sea some 200 million years ago, the plains of what would become western New Mexico emerged when the sea retreated, and eventually Bluewater Creek carved the canyon and provided life-giving water. But sometimes there was too much water. From the mid-1800s to the early 1900s, settlers wanting to irrigate farmland built a series of earthen dams, but they were all washed away. In 1925, locals established an irrigation district with an 80-foot-high concrete dam, and Bluewater Lake was created. Filled to its crest, the lake would hold 38,500 acre-feet of water, but it has rarely filled to capacity. The last time water flowed over the spillway was in April, 1941.

Maintained primarily for fishing, the 65-foot–deep lake is stocked several times each year by the New Mexico Department of Game and Fish. Rainbow trout weighing up to nine pounds have been taken from the lake, and anglers also catch cutthroat trout, German browns, and catfish. The best lakeshore fishing is in spring and fall, and boat fishing is usually preferred in June and July. Ice fishing through foot-thick ice is popular in winter, usually from December through March. Anglers also find good fishing in Bluewater Creek from mid-April through September.

Although most of the boats on the lake are fishing boats with trolling motors, water-skiers with high-powered speedboats and personal watercraft also use the lake, mostly on summer weekends, and occasionally a sailboat, sailboard, or canoe will be seen. Although there is no officially designated swim beach, swimming is permitted. It is best on the north end of the lake, a no-wake area where the beach gradually drops into the lake. Scuba divers also sometimes enjoy the clear but often chilly water.

Short trails lead to several scenic overlooks, offering views of the lake and its impressive concrete dam. A 0.25-mile trail (one-way), marked with interpretive signs on the park's plant and animal life, leads down into a rocky canyon to Bluewater Creek. The trail is relatively easy, although it is rocky and fairly steep in some sections. The return trip up the canyon wall can be tiring for those not acclimated to the 7,400-foot elevation. The trail clings to the side of the canyon, through a forest of piñon, juniper, and prickly pear cactus, providing good views of the river and high canyon walls. You can also walk for about a mile (one-way) along the creek, although there is no designated trail.

The lake is about 7 miles long by 1 mile wide at its broadest point. A rough dirt road, sometimes impassable when wet, leads from the park's

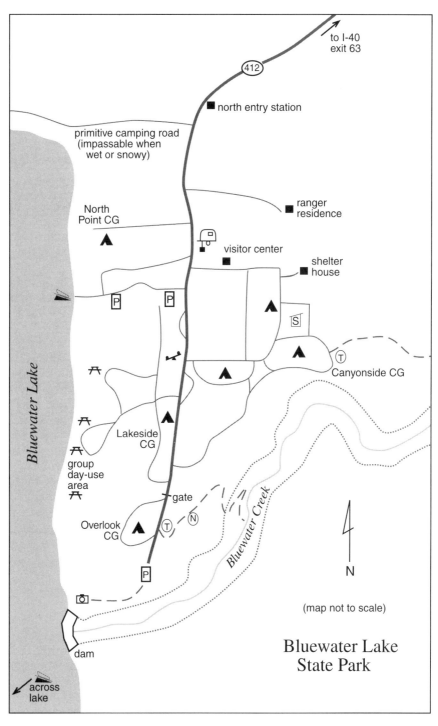

to I-40
exit 63

412

north entry station

primitive camping road
(impassable when
wet or snowy)

ranger
residence

North
Point CG

visitor center

shelter
house

P

P

S

T

Canyonside CG

Bluewater Lake

Lakeside
CG

Bluewater Creek

group
day-use
area

gate

Overlook
CG

T

N

N

(map not to scale)

P

Bluewater Lake
State Park

dam

across
lake

main section along the north side of the lake to provide fishing and primitive camping access. There is also access to the southeast section of the lake, with a boat ramp and restroom, from NM 612.

Throughout the park are an abundance of piñon jays, recognized by their bright blue color and love of the nuts of piñon trees. Bird-watchers are also apt to see pelicans in the spring, bald eagles along the west side of the lake in the winter, and great blue herons along the lakeshore year-round. Mallards and American coots nest at the lake, and Canada geese sometimes drop by. Other species you might see include mountain bluebirds, mourning doves, red-tailed hawks, dark-eyed juncos, red-headed woodpeckers, European starlings, meadowlarks, and a variety of sparrows.

Park wildlife also includes tarantulas, ground squirrels, cottontail rabbits, ringtail cats, foxes, and coyotes. The nearby national forest has all these, plus bear, elk, and mule deer.

The park offers a wide variety of camping possibilities, most with views of the lake. There are the developed sites, both with and without electric hookups, set among piñon and juniper trees, as well as make-your-own primitive sites anywhere you want along much of the lakeshore. A new visitor center has exhibits on the park's flora and fauna and offers information about activities, such as hiking and cross-country skiing, in the nearby Cibola National Forest.

The best season for boating and fishing is summer. During this time of year, especially on weekends, the park gets a lot of day users, as well as campers. Daytime temperatures are usually in the 80s, with nighttime lows in the 50s, and there are often brief afternoon thunderstorms, particularly in August. Winters are cold and can be snowy, with low temperatures well below freezing but highs sometimes climbing into the 50s. Spring is often windy, and both spring and fall have daytime temperatures in the 60s and 70s, with nights usually dropping into the 30s and 40s. An especially pleasant time in the park is October and November, when there are few people, the lake is not yet frozen over, days are warm, with temperatures in the 60s, and nights are in the 30s. It may snow, but that can be very pretty.

CORONADO STATE PARK

Hours/Season: Overnight; year-round
Area: 210 land acres
Elevation: 5,600 feet
Facilities: Picnic tables, 37 campsites (27 with electric hookups) and dispersed walk-in tent sites and overflow camping, group camping, 2 group pavilions, restrooms with showers, RV dump station, canoe and raft launch area, playground, phone: (505) 867-5589
Attractions: Canoeing, fishing, hiking, photography, bird-watching
Nearby: Coronado State Monument

Access: 15 miles north of Albuquerque via I-25 to Bernalillo (exit 242), then west on NM 44 for 2 miles to the park entrance

The view alone is worth the trip. A popular base camp for those visiting Albuquerque and central New Mexico, Coronado State Park offers a quiet retreat along the west bank of the Rio Grande. To the east, the rugged and often snow-capped Sandia Mountains stand as silent sentinels, sometimes starkly silhouetted against the black night sky, while a brilliant full moon is reflected in the slow-moving river below. In addition, the park offers camping, kayaking and canoeing, bird-watching, a bit of hiking, and an historic neighbor.

About six hundred years ago this was a busy place, with five hundred members of the Kuaua tribe living in a 1,500-room four-story adobe pueblo, ruins of which can be seen in the adjacent Coronado National Monument. These people were likely among the first American Indians to host the Spanish conquistadores who explored New Spain in the mid-1500s in search of the Seven Cities of Gold. In 1540 Don Francisco Vasquez de Coronado led an expedition of some 1,200 men to the area and is known to have spent the winter at a pueblo along the Rio Grande—quite possibly this one.

Camping is the most popular activity here; and a particularly enjoyable time can be had loafing at a campsite overlooking the river, watching ducks and geese float by, while the setting sun casts eerie shadows on the mountains. Early morning can be beautiful, too, as the sun peeks over the mountain tops.

Although not a prime destination for hikers, the park has one sandy trail, about 0.75-mile long (one-way), that follows an embankment above the Rio Grande. It offers good views of the river and mountains and provides access to walk-in tent sites.

Those with portable canoes, kayaks, and rafts can carry them to a launch area at the north end of the park. Their options then are to paddle back to the put-in site, or make arrangements for someone to meet them at one of several downstream take-out points outside the park. Each May, hundreds of boaters join the Rio Grande Raft Race, which starts here. Although the water is relatively warm, swimming is not recommended due to sinkholes and other safety factors. Anglers catch trout and pike, and night fishing for catfish is also popular.

Park visitors will often see cranes flying overhead, although they seldom land; and ducks, geese, quail, and even roadrunners are fairly common. Spring and fall visitors are apt to see a variety of raptors. This stretch of the Rio Grande is also considered a prime riparian area, so watch for muskrats and beaver; and most visitors see cottontail rabbits. One creature you would be wise to avoid is the rattlesnake, which enjoys sunning itself on rocks.

With a semi-desert terrain, the park has sunny skies and a moderate climate most of the year, although summer temperatures occasionally exceed 100 degrees F. More typical, though, are summer days in the upper 80s and low 90s, with nights in the 60s and 70s. During winter, highs are usually in the 40s and 50s, with lows in the 20s. Snow falls occasionally but usually melts quickly.

The park is popular year-round and is especially crowded during major annual events in nearby Albuquerque, such as the state fair in September and the hot air balloon rally in October.

The adjacent state monument offers an opportunity to explore the ruins of the ancient Kuaua Pueblo. There's a visitor center containing original ceremonial murals from the site, plus hands-on displays of Indian drums, grinding stones, and Spanish armor that are particularly popular with kids. Outside, a 0.25-mile self-guided loop trail leads through the pueblo ruins, with signs discussing the original residents, the Kuaua, and quoting from journals written by Spanish conquistadores when they arrived in 1540. A highlight of the monument is a reconstruction of a rare square kiva (most are round). A handmade ladder leads down into this underground ceremonial chamber, decorated with intricate wall murals, reproductions of the originals, which are in the visitor center.

El Vado Lake State Park

Hours/Season: Overnight; year-round
Area: 1,730 land acres, 3,200 lake surface acres
Elevation: 6,900 feet
Facilities: Picnic tables, restrooms with showers, group shelter, 64 campsites (19 with electric hookups), public telephone, boat ramps, RV dump station, phone: (505) 588-7247
Attractions: Boating, water-skiing, swimming, fishing, hiking, birdwatching, wildlife viewing, cross-country skiing, snowshoeing
Nearby: Heron Lake State Park
Access: 17 miles southwest of Tierra Amarilla via NM 112

Boating and hiking are the attractions at this mountain lake, created by damming the Rio Chama as part of the San Juan–Chama Diversion Project, an elaborate system of tunnels and dams that collects water from the mountains of Colorado for irrigation and domestic use throughout much of New Mexico. Located just to the southwest of Heron Lake State Park, which is also part of the project, El Vado Lake has no speed or horsepower restrictions, making it a popular destination for water-skiing and the use of personal watercraft. The rocky shoreline, studded with piñon, juniper, and sagebrush, has numerous coves and inlets, producing quiet little nooks. And because the lake level varies greatly as water is added or released, there are always new areas to explore.

While most of the boats at El Vado Lake are high-powered speedboats and fishing boats, the lake is big enough to accommodate just about anything that floats, and one also sees canoes, small inflatables, and sailboats.

Low buttes and mesas surround El Vado Lake State Park.

However, most sailing enthusiasts head to nearby Heron Lake, which allows motorboats but only at trolling speeds, producing a quieter and more peaceful atmosphere. Swimming is permitted at El Vado Lake, although there are no designated swimming areas, and water temperatures usually reach the upper 60s by the end of summer.

Spanish missionaries and explorers Fathers Atanasio Dominguez and Silvestre Velez de Escalante are believed to have passed near what is now El Vado Lake in the summer of 1776, while traveling along the Rio Chama. They had set out from Santa Fe to chart unexplored areas and make contact with local American Indians. Although they had hoped to establish an overland route to Monterey, California, they did not get beyond Arizona and Utah.

A popular and well-maintained hiking trail connects El Vado Lake with Heron Lake. The 5.5-mile Rio Chama Trail follows the Rio Chama, rising gently from the El Vado Lake trailhead to a mesa on the south side of the river, which offers tree-framed views of both El Vado and Heron Lakes. The trail then winds down the side of the canyon, through a piñon-juniper forest. It crosses the Rio Chama on a cable footbridge, built by the Young Adult Conservation Corps in the early 1980s, and leads up a steep set of redwood stairs to the Heron Lake trailhead. The trail, open to foot, mountain bike, and horse travel, is relatively flat and easy for the first 5 miles from El Vado Lake and then moderately strenuous for the last 0.5 mile.

The Rio Chama Trail offers an excellent chance of seeing wildlife. The lake is a major wintering area for the bald eagle, which is easily recognized

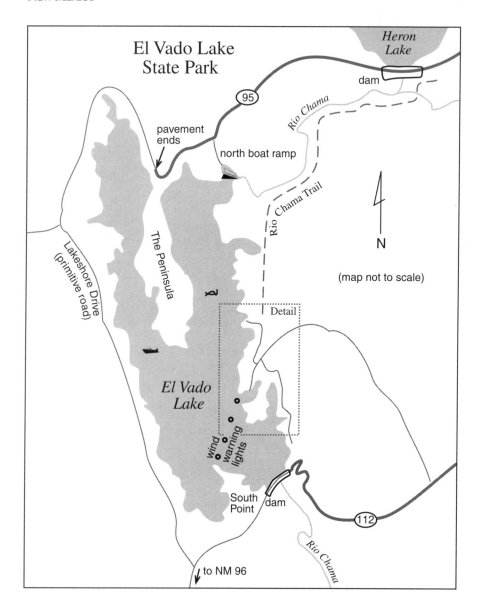

El Vado Lake
State Park

Heron
Lake

dam

95

Rio Chama

pavement
ends

north boat ramp

Rio Chama Trail

N

(map not to scale)

Lakeshore Drive
(primitive road)

The Peninsula

Detail

El Vado
Lake

Wind warning lights

South
Point

dam

112

Rio Chama

to NM 96

by its white head and tail, the flat appearance of its wings during flight, and its size—bald eagles' wingspans can reach 8 feet across. Herds of elk and mule deer are fairly common here, especially in winter. Other mammals seen in the park include tassel-eared squirrels, muskrats, striped skunks, cottontail rabbits, coyotes, bears, and mountain lions.

In addition to bald eagles, birds to watch for include wild turkeys, peregrine falcons, red-tailed hawks, ospreys, hairy woodpeckers, Clark's nutcrackers, white-throated swifts, scrub jays, mountain bluebirds, common

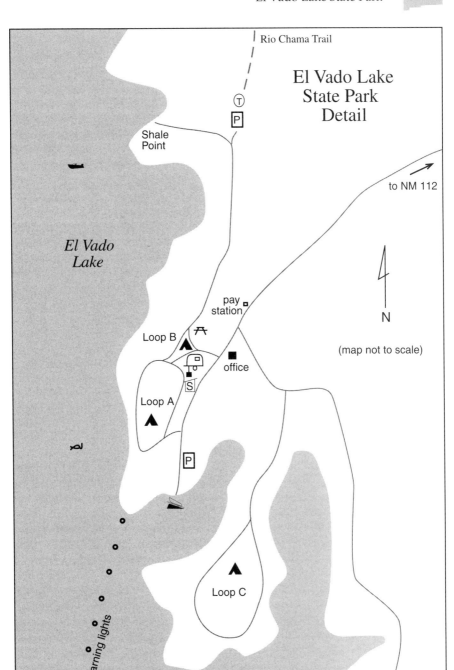

Rio Chama Trail

El Vado Lake
State Park
Detail

Shale
Point

to NM 112

El Vado
Lake

N

(map not to scale)

pay
station

Loop B

office

Loop A

Loop C

Wind warning lights

Elk are seen frequently along the Rio Chama Trail at El Vado Lake State Park.
(photo by Don MacCarter, courtesy New Mexico Dept. of Game and Fish)

flickers, and water ouzels. The prairie rattlesnake also makes its home in the park, particularly in the dry, rocky sections. Other reptiles include collared lizards, eastern fence lizards, and bullsnakes.

Anglers fish both El Vado Lake and the Rio Chama and catch rainbow and German brown trout, kokanee salmon, and sunfish. Ice fishing is popular on the lake during the winter. Also during winter there is some cross-country skiing and snowshoeing when enough snow falls.

Many of the park's campsites offer good views and easy access to the lake, but there are few trees and little shade except for the picnic table shelters. The campground rarely fills, although the electric hookup sites are usually taken first.

The park's plant life varies greatly, depending mostly on how far it is from either the lake or Rio Chama. There are dense stands of Douglas fir and ponderosa pine and rocky hillsides of piñon and juniper, and along the river banks there is a riparian area of willow and alder.

Summers here have pleasantly warm days and cool nights, with high temperatures usually in the 80s and lows in the 40s. Winters are cold—highs in the 30s and low 40s and lows near or below zero—and may be snowy, although the park does not usually get as much snow as Chama and other nearby areas. Spring can be windy, with high temperatures in the 50s and lows in the 20s; while fall has crisp days, with highs in the upper 50s and low 60s and lows dropping into the 20s.

FENTON LAKE STATE PARK

Hours/Season: Overnight; year-round
Area: 700 land acres, 35 lake surface acres
Elevation: 8,000 feet
Facilities: Picnic tables, vault toilets, group shelter, playground, 35 campsites (6 with electric and water hookups), public telephone, boat ramp, phone: (505) 829-3630
Attractions: Fishing, boating (non-motorized only), canoeing, hiking, cross-country skiing, snowshoeing, ice fishing, wildlife viewing, bird-watching
Nearby: Santa Fe National Forest, Seven Springs Fish Hatchery
Access: 33 miles northwest of San Ysidro via NM highways 4 and 126

A mellow mountain escape, set in a forest of ponderosa pine with a 35-acre fishing and canoeing lake, this isolated park has the feel of a national park or national forest, with the wind gently blowing through the trees, an abundance of birds, and an isolated, wilderness atmosphere. A fishing hole for Albuquerque residents, the park is also popular with hikers and cross-country skiers, who often use it as a base for excursions into the adjacent Santa Fe National Forest. Family-oriented, it is also an ideal spot to camp and relax. In addition to the forest of ponderosa pine, there are a few Douglas fir, spruce, and aspen, plus willows along the Rio Cebolla.

The park is named for Elijah McClean Fenton, Sr., a Presbyterian minister, missionary, land surveyor, and rancher. Fenton filed a homestead claim for what would become the core of the park in 1892, and gradually increased his holdings. The New Mexico Game Commission bought part of the land in 1940, and in 1946, the year after Fenton died, built a dam and created Fenton Lake. The state park was created in 1984, although the Department of Game and Fish continues to manage the lake itself.

Stocked with rainbow trout from fall through spring, the lake is also home to German brown trout. Although most anglers prefer the warmth and comfort of summer, the best fishing is in winter, through 2 feet of ice. There is usually about a month in late fall and another in early spring when the lake is iced over but not thick enough to support anglers, and there is no fishing at all. The lake has seven wheelchair-accessible fishing piers.

Fenton Lake is closed to sailboats, sailboards, and all powerboats—including those with electric trolling motors—but open to canoes, rowboats, and inflatable boats. Swimming is prohibited, but anglers can get into the lake in float tubes.

Camping here is just as it should be, with roomy and sometimes secluded campsites among the pines. There are no showers or flush toilets, and the park does not have an RV dump station. Campsites with RV hookups are in a loop close to the lake, just west of the dam, while non-hookup sites lie in thick woods along both sides of a dirt road that follows the Rio Cebolla. The non-hookup sites are more private, although not very level. They are closed

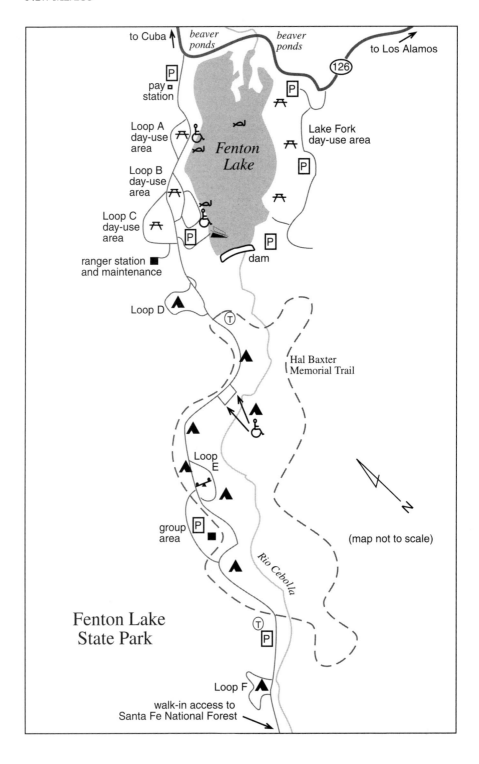

to Cuba

beaver ponds

beaver ponds

to Los Alamos

126

pay station

Loop A day-use area

Fenton Lake

Lake Fork day-use area

Loop B day-use area

Loop C day-use area

ranger station and maintenance

dam

Loop D

Hal Baxter Memorial Trail

Loop E

group area

(map not to scale)

N

Rio Cebolla

Fenton Lake State Park

Loop F

walk-in access to Santa Fe National Forest

during the winter, when this end of the road (which is not plowed) becomes part of a cross-country ski trail. There are also two wheelchair-accessible sites, reserved strictly for those with disabilities. The park has no overflow or primitive camping, although additional camping is available in nearby sections of the Santa Fe National Forest.

The park has one trail, the Hal Baxter Memorial Cross-Country Ski Trail and Biathlon Practice Area. An easy 2-mile loop, it winds through a riparian area along the Rio Cebolla and by the non-hookup campsites southwest of the lake. Thick brush can make the trail a bit difficult for hikers to follow in summer, but during the winter it is groomed by park rangers and is well-marked. Cross-country skiers also ski on the frozen lake, and along unplowed roads. Snowmobiling is not permitted.

The park has several day-use areas, including the Lake Fork day-use area on the east side of the lake, which is a bit hilly and not recommended for motor homes or trailers. It is closed to all motor vehicles from November through April but open to cross-country skiers and snowshoers.

Hikers, cross-country skiers, and snowshoers often leave the park to follow trails into the Santa Fe National Forest. One popular hike into the forest is the Ojitos Mesa Trail, a moderately strenuous hike through a ponderosa pine forest to the top of a mesa, which offers splendid views of the lake, a long valley, and the surrounding mountains. The trail is about 2 miles

Fishing at Fenton Lake State Park

long (one-way) and climbs about 1,500 feet. It can be a bit difficult to follow in spots, and hikers are advised to first discuss their plans with park rangers.

Wildlife abounds in both the park and the national forest. Animals that frequent the forest and fields include Abert's squirrels, golden-mantled ground squirrels, muskrats, beavers, racoons, deer, elk, and an occasional mountain lion or brown bear. The cattails in the northeast part of the lake are home to the meadow jumping mouse, an endangered species that has large hind legs and feet and a long tail. Birds are abundant at Fenton Lake, ranging from mallards, coots, snow geese, and osprey to bald eagles, Steller's jays, evening grosbeaks, and kingfishers.

The lake was the setting for *The Man Who Fell to Earth,* a 1976 British film starring David Bowie and Rip Torn, about a space alien who comes to Earth to try to find water for his dying planet.

The busiest time at the park is summer, and all campsites are usually claimed early in the day on weekends from April through October. Winters, however, are quiet—virtually deserted on weekdays—in part because the road into the park is often snowpacked, icy, and treacherous. Summer days are pleasant, with high temperatures ranging from 60 degrees F to 85 degrees F, but light jackets or sweaters are handy at night, when temperatures drop into the 40s and 50s. Winters are cold, with highs often not getting out of the 20s and lows below zero. Spring and fall have highs in the 40s and 50s and lows in the 20s. Fall can be beautiful, with the brilliant gold of the aspens set off by the rich darkness of the evergreens.

In addition to trips into the adjacent Santa Fe National Forest, park visitors can make an easy excursion to Seven Springs Fish Hatchery, located about 3.5 miles northwest of the park entrance via NM 126. The hatchery raises trout for Fenton Lake and other area waters. The outside rearing areas can be viewed, there are coin-operated machines that sell fish food, and there is a children's fishing pond (for children under 12 only) that is stocked from spring through fall. Fishing is also permitted in the Rio Cebolla, behind the hatchery, which is also stocked.

HERON LAKE STATE PARK

Hours/Season: Overnight; year-round
Area: 4,100 land acres, 5,900 lake surface acres
Elevation: 7,200 feet
Facilities: Visitor center, picnic tables, 300 developed campsites (4 with electric, water, and sewer hookups; 53 with electric and water hookups; and 7 with water-only hookups) and 250 primitive sites, restrooms with showers, nature trail, marina, boat ramps, boat slips and dock, public telephone, RV dump station, phone: (505) 588-7470
Attractions: Sailing, windsurfing, fishing, hiking, swimming, photography, wildlife viewing, bicycling, cross-country skiing, snowshoeing, guided hikes, interpretive programs

Nearby: Cumbres and Toltec Scenic Railroad narrow-gauge steam train
Access: 11 miles west of Tierra Amarilla via US highways 64 and 84 and
NM 95

Red sails in the sunset, and most other times, greet visitors to Heron
Lake State Park. This high-altitude haven for land-locked New Mexico
sailors offers a seemingly endless lake tucked away in a mountain forest of
ponderosa pines, piñons, and junipers. The park also boasts one of the best

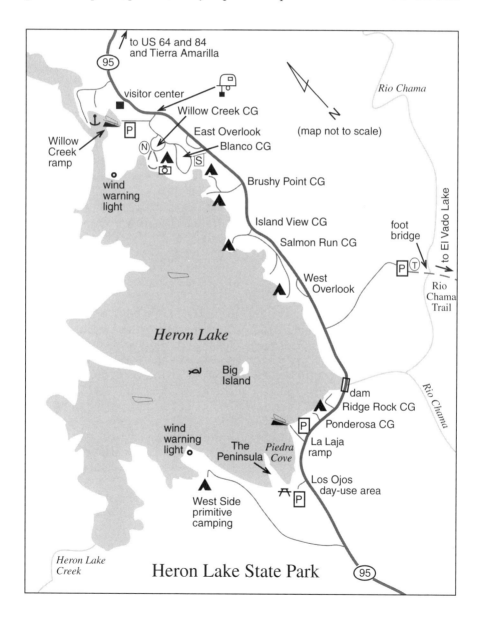

Heron Lake State Park

hiking trails in the New Mexico State Park System, which Heron shares with its neighbor El Vado Lake State Park, plus swimming, fishing, wildlife watching, bird-watching, cross-country skiing, and camping for both tenters and those with recreational vehicles.

Constructed in the late 1960s and early 1970s by the U.S. Bureau of Reclamation, a series of underground tunnels diverts an average of 110,000 acre-feet of water annually from the San Juan Mountains of Colorado to be stored in Heron Lake, behind a 263-foot-tall earth-filled dam. Water is released into the Rio Chama and flows eventually into the Rio Grande to provide domestic and irrigation water to much of the state.

Although powerboats are permitted at Heron, a no-wake policy keeps the speeds down, so water-skiers and water hot-rodders do not upset the tranquillity. Mostly seen on the lake are sailboats, plus some small fishing boats with trolling motors, and a few canoes. The New Mexico Sailing Club sponsors a series of races throughout the summer, including Fourth of July and Labor Day regattas. The sailing season is April through October, and conditions are often ideal, with mild afternoon breezes and clear skies, although there are occasional sudden summer thunderstorms with forty-knot winds. Perhaps worse, every so often a sudden stillness leaves sailboats bobbing about like abandoned rubber ducks in a bathtub—what the regulars refer to as "bob and bake on Heron Lake."

The lake is roughly 4 miles long and 3 miles wide, a broad expanse that gives sailors plenty of tacking room. A marina has a dock and slips for rent on a nightly basis but no boat rentals or supplies. However, businesses within a few miles of the park have canoe, fishing, and pontoon boat rentals, plus groceries and camping and fishing supplies. Swimming is permitted anywhere in the lake; water temperatures in summer are usually 60 degrees F to 68 degrees F.

The 5.5-mile Rio Chama Trail connects Heron Lake State Park with El Vado Lake State Park, generally following the route of the Rio Chama. Hikers from Heron Lake first descend a steep set of redwood stairs and cross the Rio Chama on a cable footbridge, both built by the Young Adult Conservation Corps in the early 1980s. The trail winds up the south slope of the Rio Chama canyon, through a piñon-juniper forest, to a mesa, which affords panoramic vistas of both Heron and El Vado Lakes through the trees. As it makes its way to El Vado Lake State Park—along an easy descent—the trail travels past a variety of plants and sometimes offers views of deer, elk, rabbits, chipmunks, and other wildlife, including an occasional bald eagle. The trail is moderately strenuous for the first 0.5 mile from Heron Lake and gets flatter and easier as it approaches El Vado Lake.

The park also has an easy 0.25-mile nature loop trail from Willow Creek Campground, leading past scrub oak, juniper, pine, and yucca to a bluff overlooking the lake. A brochure on the trail's flora and fauna was expected to be completed by 1998.

Anglers catch kokanee salmon and several species of trout; a record lake trout weighing twenty-five pounds nine ounces was caught in April 1996. Heron Lake does not freeze and is open for fishing year-round; Willow

Sailing at Heron Lake State Park

Creek, which flows into the lake, does freeze and is a popular ice fishing destination. Snagging is popular in the winter and runs from November through December when the kokanee salmon are spawning.

Those looking for wildlife will have the best luck along the Rio Chama Trail and on the west side of the lake. Winter is usually best for spotting bald eagles and larger mammals. Herds of elk and deer are fairly common, and other species seen in the park include wild turkeys, bear, and mountain lions. In addition to the bald eagle, birds to watch for include the red-tailed hawk, hairy woodpecker, Clark's nutcracker, white-throated swift, and mountain bluebird. The osprey, also called the fish hawk, can often be seen diving into the lake in search of a meal; and nesting swallows are sometimes glimpsed along the rocky cliff faces.

Winter visitors will find the bathhouses closed but most other facilities available. Although there are no established trails, cross-country skiers have numerous opportunities, including some of the lesser-used roads that are not plowed. And snowshoers can traipse along the hiking trails, or just head out across the fields and through the woods.

The visitor center has maps and brochures, plus exhibits on the dam and local wildlife, and ranger programs on plant life, wildlife, and other outdoor subjects are held periodically. In addition, ranger-led hikes and nature walks are occasionally scheduled during the summer.

Altogether there are about 550 campsites. About 250 are primitive, including some along the lake with pit toilets and little else. There are also level gravel sites with water and electric hookups (and even a few sewer hookups), plus modern restrooms with hot showers (open in summer only) at Blanco Campground and other campgrounds with varying amounts of modern conveniences. Campgrounds with the most facilities are the farthest from the lake. As in most areas in northern New Mexico's mountains,

Cumbres and Toltec Scenic Railroad's steam train near Heron Lake State Park

summer days here are pleasantly warm, with temperatures in the upper 70s or low 80s, and nights are cool, with temperatures in the 40s. Winters are cold and may be snowy, although the park does not usually get as much snow as do Chama and other nearby areas. Winter high temperatures will usually be in the 30s, with lows from zero to 10 degrees F.

About 12 miles north of the park is the town of Chama, the southern terminus of the Cumbres and Toltec Scenic Railroad, which each summer makes daily 64-mile runs between Chama, New Mexico, and Antonito, Colorado. Built in 1880 to serve the mining camps of southern Colorado and northern New Mexico, the narrow-gauge steam railroad now offers nostalgic cinders-in-your-hair excitement, as it chugs and puffs its way up mountain passes, through forests of pine and aspen, past some of the West's most rugged and beautiful scenery. Reservations are recommended.

HYDE MEMORIAL STATE PARK

Hours/Season: Overnight; year-round
Area: 350 land acres
Elevation: 8,500 feet
Facilities: Winter sports equipment rental shop, picnic tables, vault toilets, water spigots, group shelters, group-use buildings, 50 campsites (7 with electric hookups), nature trail, playground, volleyball court, public telephone, RV dump station, phone: (505) 983-7175
Attractions: Hiking, backpacking, cross-country skiing, tubing, snowshoeing, ice-skating, interpretive programs
Nearby: Santa Fe National Forest, Santa Fe Ski Area, city of Santa Fe
Access: 8 miles northeast of Santa Fe Plaza via Hyde Park Road (NM 475)

Located in the mountains above Santa Fe in a dense forest of Douglas fir, ponderosa pine, aspen, and juniper, Hyde Memorial is New Mexico's highest elevation state park, and often its snowiest. While only a few campers are willing to brave several feet of snow and temperatures that sometimes drop below zero, cross-country skiers, snowshoers, and other snow lovers flock to the park each winter, and then return to their homes or motels in Santa Fe. Then, when the snow finally melts, they make the trip back to the park, this time with tents, RVs, and, most important, hiking boots.

The park is named for archeologist Benjamin Hyde (1872–1933), a Santa Fe resident who was active in numerous youth programs and especially known for projects that helped introduce young people to the wonders of nature. After Hyde's death, his widow donated the land that would become the park to the state, asking that a park be established to serve young people. A bronze plaque set in a boulder at the park's entrance honors Hyde as "Forever serving the youth of America in stimulating love of outdoor life and nature lore." On the park grounds is a lodge from the early 1930s (used as a ski lodge in Santa Fe's early days of skiing), which can be reserved for group activities.

With elevations up to 10,000 feet, and a rustic, natural setting, the park has much the same atmosphere as a national park or national forest. Shelters for camping and picnicking are massive log Adirondack-style structures, trees and wildflowers abound, and the Little Tesuque River meanders through the park. Also running right through the park is a U.S. Forest Service National Scenic Byway, NM 475, which leads to Santa Fe Ski Area.

Winter is a busy time here. The road through the main campground is closed to cars, and, with a cover of several feet of snow, it joins with a trail along the east side of the campground to form a hilly cross-country ski loop that winds for about 2 miles through the forest. Snowshoers often head out on Hyde Park Circle Trail (described below), which is too steep for cross-country skiing. The park also has a popular sledding hill and an ice-skating rink. A concession shop (open in winter only) rents tubes, saucers, cross-country skiing equipment, and downhill skis.

The main warm-weather activity is hiking, but keep in mind that the park's elevation starts at 8,500 feet and goes up from there, so those from lower elevations will tire quickly until they become acclimated. Trails are open to foot travel only; park rangers can direct those with mountain bikes or horses to nearby trails in the Santa Fe National Forest. Good hiking boots are advised, and hikers should carry plenty of drinking water.

The best park trail, and one that receives surprisingly little use, is Hyde Park Circle Trail, which forms a 4.25-mile loop. Starting across from the ranger station, this forest trail begins by crossing the Little Tesuque River on an old stone bridge. Then it heads rather steeply up the side of the canyon, using switchbacks in some sections, before reaching a ridge that affords splendid panoramic views of the city of Santa Fe, Santa Fe Ski Area, and the mountains to the west. From the ridge, the trail drops down to the RV campground, and from there hikers can walk back to the ranger station either along the highway or through the main campground.

The trail is rocky in some areas and a bit steep, although the steepest stretches are ascending and descending the ridge, while hiking along the ridge is fairly easy. Rated moderate-to-difficult, the trail gains about 1,000 feet in elevation.

Waterfall Trail actually does lead to a pretty little waterfall, if you happen to be there at the right time. The waterfall is usually in evidence in April and May, fed by snowmelt, and again in July and August, when afternoon thunderstorms provide the water. At other times it is dry, but the hike is fun anyway.

From the old lodge, it is about 1.25 miles (one-way) along the east side of the main campground and up the side of the canyon to the waterfall, passing through the forest of pine and fir that covers most of this park. From the main campground, pick up the trail behind Group Shelter 2, and it is only a 0.5-mile hike to the falls. This trail is easier than the Hyde Park Circle Trail, although there are a few steep sections, and in some seasons you may get your feet wet crossing a stream several times.

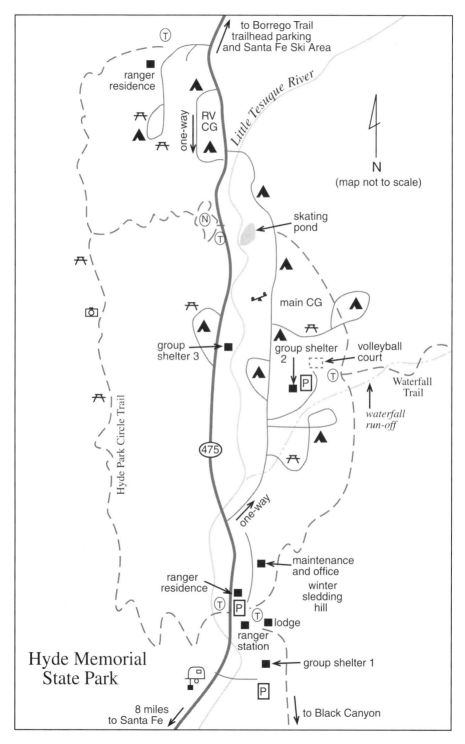

to Borrego Trail
trailhead parking
and Santa Fe Ski Area

Little Tesuque River

ranger
residence

one-way

RV
CG

N
(map not to scale)

skating
pond

main CG

Hyde Park Circle Trail

group
shelter 3

group shelter
2

volleyball
court

Waterfall
Trail

*waterfall
run-off*

475

one-way

maintenance
and office

winter
sledding
hill

ranger
residence

lodge

ranger
station

group shelter 1

Hyde Memorial
State Park

8 miles
to Santa Fe

to Black Canyon

There is also an interpretive nature trail—an easy 0.5-mile loop—that was built by a local Girl Scout troop in 1959. Signs identify the park's various plants and trees. A spur off the west side of the loop connects with the Hyde Park Circle Trail.

The main campground is rugged and hilly, with tall ponderosa pines and an abundance of shrubs and wildflowers; running along the edge is the Little Tesuque River. This is forest camping at its best for those with tents or small, maneuverable RVs, but it is difficult for those with large trailers or large motor homes. The RV campground, across the highway, is more open, with fewer trees, but does provide seven sites with electric hookups. In the forest above the RV campground, there are additional non-hookup campsites that are somewhat larger and more accessible than those in the main campground. Although there are no showers in the park, and not even any swimming, those who insist on being clean can find showers (for a fee) within 7 or 8 miles, with directions available from park rangers.

There is no fishing in the park—the streams do not have enough water to support fish—but there is plenty of wildlife to be seen, especially in winter.

Among the larger animals to watch for are mule deer, coyotes, and an occasional bobcat. Every once in a while a bear or cougar is spotted. There are also foxes and kit foxes, racoons, and Abert's tassel-eared squirrels. Birds here include several species of hummingbirds, Steller's jays, scrub jays, American robins, downy woodpeckers, great horned owls, red-tailed hawks, ravens, and golden eagles.

During summer, rangers and volunteers present talks and slide shows at the old lodge on Friday or Saturday evenings, covering topics on the area's

Camping and picnic shelter at Hyde Memorial State Park

wildlife, plants, and history. Annual events include the Snowshoe Classic in early January, a race that is based in the park but actually takes place just outside the park in the national forest. Various activities, including tree planting, are scheduled in April for Earth Day. Benjamin Hyde Day, which takes place in early October, includes activities on history and nature; and several Cub Scout Days are planned each year, usually in April and May.

The weather here is what one would expect at a park that is next door to a downhill-ski resort. Winters are sunny but cold, with lows often at or below zero and high temperatures usually below freezing. Up to 6 feet of snow has been measured at one time in the park, and it can snow anytime between Halloween and mid-May. Spring comes late and can be unpredictable, but days often warm up into the 60s. Summers are very comfortable, with highs usually in the 70s, but you will want a jacket or sweater at night, when temperatures drop into the 40s and 50s. Fall is among the nicest times in the park, when the aspen turns brilliant gold, with the best time to see the colors usually about the second week of October. There is often frost by mid-September, and fall temperatures usually range from nights in the 20s to afternoons in the 50s and 60s.

Because of its proximity to the city of Santa Fe, Santa Fe National Forest, and Santa Fe Ski Area, Hyde Memorial State Park is often a base of operations for area visitors. The culturally inclined will want to take advantage of at least some of the art galleries, museums, historic buildings, and fine restaurants that have made Santa Fe famous worldwide.

Skiers with well-insulated recreational vehicles sometimes camp in the park while downhill skiing at nearby Santa Fe Ski Area, about 7 miles north, and cross-country skiers and snowshoers often use the park as a base for exploring trails in the Santa Fe National Forest, which surrounds the park. During warmer weather, hikers often head out of the park for day trips into the national forest, and backpackers often make arrangements with park rangers to leave their vehicles in the park while taking extended trips into the national forest and nearby Winsor Wilderness Area. One popular national forest trail is the Borrego Trail, with a trailhead just outside the north boundary of Hyde Memorial State Park. Considered moderate, the trail wanders through the forest to Tesuque Creek, connecting with several other trails and opening up miles of hiking possibilities through the national forest. The trail is also used by mountain bikers and horseback riders in summer and cross-country skiers and snowshoers in winter.

NAVAJO LAKE STATE PARK

Hours/Season: Overnight; year-round
Area: 21,000 land acres, 13,000 to 15,000 lake surface acres
Elevation: 6,100 feet
Facilities: Visitor center, interpretive exhibits, marinas, store, restaurant, boat ramps, courtesy docks, picnic tables, group shelters, 248 camp-

sites (89 with electric hookups and 9 with electric, water, and sewer hookups), primitive lakeshore camping, restrooms with showers, public telephone, airstrip (administered by State Aviation Department), RV dump stations, phone: (505) 632-2278

Attractions: Boating, fishing, water-skiing, swimming, scuba diving, hiking

Nearby: Aztec Ruins National Monument

Access: 25 miles east of Bloomfield via US 64 and NM 511

New Mexico's second largest state park, remote Navajo Lake is being discovered as a prime boating and fishing destination and an excellent place for water-skiing, swimming, scuba diving, and camping. Hillsides covered with piñon and juniper create a forest atmosphere and, along with the cottonwoods and willows closer to the water, provide the right habitat to attract a variety of wildlife. The San Juan River, just below Navajo Dam, is considered one of America's premier trout-fishing waters.

Located at the base of the San Juan Mountains, the lake has almost 150 miles of shoreline and at full capacity is 35 miles long, covering more than 15,000 surface acres. It is the only major lake shared by New Mexico and Colorado, with New Mexico claiming 80 percent of its surface area. Fed primarily by mountain snowmelt, the lake was formed in 1962 with the construction of Navajo Dam, an earth-and-rock-filled structure 400 feet high and almost 0.75 mile long. Its main purposes are to generate electricity and provide irrigation water for the Navajo Indian Reservation. Water is also released into the San Juan River for downstream irrigation and municipal and industrial uses.

There are four recreation sites on the lake, and one along the San Juan River. Two of the lake sites—Pine and Sims Mesa—and the river site comprise New Mexico's developed sections of Navajo Lake State Park. Another site in New Mexico, near the Colorado border—Miller/Sambrito—is operated by a concessionaire and offers primitive camping only. The one site in Colorado is in a totally separate Navajo State Park, operated by the Colorado State Park System. Following are details of the developed areas in New Mexico; the Colorado park has similar facilities, although on a smaller scale, and is discussed fully in the book *Colorado State Parks,* also published by The Mountaineers.

In many ways, Navajo Lake resembles Lake Powell (to the west in Arizona and Utah), with its numerous narrow channels and prominent rock formations, although Navajo Lake's rocks are less colorful. Being a big lake, its facilities are spread out. The Pine site is the most developed, with the visitor center and park offices, and is located 0.5 mile north of the dam on NM 511. The more remote Sims Mesa site is within sight of Pine across the lake, but its road access takes you on a loop of about 42 miles, heading first east of the dam about 25 miles on NM highways 511 and 539 and US 64, and then northwest for another 17 miles on NM 527 to Sims Mesa. The San Juan River site runs for about 6 miles along the river below the dam and is accessed from NM highways 511 and 173.

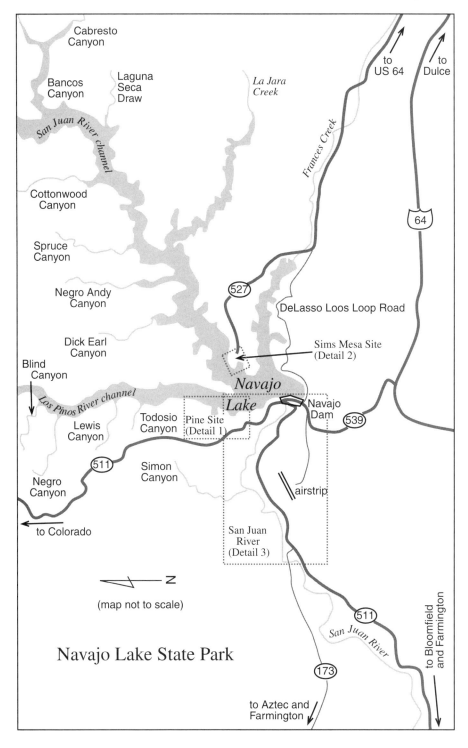

Cabresto
Canyon

Bancos
Canyon

Laguna
Seca
Draw

*La Jara
Creek*

to
US 64

to
Dulce

San Juan River channel

Frances Creek

64

Cottonwood
Canyon

Spruce
Canyon

Negro Andy
Canyon

527

DeLasso Loos Loop Road

Dick Earl
Canyon

Sims Mesa Site
(Detail 2)

Blind
Canyon

Navajo

Los Pinos River channel

Lake

Navajo
Dam

539

Todosio
Canyon

Pine Site
(Detail 1)

Lewis
Canyon

511

Simon
Canyon

airstrip

Negro
Canyon

San Juan
River
(Detail 3)

to Colorado

N

(map not to scale)

511

San Juan River

to Bloomfield
and Farmington

Navajo Lake State Park

173

to Aztec and
Farmington

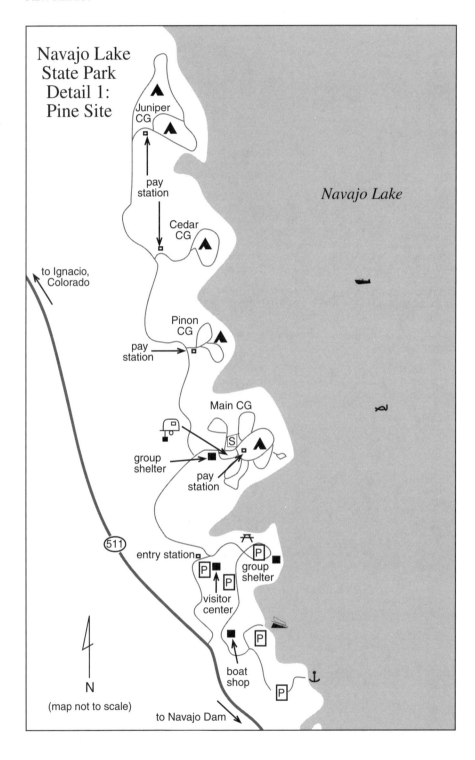

Navajo Lake
State Park
Detail 1:
Pine Site

Juniper
CG

pay
station

Cedar
CG

to Ignacio,
Colorado

Navajo Lake

Pinon
CG

pay
station

Main CG

group
shelter

pay
station

511

entry station

P

P

visitor
center

group
shelter

P

P

boat
shop

P

N

(map not to scale)

to Navajo Dam

44

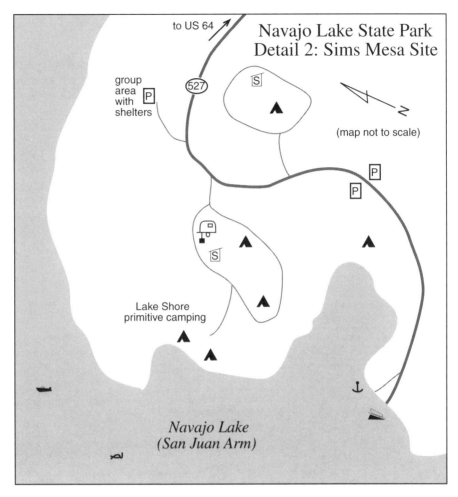

Navajo Lake State Park
Detail 2: Sims Mesa Site

to US 64

527

group
area
with
shelters

(map not to scale)

Lake Shore
primitive camping

*Navajo Lake
(San Juan Arm)*

All types of boats are welcome on the lake, and there are several no-wake and no-skiing sections. The upper end, near the state line, is particularly popular for sailing. The lake is also experiencing growing use of personal watercraft. The lake's two marinas offer boat rentals—mostly ski boats, personal watercraft, and houseboats.

The water is clear—good for swimming and scuba diving—and the water temperature usually warms into the 70s by mid-July. Although there are no designated swimming areas and much of the shoreline is rocky, there are a number of sandy beaches, particularly when the lake level is low. Especially nice are some of the small beaches accessible only by boat.

Record-breaking kokanee salmon have been taken from the lake, and anglers also catch rainbow and brown trout, channel catfish, crappie, northern pike, bluegill, and largemouth and smallmouth bass. During their spawning season—October through December—kokanee can be legally snagged. The lake does not freeze, and fishing is good year-round.

The San Juan River is rated as one of America's top-ten trout-fishing waters. A section of the river for 6 miles south of the dam is in the state park, flowing through a scenic sandstone canyon. The river's first 3.75-mile section from the dam is listed as "special trout water," with stringent fishing requirements and limits. Anglers are allowed only one trout, at least 20 inches long, in possession at any time. There is also a 0.25-mile section of the river that is catch-and-release only. There are four wheelchair-accessible fishing piers along the river.

As is the case for all public waters in the state, a current New Mexico fishing license is required to fish both the river and the section of the lake that is in New Mexico. Anglers who plan to fish in the Colorado portion of the lake will also need a Colorado license, which can be purchased at various locations in Colorado.

The two lake camping areas—Sims Mesa and Pine—are in forests of piñon and juniper, offering some shade and good views of the lake, and

Boating at Navajo Lake State Park

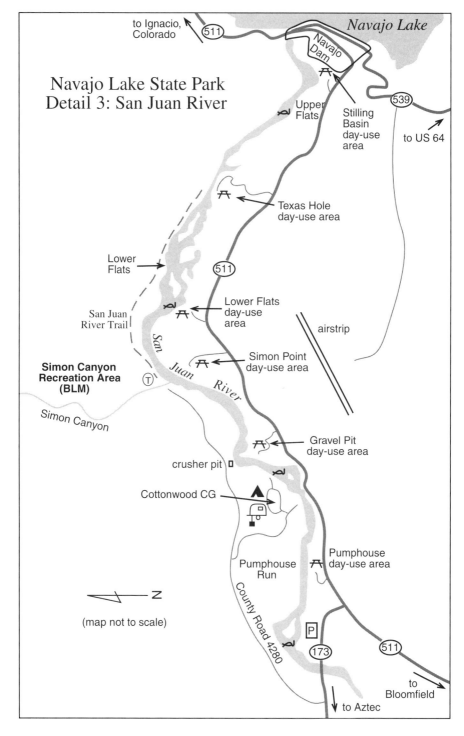

Navajo Lake State Park
Detail 3: San Juan River

to Ignacio, Colorado

511

Navajo Lake

Navajo Dam

539

to US 64

Upper Flats

Stilling Basin day-use area

Texas Hole day-use area

Lower Flats

511

Lower Flats day-use area

San Juan River Trail

Simon Point day-use area

Simon Canyon Recreation Area (BLM)

San Juan River

airstrip

Simon Canyon

Gravel Pit day-use area

crusher pit

Cottonwood CG

Pumphouse day-use area

Pumphouse Run

County Road 4280

N

(map not to scale)

P

173

511

to Bloomfield

to Aztec

47

both have paths to the lake. Sims Mesa is somewhat less developed, with gravel rather than paved roads, and the sites are a bit farther apart. Primitive lakeshore camping is also permitted, and you can also sleep on your boat or rent a houseboat. The Cottonwood Campground, on the San Juan River, is set in a large cottonwood grove, and is within easy walking distance of several good fishing holes.

An easy hiking trail runs for about 1.5 miles (one-way) along the north side of the San Juan River, and a number of paths lead to popular fishing spots along the river and the lake. Outside the park, on property administered by the Bureau of Land Management (BLM), there are opportunities for hiking and horseback riding. The Simon Canyon Recreation Area runs north onto BLM land from the Cottonwood Campground Road in the San Juan River section of the park. A sandy trail leads about 1.5 miles (one-way) to a rock shelter built by Navajos in the 1700s. Backpacking, tent camping, and horseback riding are permitted in the recreation area, although the trail should be avoided during rain because of the danger of flash floods.

The San Juan River section of the park offers the best wildlife viewing, including a good chance of seeing bald eagles from November through March. There are also turkey vultures, osprey, mallards, cinnamon teal, blue-winged teal, common mergansers, piñon jays, and violet-green swallows. Canada geese sometimes nest in the rocks above the river. Seen throughout the park are deer mice, which are gray to reddish-brown with a two-tone tail. Although the mouse's body is only about 3 inches long, its tail can be up to 5 inches long. Also spotted frequently are black-tailed jackrabbits and Colorado chipmunks, recognized by the white stripes on their faces and backs. The park is also home to mule deer, elk, beaver, muskrats, bobcats, racoons, rock squirrels, and porcupines. Southern plateau lizards are often seen in summer, perched on sandstone ledges in the canyons. They are about 2 inches long, brown, and have striped markings along their flanks.

A visitor center in the Pine Recreation Area has interpretive displays on the lake's creation, history, wildlife, and fish. Nearby is a 5,000-foot paved airstrip, operated by the State Aviation Department, that is seasonal and daytime use only. Bass tournaments take place in July and August, and there is also a fly-fishing tournament in August. Each September, local scuba diving groups do an underwater cleanup of the lake.

The park gets about 500,000 visitors each year. Weekends are usually busy from mid-April through November, and it is often difficult to find an electric hookup campsite anytime in June and July, the park's busiest months. Summers are warm but not hot, with highs usually in the 80s and low 90s, and lows in the 50s and 60s. Fall is particularly nice, with the cottonwoods turning brilliant gold, and days in the 70s and nights in the upper 30s and low 40s. Winters are brisk, with nights in the teens but days in the 40s; and spring brings high temperatures mostly in the 60s, with lows in the 30s.

Nearby attractions include Aztec Ruins National Monument, about 28 miles west of the park visitor center via NM highways 511 and 173. A worthwhile side trip, the monument contains the ruins of a twelfth-century American Indian pueblo with a fully restored Great Kiva.

RIO GRANDE NATURE CENTER STATE PARK

Hours/Season: Trails open 24 hours year-round; visitor center open 10:00 A.M. to 5:00 P.M. daily year-round, until 8:00 P.M. Fridays May through October; parking lot opens at 7:00 A.M. weekdays and 8:00 A.M. weekends and is padlocked shut when the visitor center closes; visitor center and parking lot closed Thanksgiving, Christmas, New Year's Day

Area: 270 land acres

Elevation: 4,650 feet

Facilities: Visitor center, interpretive exhibits, library, observation room, nature trail, demonstration gardens, viewing platform, restrooms, gift shop, phone: (505) 344-7240

Attractions: Nature study, interpretive programs, hiking, nature walks, bird-watching, mountain biking, horseback riding

Access: In Albuquerque at the west end of Candelaria Road Northwest; from I-40 take exit 157A onto Rio Grande Boulevard north for 3 blocks, and turn left onto Candelaria Road; from I-25 take exit 227 (Frontage Road) and turn right onto Candelaria Road

A peaceful oasis and escape from the hustle and bustle of New Mexico's largest city, the Rio Grande Nature Center's main reason for being is environmental education. Nestled among the cottonwoods and willows along the Rio Grande, a few miles northwest of Albuquerque's historic Old Town, the nature center offers two interpretive nature trails, demonstration gardens, numerous exhibits on the area's natural environment, guided walks, and an abundance of birds and other wildlife.

The center is located in what is called a *bosque.* The word is Spanish for forest, but in New Mexico it is often used to describe the wetlands along rivers, and particularly along the Rio Grande. At the center are some 270 acres of woods and meadows, with native grasses, wildflowers, willows, tamarisk, Russian olives, and century-old cottonwoods. There is also a 3-acre pond surrounded by cattails, which helps the center attract over 260 species of birds.

The main activities here are walking the trails—either on your own or on a guided walk—and examining the displays in the visitor center, including a number of hands-on exhibits for children. This is such a tranquil spot that it is also perfect for a leisurely stroll, or simply as a place to sit and contemplate nature. The purpose of the nature center is to preserve the *bosque* and teach people about their relationship with the river, and the idyllic setting makes it an immensely enjoyable learning experience.

The Riverwalk Trail is an easy 1-mile loop that meanders through the *bosque* and along the river, passing through open meadows and heavily wooded areas. A booklet or audio tape, keyed to numbers along the trail, describes the terrain and some of the plant life and other natural features, points out evidence of beavers, and discusses the effects of human activity. Although mostly flat, the trail has a few grades and uneven sections.

The Bosque Loop Trail, about 0.8 mile, is an easy walk through the *bosque*, with a spur to the river. A booklet or audio tape, again keyed to numbered markers, is geared more to families than the Riverwalk Trail booklet or tape, suggesting subjects that parents can discuss with their children as they walk the loop, such as what it feels like to be a tree, the needs of wildlife, and the sounds of the *bosque*. This trail is almost completely flat and has a bit more shade than the Riverside Trail.

Pets and bikes are prohibited on the above trails but are permitted on a 1.25-mile paved loop that runs along a flood-control ditch between the visitor center and river. Park officials can also direct mountain bikers to several other nearby trails.

The 3-acre pond behind the visitor center is closed to the public (except on guided walks) but can be easily seen from an observation room in the visitor center, complete with a sound system that brings the noise of the pond into the room. There are also blinds just outside the visitor center that allow

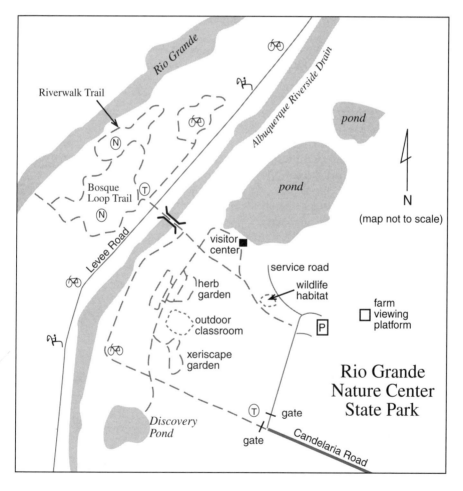

people to observe the numerous birds and other wildlife without scaring them off.

The smaller Discovery Pond is aimed at children, and lets them get a close-up look at aquatic life—from a boardwalk or by wading in—and then take their finds to microscopes for an even closer look.

Numerous birds make their homes in the park, although the greatest number of species can be seen from November through February. Among birds likely to be observed in winter are waterfowl, such as ring-necked ducks, American wigeons, and cinnamon teal, plus northern harriers, ruby-crowned kinglets, hermit thrushes, chipping sparrows, song sparrows, dark-eyed juncos, western meadowlarks, sandhill cranes, and an occasional bald eagle. Summer migrants include numerous species of warblers, western meadowlarks, black-chinned hummingbirds, brown-headed cowbirds, black phoebes, and western kingbirds. Year-round residents include Cooper's hawks, great horned owls, American coots, Canada geese, Gambel's quail, ring-necked pheasants, Mandarin ducks, mallards, wood ducks, black-capped chickadees, great blue herons, northern flickers, and both downy and hairy woodpeckers.

Also in the park are turtles, toads, lizards, bullsnakes, dragonflies, beavers, muskrats, cottontail rabbits, pocket gophers, rock squirrels, and coyotes. Demonstration gardens grow herbs and a variety of drought-tolerant plants, and a viewing platform provides a look at the nature center's farm, where corn is grown for bird feed.

There are no picnic areas at the nature center, but shaded benches provide a spot where you can have your picnic lunch, if you brought one. No food or beverages (except water) are available at the center, and walkers are discouraged from taking food and drink (except water) on the trails.

Once you get inside the visitor center, another world opens up. There are exhibits describing the *bosque*'s plants and animals, including a large turtle skeleton and a series of river photos by well-known New Mexico photographer Laura Gilpin. The Discovery Room has hands-on exhibits for children, including stamps for making footprints of park birds and animals in a sandbox, and a drawing and coloring table. A "Please Touch" display lets kids feel the scaly skin of a bullsnake.

The glass-walled semi-circular observation room, which overlooks the pond, contains a library, with publications on birds, herbs, trees, and other aspects of natural history that can be used on the premises. The center's gift shop has various souvenirs, plus a good selection of nature books, on topics ranging from bird identification to desert landscaping, and will search for hard-to-find books.

Also at the visitor center are park trail guides, available either in printed or audio cassette form, plus tape players, binoculars, birding books, and similar items that can be borrowed.

The center offers a variety of guided walks, classes, programs, and special events. Guided nature walks—some geared to adults and some to children—are presented Saturdays and Sundays year-round and usually last about

Canadian geese at Rio Grande Nature Center

1.5 hours. Guided bird walks are offered Saturday mornings year-round and can last up to 3 hours, depending on the interests of the group. Special nature walks for senior citizens are planned the third Wednesday of each month. Special programs are also scheduled periodically, with subjects such as nesting birds of the park, wilderness survival for children, orienteering, and endangered species.

During the summer there are a number of children's programs, classes, and field trips, ranging from activities lasting several hours to one- and two-week sessions.

Annual events include the Herb Festival in mid-May, with speakers, demonstrations, plant sales, and children's activities. The Hummerfest, which takes place in early August, is the nature center's celebration of humming-birds, which, incidentally, are the only birds known to fly backwards. It includes guided walks, storytelling, and demonstrations of bird-banding and identification. The Winter Bird Festival, in late January, concentrates on waterfowl and other birds that spend winters at the center, with guided walks, demonstrations, lectures, and similar activities. The center also celebrates Earth Day in April and *Día del Rio* (Day of the River) in October.

Visitors to the nature center will find something to see at any time of the year. Summers can be hot, though, with afternoon temperatures reaching the upper 90s and occasionally breaking 100 degrees F, so it is best to go out on the trails in the morning or evening. Summer lows are usually in the 60s. Winter days are mostly sunny and comfortable, with highs in the 40s and 50s, while nights drop into the 20s. Although it occasionally snows, the snow usually melts within a few hours. Fall is beautiful, with the cotton-woods turning a magnificent gold and daytime temperatures in the 70s; and spring, although often windy, sees new growth, wildflowers, and daytime highs in the 60s and 70s.

NORTH-EASTERN NEW MEXICO

Running from the Sangre de Cristo Mountains of the Rocky Mountain chain east to the Great Plains, this area includes a vast variety of terrain. Here are high-elevation parks in rugged mountains covered by forests of piñon, juniper, ponderosa pine, and Douglas fir. There are lakes and rivers, huge rock formations carved by millions of years of erosion, and historic sites from New Mexico's wilder days. Mountain parks offer some of the state's best hiking trails, which often become cross-country skiing and snowshoeing trails in winter. As elevation decreases, the wide-open ranching country of the Plains appears, sparsely populated and semiarid, except where people have created lakes to provide irrigation water, as well as boating and fishing at several state parks. This area's largest city is Las Vegas (not to be mistaken for Las Vegas, Nevada), an historic community that during its nineteenth-century heyday attracted the likes of Doc Holliday, Bat Masterson, and Billy the Kid.

CIMARRON CANYON STATE PARK

Hours/Season: Overnight; year-round
Area: 3,600 state park land acres; 33,000 state wildlife area land acres
Elevation: 8,000 feet
Facilities: Picnic tables, restrooms (no showers), 100 campsites (no RV hookups or dump station), corrals, phone: (505) 377-6271
Attractions: Fishing, hiking, mountain biking, horseback riding, wildlife viewing, bird-watching, rock climbing, hunting
Nearby: Eagle Nest Lake
Access: 3 miles east of Eagle Nest along US 64

Opposite: *Coyote Creek flows through its namesake state park.*

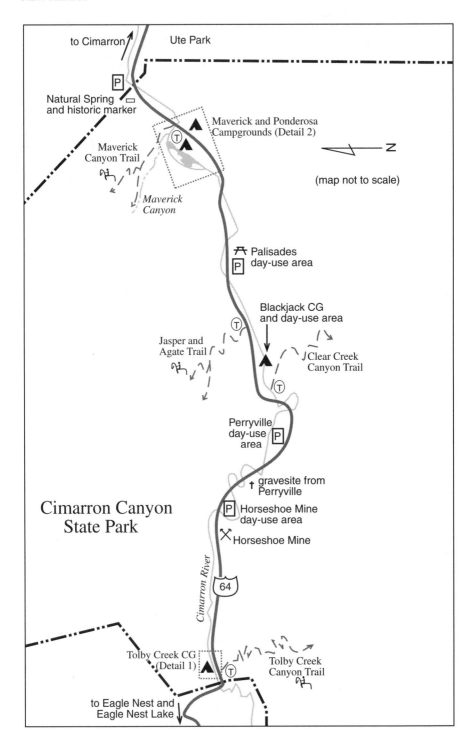

to Cimarron

Ute Park

P

Natural Spring
and historic marker

Maverick and Ponderosa
Campgrounds (Detail 2)

Maverick
Canyon Trail

N

(map not to scale)

Maverick
Canyon

Palisades
day-use area

P

Blackjack CG
and day-use area

Jasper and
Agate Trail

Clear Creek
Canyon Trail

Perryville
day-use
area

P

gravesite from
Perryville

P

Horseshoe Mine
day-use area

Horseshoe Mine

Cimarron Canyon
State Park

Cimarron River

64

Tolby Creek CG
(Detail 1)

Tolby Creek
Canyon Trail

to Eagle Nest and
Eagle Nest Lake

Once the domain almost exclusively of hunters and anglers, Cimarron Canyon State Park is attracting a growing number of hikers, mountain bikers, campers, and wildlife watchers. The park runs for 8 miles along the Cimarron River, through a spectacularly scenic section of Cimarron Canyon known for its towering rock cliffs called the Palisades.

Located at an elevation of 8,000 feet, in a forest of cottonwood, alder, willow, oak, ponderosa pine, piñon, juniper, and aspen, the park is part of the Colin Neblett Wildlife Area, managed by the New Mexico Department of Game and Fish. Until recently, a valid New Mexico hunting or fishing license was required for use of the park's campgrounds, but times have changed, and although trout fishing remains a major activity and hunters often camp in the park, anyone can now use the campgrounds, if they can find a space.

Camping is first-come, first-served, and the 100 sites in the park's three shady but somewhat cramped campgrounds often fill by early afternoon in summer, even though there are no showers or RV hookups. The park has no overflow camping, no backcountry camping, and overnight parking in day-use areas or along US 64 through the park is prohibited.

This is intentional. The main reason for the park's existence is wildlife habitat, according to park officials, and camping is restricted to protect the wildlife. Day-use hours are 6:00 A.M. to 9:00 P.M. Those who cannot find a campsite in the park often stay in commercial campgrounds in the nearby communities of Eagle Nest or Cimarron. There are also two undeveloped campgrounds in the Colin Neblett Wildlife Area, used mainly by elk hunters each fall.

The Cimarron River is stocked with trout—usually rainbows—from May through September, with the best fishing in April and May and again in September and October. A 1.5-mile section is designated a "special trout water," with stringent bait and limit restrictions.

Some park visitors, however, don't care about fishing and simply want to escape civilization and enjoy the canyon's beautiful scenery, either sitting along the river or hiking its trails. The park's most popular hike is the 7-mile round-

Fishing the Cimarron River at Cimarron Canyon State Park

trip Clear Creek Canyon Trail, which is considered to be moderately difficult. Following Clear Creek through a forest of ponderosa pine and fir, with mountain wildflowers scattered about liberally, it leads to several picturesque waterfalls and small pools. Open to hikers only, the trail is relatively easy to follow, has lots of shade, and crosses the creek on a log bridge.

Most of the park's other trails are old logging roads—they are wide but rocky, steep, and sometimes hard to follow as they head from the valley floor up the steep canyon walls—but the views are wonderful. These are generally more difficult than Clear Creek Trail but go through similar terrain and are open to mountain bikes and horses. Corrals are located at each end of the park; each set has four corrals, measuring 20 feet by 20 feet each.

Logging road trails include Tolby Creek Canyon Trail, which is about 14 miles round-trip; Maverick Canyon Trail, about 10 miles round-trip; and Jasper and Agate Trails, which combine for about a 4-mile round-trip hike. These distances are based on following the trails until they peter out, and then returning along the same route. Those with good mountaineering skills can usually find side trails that connect these old logging roads, turning them into lengthy loops. Area topographic maps can be purchased at sporting goods stores in Eagle Nest and Cimarron.

Cimarron River and its various tributaries are not deep enough for swimming, but weary hikers can sit on the rocks and cool their feet in the

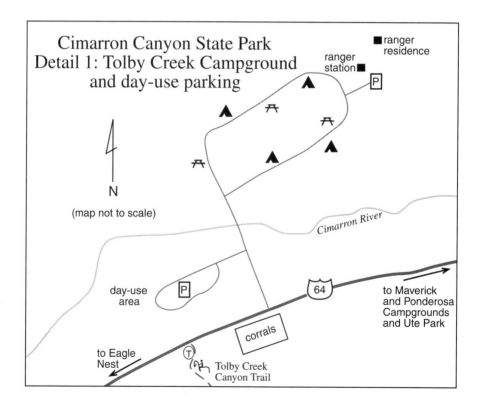

Cimarron Canyon State Park
Detail 1: Tolby Creek Campground and day-use parking

ranger residence

ranger station

N

(map not to scale)

Cimarron River

day-use area

P

64

to Maverick and Ponderosa Campgrounds and Ute Park

to Eagle Nest

corrals

Tolby Creek Canyon Trail

snow-fed water. The Gravel Pit Lakes are about 10 feet deep, but swimming and boating are prohibited.

Since this is a wildlife area, it comes as no surprise that the state park is a good place to see wildlife. Sightings of black bears are fairly common, and the park is also home to mule deer, elk, mountain lions, bobcats, coyotes, racoons, badgers, long-tailed weasels, cottontail rabbits, Colorado chipmunks, Abert's squirrels, golden-mantled ground squirrels, and pocket gophers. Birds include wild turkeys, red-tailed hawks, golden eagles, great horned owls, rock wrens, mourning doves, song sparrows, black-chinned hummingbirds, dusky flycatchers, and violet-green swallows.

Rock climbers are fascinated by the dramatic Palisades, a 400-foot-high crenellated granite formation. It was created by the Cimarron River as it cut through an igneous rock sill that was uplifted some forty million years ago. However, climbers are warned that the rock is not stable and climbing here requires advanced skills. Beginners are directed to a safer section near the east end of the canyon. All rock climbers should obtain special use permits from park officials.

More than one hundred years ago, the community of Perryville was located here. Founded in 1877 and named for a blacksmith named Perry, the village had its own post office in 1894 and 1895 and reportedly had a school, store, hotel, and a number of homes. All that remains today is the grave and

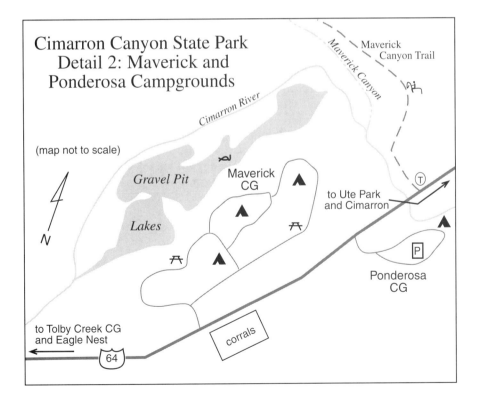

Cimarron Canyon State Park
Detail 2: Maverick and
Ponderosa Campgrounds

(map not to scale)

N

Maverick
Canyon Trail

Maverick Canyon

Cimarron River

Gravel Pit

Lakes

Maverick
CG

to Ute Park
and Cimarron

T

P

Ponderosa
CG

to Tolby Creek CG
and Eagle Nest

64

corrals

tombstone of one Jessie Phillips, who lived from 1879 to 1894. The grave site is located in the middle of the park, across the road from the Perryville Day-Use Area.

Also in the park are several old mines. Although gold was found in other sections of northern New Mexico, there are no reports that any of the holes dug here resulted in anything more than tired muscles. One such mine, along the south side of the highway on a curve just west of the Horseshoe Mine Day-Use Area, goes back about 30 feet into the canyon wall and often contains standing water. There are several other mine shafts in the park, but no old mining equipment has been located.

At the eastern edge of the park, on the north side of the road near an historical marker, is a natural spring, captured in a small brick enclosure with a pipe out of the side, which provides a year-round supply of good-tasting, tested drinking water.

The park is busiest in summer, when residents of Texas, Oklahoma, and Kansas leave the heat of their home states for the northern New Mexico mountains. Summer temperatures range from nighttime lows in the low 40s to daytime highs in the 80s, and afternoon thunderstorms are common, especially in August. Fall colors can be especially pretty in the canyon. Days often warm into the 60s, while nights often drop into the upper 20s and low 30s, and snow may fall, even in early October. Hunters often use the park as a base camp from September through December.

The quietest time at the park is in January and February, when daytime highs are usually in the mid-30s and nights drop to single digits, although cold spells with temperatures 20 degrees F to 30 degrees F below zero are not uncommon. Winters can be snowy, but there is not usually enough snow in the right places for much cross-country skiing or other winter sports. Spring temperatures are similar to those in autumn, and snow may fall into early May. Water is turned off in the campgrounds, and only portable toilets are available from September 15 through April.

Several miles west of the state park is 2,200-acre Eagle Nest Lake, created by the construction of a dam across Cimarron River. Leased by the New Mexico Department of Game and Fish, the lake has good bank and boat fishing for rainbow trout and kokanee salmon, plus ice fishing in winter. It is also popular with windsurfers, who brave the chilly water in spring, when the winds are best. A spectacular fireworks display over the lake takes place each Independence Day.

CLAYTON LAKE STATE PARK

Hours/Season: Overnight; year-round
Area: 420 land acres, 150 lake surface acres
Elevation: 5,100 feet
Facilities: Interpretive exhibits, picnic tables, restrooms with showers, playground, group shelter, 43 campsites (8 with electric and water

hookups), public telephone, docks, boat ramp, phone: (505) 374-8808
Attractions: Boating, fishing (except in winter), hiking, swimming, wild-
life and bird viewing, dinosaur tracks
Access: 12 miles north of Clayton via NM 370

▲ Dinosaurs, trout, geese, and ducks are the main draws at this quiet park
⊥ on the plains of eastern New Mexico. Created in 1955 as a fishing lake
and winter stop for migrating waterfowl, the park's focus expanded greatly
some thirty years later with the discovery of more than five hundred dinosaur footprints, in what is now considered one of the best dinosaur
trackways in America.

No one knew the dinosaur tracks existed when dynamite was used to
create the lake in the 1950s, and it apparently was an amateur paleontolo-
gist who actually discovered them. State park officials were unaware of the
tracks until 1982, when they spotted several people carrying what turned
out to be positive in-fillings of dinosaur tracks to their cars. The in-fillings
were confiscated, charges of vandalism were filed, and officialdom took
charge of the site.

Paleontologists from the New Mexico Museum of Natural History found
almost 500 footprints, left in the mud by at least eight different types of dinosaurs about 100 million years ago. At that time, this area was along the
western coast of a large sea, with a warm and humid climate and an abundance of plant life.

Dinosaur tracks at the lake are
from both carnivores and herbi-
vores. The meat-eaters' tracks are
smaller than the ones left by herbi-
vores, and most are bird-like, with
thin toes, sharp claws, and pointed
heels. The majority of the tracks at
the site are from large plant-eating
dinosaurs. These prints have three
toes, squared-off heels, and no claw
marks. Herbivore footprints are
also easily identified by the long
middle toe, often about twice the
length of the two side toes.

Among the more interesting
tracks are those of a web-footed dinosaur, a baby dinosaur, and a
winged pterodactyl. There is one
set of tracks that appears to show a
dinosaur slipping in the mud and
dragging its tail to help keep it
from falling.

The tracks are on the dam spillway, at the end of an easy 0.5-mile

*Footprint of meat-eating dinosaur at
Clayton Lake State Park*

A view of Clayton Lake at Clayton Lake State Park

trail along the lake's east side. A boardwalk meanders among the tracks, and a gazebo contains information on the trackway. The tracks are easiest to see when the sun is low in the sky during early morning and late afternoon, when shadows throw them into relief.

The park's only real hiking trail is the North Trail, which meanders for about 0.75 mile through grasslands and woods to the top of a ridge, providing panoramic views across the lake. Along the way, it crosses a seepage that feeds the lake, skirts rock pens built by pioneer sheepherders, and passes through a small canyon with numerous picturesque rock formations. The trail is moderately difficult at the beginning but soon becomes relatively easy. It offers a good chance of seeing a variety of birds and wildlife, plus wildflowers in late spring and summer, and can usually be hiked year-round. Future plans call for continuing the trail around the lake for another 3.5 miles to the dinosaur trackway.

The Rock Garden, a favorite of kids, is a smaller and somewhat subdued version of Bryce Canyon National Park. Dakota sandstone in shades of orange, tan, and brown has been molded by wind and water to form a variety of stone sculptures, similar to the hoodoos of Bryce but shorter and fatter.

The 170-acre Clayton Lake is open to all types of boats, although a no-wake speed limit is enforced. The lake is popular with canoeists and those with small inflatable boats, and for windsurfing in the spring. However, because this lake offers excellent fishing, it is essentially the domain of trailer-size fishing boats. No boat rentals are available at the lake. Swimming is permitted, but there are no designated swimming areas.

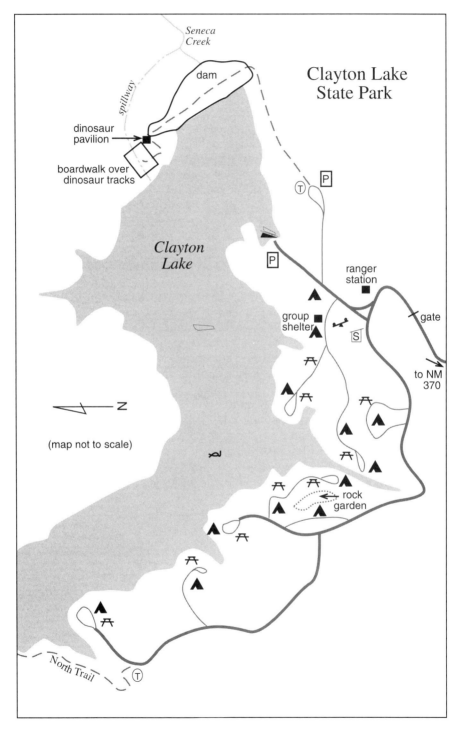

Seneca Creek

spillway

dam

Clayton Lake
State Park

dinosaur
pavilion →

boardwalk over
dinosaur tracks

T   P

P

Clayton
Lake

ranger
station

group
shelter

S

gate

to NM
370

N

(map not to scale)

rock
garden

North Trail

T

The fishing season generally runs from April through October, with both cold-water species, such as rainbow trout, walleye, and bluegill, and warm-water species, including channel catfish and largemouth bass.

The lake is closed to fishing during winter, when it attracts migrating waterfowl that often spend their nights at the lake but daily fly across the state line to feed in the fields north of Dalhart, Texas. Species of ducks you are apt to see include mallards, pintails, canvasbacks, and teals; and the lake is also a winter home for Canada geese and snow geese. The best time to see waterfowl is usually from mid-December through mid-January, although there likely will be some there throughout the winter.

Pronghorn antelope can often be seen year-round, just outside the park's entrance; and mule deer also frequent the park year-round, although the best time to see them is from November through March. The park is also home to coyotes, racoons, foxes, porcupines, and bobcats. There are a few rattlesnakes in residence, but they are seldom a problem, and both brown recluse and black widow spiders are sometimes seen.

Winter visitors to the park should be on the watch for bald eagles, spotted occasionally from fall through early spring. Other bird species seen at Clayton Lake in recent years include the common loon, several varieties of grebes, turkey vultures, red-tailed and Swainson's hawks, swallows, wrens, northern mockingbirds, American robins, a variety of sparrows, yellow warblers, starlings, and an occasional white pelican.

Campers will find spacious and sunny sites, some with views of the lake and others scattered among the scenic rock garden. Of the eight campsites with RV hookups, there are five pull-throughs and three back-ins. Plans call for construction of an RV dump station, as well as a visitor center.

Summer temperatures are pleasant—generally 80 degrees F to 90 degrees F during the day and dropping into the low 60s at night. Fall days are comfortable, with highs about 70 degrees F, and nights reach the low 40s. Winters are cold, but not unbearably so, with daytime temperatures in the upper 40s and 50s, and lows in the teens and low 20s. Spring winds can be annoying, but temperatures are moderate, with highs usually in the 60s, and lows in the upper 30s. Average precipitation is less than 10 inches a year.

CONCHAS LAKE STATE PARK

Hours/Season: Overnight; year-round
Area: 290 land acres, 9,600 lake surface acres
Elevation: 4,200 feet
Facilities: Visitor center, marina, restaurant, store, bait shop, lodge, golf course, picnic tables, playground, restrooms with showers, 106 campsites (33 sites with electric and water hookups, 29 with water hookups only) and primitive camping, public telephone, boat ramps, RV dump

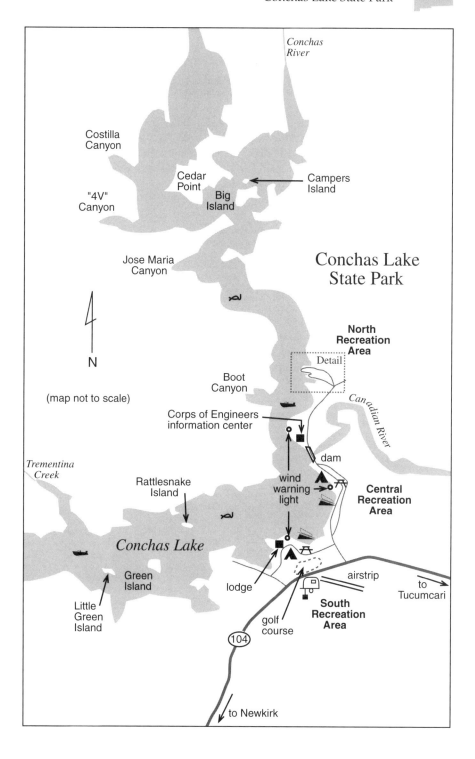

Conchas River

Costilla Canyon

Cedar Point

"4V" Canyon

Big Island

Campers Island

Jose Maria Canyon

Conchas Lake State Park

North Recreation Area

Detail

N

(map not to scale)

Boot Canyon

Corps of Engineers information center

Canadian River

dam

wind warning light

Central Recreation Area

Trementina Creek

Rattlesnake Island

Conchas Lake

Green Island

lodge

airstrip

to Tucumcari

Little Green Island

golf course

South Recreation Area

104

to Newkirk

station, airstrip, phone: (505) 868-2270, recorded lake information: (505) 868-2961

Attractions: Boating, fishing, water-skiing, swimming, bird-watching, golfing

Access: 34 miles northwest of Tucumcari via NM 104

One of New Mexico's largest lakes, Conchas is administered by both the State Parks Department and the U.S. Army Corps of Engineers, providing ample opportunities for boating of all kinds, fishing, swimming, camping, hiking, and even golf. Created as a flood-control and irrigation project in the late 1930s, at a cost of $15.8 million, Conchas Lake became a state park in 1943. The dam is 200 feet high and 1,250 feet long. When full, the lake covers about 15 square miles. There are three developed sections in the park. North Recreation Area includes state park offices, much of the camping, and a marina. There is additional camping in the Central Recreation Area. A golf course and airstrip are located in the South Recreation Area, which is under the jurisdiction of the Army Corps of Engineers.

As one would expect at one of the state's largest lakes, boating and fishing are the main activities. Conchas Lake is particularly popular with families and retirees, and boats here range from canoes to sailboats to large cabin cruisers and houseboats. Water-skiing and the use of personal watercraft are popular in summer, and because the wind blows at 15 mph more than half the time, the lake is being discovered by windsurfers. Those with canoes usually head for one of the many protected coves, but even there the

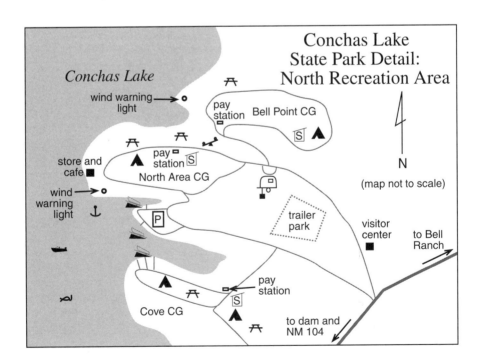

water is often choppy. A system of flashing white lights warns boaters to stay out of open water when winds exceed 15 mph.

The lake has about 60 miles of shoreline, with numerous little coves, inlets, and secluded beaches that make it easy for boaters to get away from the crowds. Although there are no designated swimming beaches, swimming, snorkeling, and scuba diving in the clear water are permitted in most areas. Swimmers usually prefer the beaches in the Central Recreation Area and near Cove Campground in the North Recreation Area, where drop-offs are more gradual than in other parts of the lake.

The lake is regularly stocked by the New Mexico Department of Game and Fish. The best times to catch walleye and crappie are spring and fall, and anglers catch channel catfish, bluegill, largemouth bass, bullhead, and sunfish year-round. There is a wheelchair-accessible courtesy dock at the North Recreation Area. Spear-fishing is gaining in popularity. In winter, the lake occasionally has a light skim of ice but does not freeze sufficiently for ice fishing. Concessionaires operate a full-service marina, bait shop, store, restaurant, lodge, nine-hole golf course, swimming pool, and cabins. There are docks, slip rentals, and an unlighted paved airstrip of just under 1 mile, with tie-downs. Boat rentals are not available at the park.

Throughout the park are piñon and juniper trees, and there are also elms and cottonwoods along the shore in some areas. Wildflowers will be seen—mostly in April and May—and there are also several species of cacti, including prickly pear, cholla, and barrel. The park has no designated hiking trails, although there are miles of beach, dirt roads, and open space for those who want to stretch their legs or simply get from point A to point B. Campgrounds offer a variety of facilities, from unlimited primitive camping along the shore to developed sites with water and electric hookups, shelters, picnic tables, and fire grills. There is also a commercially operated trailer park.

Conchas Lake is growing in popularity as a bird-watching destination, especially in winter, when the lake attracts an abundance of waterfowl, including Canada and snow geese, ring-necked ducks, cinnamon teal, green-winged teal, blue-winged teal, pintails, American wigeons, shovelers, mallards, canvasbacks, and redheads. There are also American robins, swallows, yellow-headed blackbirds, golden and bald eagles, sandhill cranes, several species of owls, red-tailed hawks, and northern harriers (also called marsh hawks).

Tarantulas live in the park and are often seen in August and September. Signs along the roads warn motorists to use extra care at tarantula crossings, and despite their rather unsavory reputations, most tarantulas are not poisonous—although their bite may sting a bit—and will go to great lengths to avoid confrontations with people. Just try not to step on them. Other park wildlife includes mule deer, which are sometimes spotted walking along the dam, plus coyotes, cottontail rabbits, jackrabbits, beaver, porcupines, muskrats, badgers, racoons, chipmunks, and turtles. Snakes include rattlers, bullsnakes, and racers, and the park is home to a variety of lizards.

Tarantula crossing sign at Conchas Lake State Park

A state park visitor center in the North Recreation Area has a few exhibits on the park's plants and animals and provides information on state park facilities and activities. The Army Corps of Engineers has offices and an information center north of the Central Recreation Area. Park officials warn that although the entire lake is open to the public, parts of the shoreline are on private property, and boaters should be careful to avoid trespassing.

Activities at the park include some thirty fishing tournaments each year, such as the American Legion Fishing Derby in early May. An organization called Sky Dive New Mexico does sky diving certifications in mid-September, with jumps over the lake as well as land areas of the park.

Open all year, the park's main season is from late March through October, with the busiest time between Memorial Day and Labor Day, when throngs of boaters and anglers invade. Summer temperatures usually hit the 90s during the day, with about a week each summer of temperatures topping 100 degrees F. Summer nights usually drop into the 50s. Winter days can vary greatly, with temperatures usually in the 50s, but highs in the 20s or 60s are not uncommon. Winter lows are usually in the teens and 20s. Snow does not usually stay on the ground for more than a day or two. Spring and fall typically have daytime temperatures in the 60s and 70s, with nights in the upper 30s and 40s.

COYOTE CREEK STATE PARK

Hours/Season: Overnight; year-round
Area: 80 land acres
Elevation: 7,700 feet
Facilities: Picnic tables, group shelter, playground, restrooms with showers, 60 campsites (13 with electric and water hookups, 4 with electric hookups only), public telephone, RV dump station, phone: (505) 387-2328
Attractions: Fishing, hiking, wildlife viewing, bird-watching, historic exhibits
Nearby: Morphy Lake State Park
Access: 17 miles north of Mora via NM 434

A secluded getaway in a quiet mountain valley, Coyote Creek State Park is best known as a place to relax, listen to the wind moving through the tall ponderosa pines, and admire the delicate blossoms of wildflowers that blanket the fields and roadsides. Those craving a bit more excitement can fish, get out the binoculars for some bird-watching, or hike the park's trail.

The park's namesake, Coyote Creek, provides good trout fishing—rainbows and German browns—and most anglers catch their limits. The shallow creek ranges from 5 to 15 feet across, with several good fishing ponds created by beaver and human-made dams. There are no areas appropriate for swimming or boating.

The campground is attractive and heavily wooded. The sites with RV hookups are the most open, fairly level, but a bit close together; while the non-hookup sites are dispersed among the trees over a large part of the park. Close and low-hanging trees make some of the non-hookup sites inappropriate for large RVs. Ground fires are permitted, and firewood is usually available for a fee.

The 1-mile Coyote Creek Trail (one-way) follows the park perimeter through a forest of ponderosa pine, scrub oak, juniper, spruce, and willow and twice crosses the picturesque creek on footbridges. Mostly moderate, with a few steep sections, it climbs to a ridge that offers good panoramic views of the Rincon Mountains, part of the Sangre de Cristo (Blood of Christ) chain, so-named because of the deep red color often seen when winter sunsets are reflected on the snow-covered peaks. The trail starts just east of the campground's RV hookup sites and returns to the developed part of the park a little to the south of the starting point, near a reconstructed 1930s moonshiner's shack and an old cattle watering trough.

Some claim the wildflowers here are the best in the state. Numerous species bloom from late spring through early fall, although the best display is usually in August. Watch for deep pink or purple mountain geraniums, delicate purple flowers of the Rocky Mountain iris, the yellow bell-shaped flower of the fringed gromwell, various members of the sunflower family,

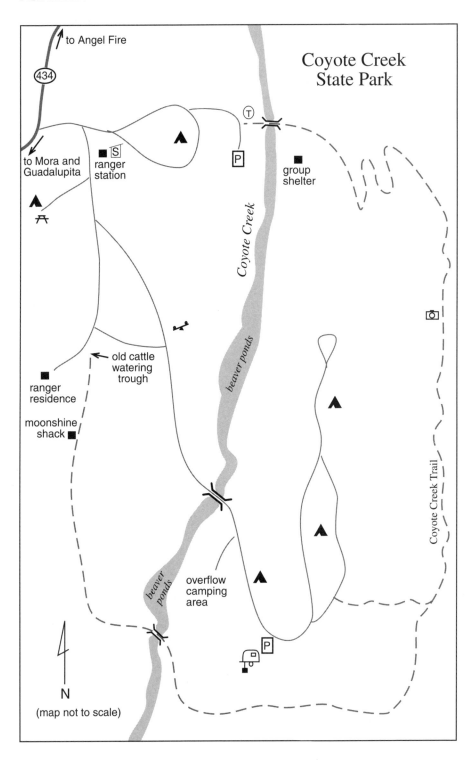

Coyote Creek State Park

to Angel Fire

434

to Mora and
Guadalupita

ranger
station

group
shelter

Coyote Creek

ranger
residence

old cattle
watering
trough

moonshine
shack

beaver ponds

beaver ponds

overflow
camping
area

Coyote Creek Trail

N

(map not to scale)

including cutleaved coneflowers, and the bright yellow evening primrose. One plant to avoid is poison ivy, which grows along the trail and in other areas of the park.

Anyone who walks anywhere in the park, especially in the early morning or late evening, is almost guaranteed to see some form of wildlife, such as beavers, skunks, racoons, porcupines, squirrels, and of course coyotes. There are also black bear in the park, and elk in winter.

Among the birds frequently seen and heard are western flycatchers, belted kingfishers, red-winged blackbirds, Steller's jays, western tanagers, common grackles, warbling vireos, western bluebirds, American robins, yellow warblers, red-shafted flickers, and violet-green swallows. The many hummingbirds seen each summer include rufous, broad-tailed, and black-chinned.

The park hosts a fiesta the second Sunday of August each year, with music, dancing, contests, and other activities.

Summer is the busiest time in the park. Daytime temperatures are usually in the 80s—only rarely hitting 90 degrees F—and nights routinely drop into the 40s and 50s. Afternoon thunderstorms are common in August but usually last only a short time and are gone by dinner. Fall comes early, with brisk days and cold nights; and winters are serious, with highs in the 30s and lows often near or below—sometimes far below—zero. Heavy snows sometimes limit access to and use of the park, although that is a good time for cross-country skiing and snowshoeing and the best time to see some of the larger wildlife, such as elk. Spring comes late, with snow a possibility as late as Memorial Day. Spring brings highs in the 60s and low 70s, and lows usually in the 30s, although 20s are possible into May.

Hiking the Coyote Creek Trail at Coyote Creek State Park

For those who find Coyote Creek State Park too modern and developed, Morphy Lake, about 28 miles to the southeast, is a pretty high-mountain lake with limited facilities. Morphy Lake State Park is described in the next section of this book.

71

MORPHY LAKE STATE PARK

Hours/Season: Overnight; year-round
Area: 20 land acres, 15 lake surface acres
Elevation: 7,800 feet
Facilities: Picnic tables, portable toilets, 60 campsites (no hookups), boat ramp, phone: (505) 387-2328
Attractions: Boating (no gasoline motors), fishing
Nearby: Coyote Creek State Park
Access: From Mora, take NM 94 south 7 miles to Ledoux and then go 4 miles west on a dirt road

This is the park for people who think state parks have gotten too comfortable and want to return to the days when camping meant roughing it. This pretty little park has no paved RV campsites. Also, there are no flush toilets, no showers, no telephone, no trash cans, and not even drinking water.

What Morphy Lake does offer is a delightful mountain lake, hidden among tall ponderosa pines in a rugged forest, where the birds sing, the wind gently blows through the trees, and the fish bite—at least most of

Large boulders and ponderosa pines set a tranquil mood at Morphy Lake State Park.

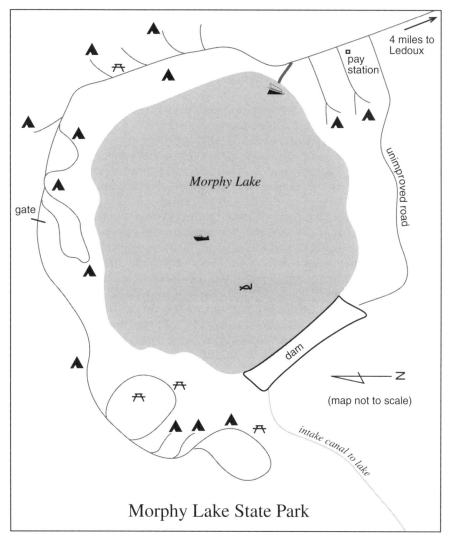

4 miles to Ledoux

pay station

unimproved road

Morphy Lake

gate

dam

N

(map not to scale)

intake canal to lake

Morphy Lake State Park

the time. There are massive boulders along the shore, panoramic views of the Jicarita Mountains, and the smell and feel of the wilderness.

The only paving in the park is the concrete boat ramp. There are campsites and picnic tables scattered among the trees overlooking the lake, some portable toilets, and a self-pay station. There is no trash pickup; this is strictly pack it in, pack it out. Although there is no ranger in residence at the park, which is managed from nearby Coyote Creek State Park, plans are in the works to have a volunteer campground host during the summer.

The main activity year-round is fishing, and the lake is stocked with trout by the New Mexico Department of Game and Fish. Boats are mostly of the small fishing variety, and gasoline motors are prohibited (electric or self-propelled only). Sometimes canoes and rowboats appear on the lake. During winter, the lake is popular for ice fishing. There are no developed hiking trails, although a number of trails have evolved as anglers have made their way to the lake, and you can always walk around the lake, which is a distance of about a mile.

Park visitors should take drinking water and whatever else they need. The park does not have an on-site office or resident staff, and the nearest public telephone is in Mora, about 11 miles away.

Ducks and geese enjoy the lake, and other birds you are likely to see include ravens, crows, Brewer's blackbirds, piñon jays, and American robins. There are also squirrels, racoons, porcupines, coyotes, and an occasional black bear.

Although this park is isolated, and definitely out of the way, it does get a surprising amount of day use, and it sometimes gets crowded on weekends when anglers come from Las Vegas, New Mexico, and other nearby communities. Summer weekends are the busiest times, but sunny winter weekends after the roads have been cleared of snow can bring out the ice fishermen in droves.

Daytime temperatures in summer are usually in the upper 70s and low 80s, while nights often cool down to the 40s. Afternoon thunderstorms are common during August. Fall comes early, with brisk days and cold nights; and winters are cold, with lows often well below zero, and highs in the 30s. Heavy snows sometimes block the park access road. Spring comes late, with high temperatures in the 60s and lows in the 20s and 30s, and snow a possibility as late as Memorial Day.

Nearby, about 28 miles northwest, Coyote Creek State Park has a developed campground with RV hookups, a fishing stream, and a 1-mile hiking trail. Coyote Creek is discussed in the previous section of this book.

STORRIE LAKE STATE PARK

Hours/Season: Overnight; year-round
Area: 80 land acres, 1,500 lake surface acres
Elevation: 6,500 feet
Facilities: Visitor center, historical exhibits, picnic tables, group shelters, playground, playing field, restrooms with showers, 43 campsites (20 with electric and water hookups), public telephone, boat ramp, RV dump station, phone: (505) 425-7278 (office) and (505) 425-0425 (automated temperature and wind report)
Attractions: Boating, windsurfing, water-skiing, fishing, swimming, winter sports
Nearby: Las Vegas, New Mexico; Fort Union National Monument; Coyote Creek and Morphy Lake State Parks
Access: 4 miles north of Las Vegas, New Mexico, via NM 518

Camping, fishing, and water sports are the attractions at this busy lake, which sits on the high plains just east of the southern edge of the Rocky Mountains. Manicured lawns of native grasses, cottonwood and juniper trees, yucca, rabbitbrush, a variety of wildflowers, and an abundance of cactus cover the grounds; and campers can park their RVs or pitch their tents at the water's edge.

Storrie Lake was created in 1916 when Robert Storrie built a 1,400-foot earth-filled dam across the Gallinas River to provide irrigation water for vegetable farms. Although large-scale farming was not successful, the lake proved popular for recreation, and in 1960 it became a state park.

Open to all types of boats, with no horsepower restrictions, the lake is popular with pleasure boaters out for a cruise, as well as water-skiers, those with personal watercraft, and canoeists. Windsurfers from throughout the state begin arriving in early spring, sometimes wearing wet suits, and can be seen whenever the winds are blowing. Sailboats, on the other hand, are rare. Swimming is permitted in most parts of the lake, although there are no designated swimming beaches, and the water tends to be a bit cool.

Anglers can usually fish year-round, although the lake may freeze over for several weeks in winter. The ice is just thick enough to prevent boat and shore fishing but is very seldom thick enough for ice fishing. The lake is periodically stocked with rainbow trout, and anglers also catch German brown trout, crappie, and catfish. There is one wheelchair-accessible fishing dock.

Campers can enjoy the park year-round, although showers and some of

Clouds reflected in the water at Storrie Lake State Park

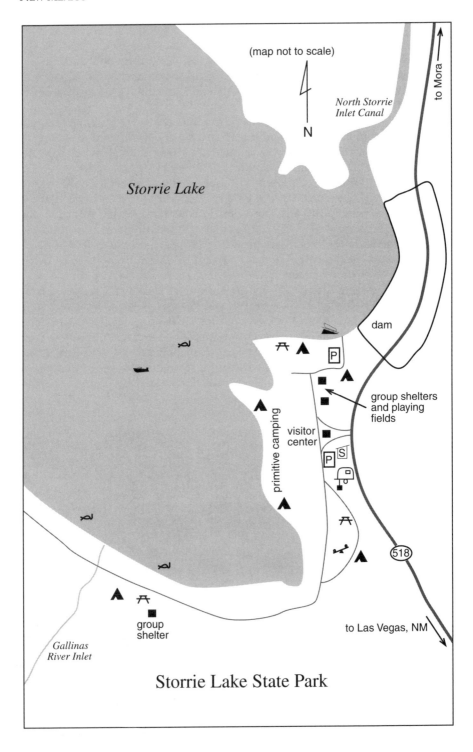

(map not to scale)

N

North Storrie
Inlet Canal

to Mora →

Storrie Lake

dam

P

group shelters
and playing
fields

primitive camping

visitor
center

P S

group
shelter

Gallinas
River Inlet

518

to Las Vegas, NM

Storrie Lake State Park

the water spigots are shut off in winter. There are developed tent and RV sites (without RV hookups) within several feet of the lake; and there is a large lakeshore area for primitive camping that practically allows anglers to fish from the comfort of their RVs or tents. RV sites with electric hookups are back a bit from the lake, but they offer good views of the lake and are within easy walking distance. Many of the developed sites have cabana-style shelters and are also shaded by cottonwoods; the primitive camping is along a shoreline that is grassy but has few trees. Nights are almost always quiet; the entry gate is locked at sundown year-round.

There are no designated hiking trails, although walkers can stretch their legs on the several miles of gravel road that circle the lake or go cross-country anywhere in the park. There are also horseshoe pits and a volleyball court at the group area, with equipment available from park rangers.

The lake attracts waterfowl, especially during migrations in late fall and winter when you are apt to see Canada geese and a variety of ducks. Winter is also the best time to catch a glimpse of a bald eagle. Other birds that have been seen in the park include falcons, burrowing owls, doves, and red-winged blackbirds. The park has cottontail rabbits, ground squirrels, and an occasional mule deer.

At the visitor center, there are exhibits on the history of the Santa Fe Trail, which passed near here, and the community of Las Vegas in the nineteenth century.

Summer is the busiest time at Storrie Lake, especially on weekends when the park fills with area boaters and anglers. From late October through February, the park is very quiet except for a few anglers; and windsurfers start arriving in early spring. The wildflowers usually begin to bloom by May, and the show often continues through August. High temperatures in summer are usually in the 80s, and lows dip into the upper 40s. In winter, daytime highs seldom get out of the 40s, with lows usually in the teens and upper 20s. Fall and spring often have highs in the 60s and low 70s, and lows in the 30s and low 40s. Snow can fall anytime from October through May.

The city of Las Vegas, just 4 miles south of the park, was one of New Mexico's wildest frontier towns in the late nineteenth century, when famed gunfighter and dentist Doc Holliday was a resident, and Billy the Kid and even Jesse James occasionally stopped by. Today, there are over 900 buildings listed on the National Register of Historic Places. Brochures outlining walking and driving tours are available from the chamber of commerce, and there is also a small historical museum.

About 26 miles northeast of Las Vegas via I-25 is Fort Union National Monument, with the ruins of a military fort that was established in 1851 to protect wagon trains from Indian attacks and also proved valuable to the Union during the Civil War. To the north of Storrie Lake via NM 518 are two other state parks, Coyote Creek and Morphy Lake, that offer mountain fishing, hiking, and camping. Both are described in their own sections of this book.

SUGARITE CANYON STATE PARK

Hours/Season: Overnight; year-round
Area: 3,600 land acres, 123 lake surface acres
Elevation: 7,000 feet
Facilities: Visitor center/museum, picnic tables, 41 campsites (8 with electric and water hookups and 4 with electric, water, and sewer hookups), restrooms (no showers), public telephone, group campsite, group shelter, amphitheater, boat ramps, RV dump station, dock, phone: (505) 445-5607
Attractions: Hiking, mountain biking, horseback riding, rock climbing, wildlife viewing, bird-watching, boating, photography, cross-country skiing, sledding, tubing, historic exhibits, lake and ice fishing, bow hunting
Nearby: Lake Dorothey and Colorado State Wildlife Area
Access: Take I-25 exit 452 at Raton, follow NM 72 east for 3.5 miles, and then go north on NM 526 for about 2 miles to the visitor center

▲ Deep forests, peaceful lakes, and among the greatest variety of activities of any New Mexico state park are the attractions at Sugarite Canyon, perched high along the New Mexico–Colorado border. About 10 miles of well-maintained multiuse trails meander through the park, providing views of wildlife, wildflowers, and rugged mountain scenery. There are two lakes—120-acre Lake Maloya and 3-acre Lake Alice—in the park, plus Lake Dorothey, also about 3 acres, just north of the park in the adjacent Colorado State Wildlife Area. There are good campgrounds and picnic areas, and an early twentieth-century ghost town.

Prehistoric humans hunted here about ten thousand years ago, and nomadic tribes including the Apaches, Utes, and Comanches often stopped here. The Santa Fe Trail passed by in the nineteenth century, and the Sugarite Coal Camp flourished at this site from 1910 to 1941. The park was established in 1985. The name Sugarite (pronounced sugar-reet) is believed to be a corruption of the Comanche word *chicorica*, which translates to "an abundance of birds"—an appropriate name for a park that is home to more than sixty bird species.

Your first stop should be the visitor center/museum at the entrance to the park, where you can get current information on trail conditions and other activities and learn about the animals and history of the area. In addition to displays on coal mining and the Sugarite Coal Camp, there are several hands-on exhibits that are especially popular with kids. These include an opportunity to use a stamp to make and identify various animal tracks in the sand and a "Guess Whose Hair" display to help learn about the park's many mammals. Visitors are asked to log in their wildlife sightings on a blackboard, and it is not uncommon to see listings of deer, wild turkeys, bear, elk, and mountain lions that have been spotted throughout the park.

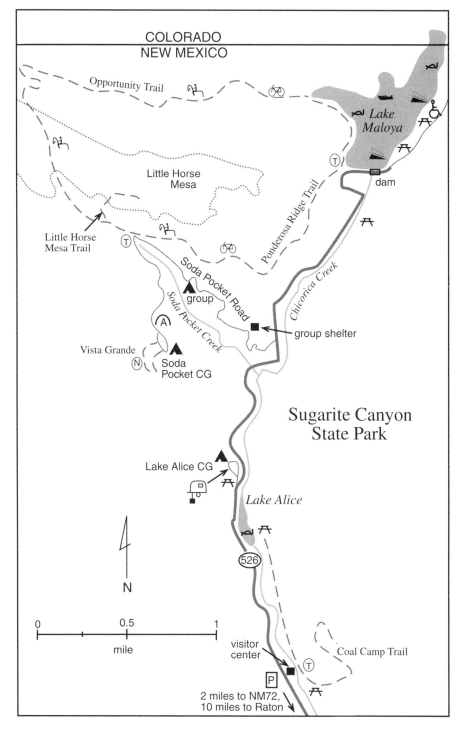

COLORADO
NEW MEXICO

Opportunity Trail

Lake Maloya

dam

Little Horse Mesa

Ponderosa Ridge Trail

Little Horse Mesa Trail

Soda Pocket Road

Chicorica Creek

group

Soda Pocket Creek

group shelter

Vista Grande

(A)

(N) Soda Pocket CG

Sugarite Canyon State Park

Lake Alice CG

Lake Alice

526

N

0   0.5   1

mile

visitor center

Coal Camp Trail

P

2 miles to NM72, 10 miles to Raton

More than a half dozen trails crisscross the park, winding through grassland meadows, rich with wildflowers in spring and summer, and deep into forests of ponderosa pine. Trails are well-marked and well-maintained but can be a bit muddy in early spring, as winter snows melt. Most trails here are shared by hikers, mountain bikers, horseback riders, and, in winter, cross-country skiers.

A relatively easy 3-mile round-trip hike, which starts just outside the visitor center, meanders through the remains of the coal camp, which during its heyday was a fairly substantial town, with a population of about 1,000, a two-story schoolhouse, a company store, a social hall, a music teacher, its own doctor, and rows of solid concrete and stone houses perched on the hillsides. The trail takes hikers to a number of ruins, many little more than a foundation or a section of stone wall, and to interpretive signs, some with historic photos of the buildings and their occupants.

If the wonders of nature are what you seek, try one of several trails above Lake Maloya at the north end of the park. Ponderosa Ridge Trail connects with Opportunity Trail to produce a splendid easy-to-moderate 6-mile loop. Starting at the Lake Maloya spillway, the trail climbs steeply through a forest of ponderosa pine and Gambel oak onto a mesa covered with aspen and fir trees, rewarding hikers with spectacular views of the distant Kiowa Hills to the south. The trail then drops down a series of switchbacks to a little valley and finally makes its way back to the starting point. Along the way, hikers will likely see an abundance of wildflowers in summer, lots of birds, and quite possibly mule deer and other wildlife. The trail, which ranges from 7,500 feet to 8,200 feet in elevation, is easiest if hiked or biked in a clockwise direction.

A bit more strenuous is the 2-mile round-trip Little Horse Mesa Trail, with a trailhead on Soda Pocket Road, north of Soda Pocket Campground. The steep trail leads up onto Little Horse Mesa, the highest point in the park, where hikers are rewarded for their efforts with a meadow loaded with wildflowers, a good chance of seeing deer and other wildlife, and beautiful views in all directions.

Lake Maloya is open to oar, paddle, sail, and electric-powered boats, but it is off limits to gasoline engines because it is a source for local residents' drinking water. Swimming is also prohibited. Both lakes are stocked with rainbow trout and are popular with anglers fishing from shore or boats, as well as for ice fishing in winter. There is also growing use by canoeists and kayakers, who especially enjoy exploring the narrow fingers that jut out from Lake Maloya. Each August, the park hosts the Poor Man's Yacht Race, a colorful and fun competition open only to muscle-powered home-made boats.

Technical rock climbers have recently discovered the park. Bolting is not permitted, and climbers are asked to check in first at the visitor center. Bow hunting is permitted in the park during the state's annual fall deer hunt.

The park is quiet—practically deserted—in winter, except for anglers, who set up their folding chairs out on the thick ice that covers Lake Maloya. Although it has not caught on yet, cross-country skiing conditions are excellent in most years, particularly on Opportunity Trail in the northern part of the park. Kids also enjoy sliding down the snow-covered hills on sleds, inner tubes, and even old cardboard boxes.

A prime location for wildlife viewing and bird-watching, it is highly unlikely that any park visitor will leave without seeing at least one furry, feathered, or scaly creature. Wild turkeys and the tasseled-eared Abert squirrels are abundant year-round, and practically every camper encounters mule deer in summer. Muskrats and beavers can often be spotted in

Paddling across Lake Maloya at Sugarite Canyon State Park

warmer weather, and visitors occasionally see mountain lions and foxes. Elk are sometimes seen, usually in herds of twenty-five or more, in the northern part of the park along the Colorado border. Black bears also live in the park and occasionally cause problems. Campers should be especially careful about not leaving food out and should check with rangers to see if any special precautions, such as hanging food from trees, are advised. One creature to avoid is the prairie rattlesnake, which inhabits rocky areas.

While looking for wild things, try to not forget the park's wildflowers—all seventy or so species. The best time to see them in all their colorful glory is from late spring through midsummer, although exact bloom times depend on temperature and water availability. However, if the timing is right, you cannot miss the meadows' blanket of deep blue Rocky Mountain iris, purple wild oregano (also called horse mint), orange and red Indian paintbrush, woodland sunflowers, and delicate white aster. Those who have been reading too many Agatha Christie mysteries might want to keep an eye out for poison hemlock, with its delicate, innocent-looking white flowers.

Campers will find RV hookups at the small Lake Alice Campground, in a protected area along the main park road. The shady campground has plenty of trees, but some sites are a bit close to each other. Those looking for panoramic vistas and lots of elbow room should head up the hill to the larger Soda Pocket Campground, which is close to hiking trails but has no RV hookups. The Soda Pocket section of the park was named by early pioneers, who mistakenly thought the numerous springs in the area were carbonated. Soda Pocket Campground is closed in winter, but Lake Alice Campground is open year-round. No backcountry camping is permitted.

Cooking the breakfast bacon at Sugarite Canyon State Park

The *Raton Daily Range* newspaper publishes current park information, including trail and fishing conditions and wildlife viewing, each Friday, year-round. From June through Labor Day, there are campfire programs each Friday and Saturday evening at the park's amphitheater, near Soda Pocket Campground. Friday programs usually consist of a ranger discussing the history of the park, wildlife, wildflowers, or similar subjects; while talks Saturday evenings are often given by area residents or visitors, when the topic could be practically anything, from mountain climbing to the West's Victorian mansions to migrating waterfowl.

Many consider summer the best time to visit, when days are pleasantly warm, with daytime highs usually in the 80s and nights in the upper 40s and 50s. Fall can be beautiful, as the aspen turn a brilliant gold. Fall days are usually warm, often in the 70s, but be prepared for cold nights, sometimes below freezing. Winters are cold, with temperatures sometimes dropping below zero, and may be snowy, although daytime temperatures often warm into the 50s. Spring comes late, usually not until late April, and can be windy, with temperatures similar to those in fall.

Just north of the park, over the state line in Colorado, are more fishing and hiking opportunities at the Colorado State Wildlife Area and Lake Dorothey.

UTE LAKE STATE PARK

Hours/Season: Overnight; year-round
Area: 1,500 land acres, 8,200 lake surface acres
Elevation: 3,900 feet
Facilities: Visitor center, marina, picnic tables, group shelter, nature trail, restrooms with showers, 200 campsites (80 with electric hookups) and abundant primitive camping, boat ramps, RV dump stations, phone: (505) 487-2284
Attractions: Boating, swimming, water-skiing, fishing, hiking, bird-watching, off-road-vehicle use
Nearby: Conchas Lake State Park
Access: 3 miles west of Logan via NM 540

Known for its numerous little coves and inlets, Ute Lake is among the state's longest lakes—almost 13 miles—but it is also skinny, only 1 mile across at its widest point. A popular family-camping destination, this boating and fishing park also has good swimming, a hiking/nature trail, wildlife, and something rare in the state park system—an area for off-road-vehicle use.

Created in 1963 with construction of the 5,750-foot-long earth-filled Ute Dam, the lake was enlarged in 1984. A subsequent lawsuit claimed that New Mexico was taking too much water from the Canadian River, which eventually flows into Texas and Oklahoma. This was eventually settled by the United States Supreme Court, in a ruling that barred a number of New Mexico communities from tapping into the lake for drinking water. A side effect of that ruling is that unlike most other reservoirs, Ute Lake's water level fluctuates very little, which pleases boaters and anglers.

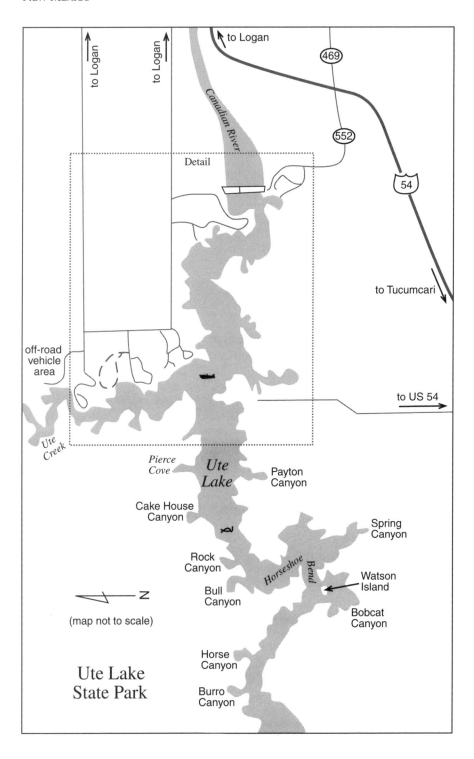

The deep-blue lake attracts a variety of boaters, and, especially during summer, you are apt to see a mix of fishing boats, ski boats, personal watercraft, and sailboats. Windsurfing is particularly popular in spring. The only restricted area is Ute Creek, where water-skiing is prohibited. A concessionaire-operated marina rents small fishing boats and pedal-boats and sells fishing and boating supplies. Although there are no designated swimming areas, there are a number of sandy beaches, especially in the North Area. Water temperatures during summer are usually in the 70s. One potential hazard is sand burrs, which stick to clothing and skin and can be quite painful.

Anglers are here year-round, although the best fishing is in spring and fall. The lake is known for excellent walleye fishing, and anglers have also caught record-breaking smallmouth bass, plus crappie, bluegill, and channel catfish.

The Cedar Valley Nature Trail is a 1.5-mile loop that is mostly moderate but has a few relatively steep and difficult sections. It climbs through rugged terrain of loose rock, passing yucca, cactus, juniper, and a few piñon, and provides panoramic views of the lake. Planned for the near future is a 1-mile walking/fitness trail. Those who prefer their trips on the trail to be motorized can dig their way through several miles of loose sand in the Rogers Park section of the state park, where numerous trails crisscross the sandy hills. The area is best for small all-terrain vehicles and dirt bikes, although full-size four-wheel-drive vehicles are also permitted. Those attempting to drive two-wheel-drive vehicles on these trails usually get stuck.

Marina at Ute Lake State Park

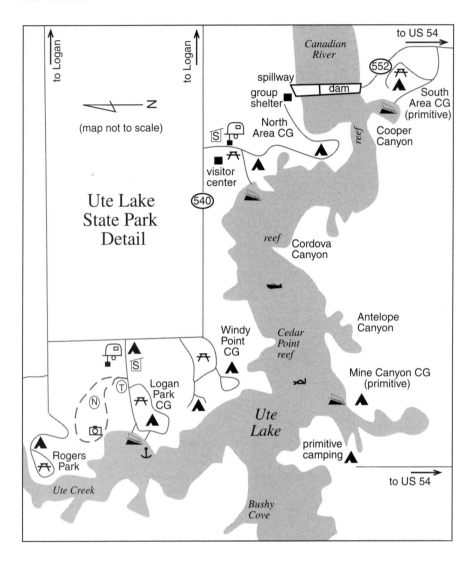

Visitors looking for wildlife will see migratory birds, including ducks and geese, from late fall through early spring. Bald and golden eagles often roost in the northern sections of the park from January through early March, and there are also doves, quail, and pheasants. Roadrunners are often spotted in the campgrounds. Deer are sometimes seen in the Rogers Park area, plus the park is home to racoons, rabbits, squirrels, and a variety of snakes, including bullsnakes and rattlesnakes. Tarantulas—the biggest and hairiest spiders in the United States—are often seen in spring and fall, as the males make their stately trek in search of a mate.

The park has practically unlimited camping, with facilities that range

Diving for dinner at Ute Lake State Park

from RV sites with hookups to isolated developed sites without hookups to primitive camping. Most camping areas have good views and fairly easy access to the lake. Showers and RV hookups are located in both the North Area and Logan Park. A small visitor center has exhibits and can provide information on park activities.

The busiest times at Ute Lake are on summer holiday weekends, but the large park is seldom really crowded. Early fall is a particularly pleasant time, because air and water temperatures remain warm, there are few people, and there is a greater chance of seeing wildlife. Summer high temperatures are usually in the 90s, with lows in the 60s; while winter highs are often in the 50s with lows in the 20s. Although it occasionally snows, the snow usually melts within a day. Fall temperatures range from daytime highs in the 60s and 70s to lows in the 40s; and during the windy spring, highs are usually in the 70s, while lows drop into the 40s.

About 60 miles west of Ute Lake is Conchas Lake State Park, which also offers a variety of water sports, fishing, and bird-watching and even has a nine-hole golf course. Conchas Lake is discussed in its own section of this book.

VILLANUEVA STATE PARK

Hours/Season: Overnight; year-round
Area: 1,679 land acres
Elevation: 5,600 feet
Facilities: Visitor center, interpretive garden, picnic tables, group shelter, playground, restrooms with showers, 29 campsites (12 sites with electric hookups), public telephone, RV dump station, phone: (505) 421-2957
Attractions: Hiking, canoeing, fishing, wildlife viewing, historic sites
Nearby: Las Vegas, New Mexico; Storrie Lake State Park
Access: From Las Vegas, take I-25 south for 23 miles to exit 323, and then go 15 miles south on NM 3

A picturesque little park along the banks of the Pecos River, Villanueva sits at the base of 400-foot sandstone cliffs, whose shades of tan and reddish-brown are a handsome backdrop to the rich green of the piñon and juniper that grow among the rocks. Tall cottonwoods shade anglers, and rocky trails climb past ruins of a nineteenth-century Spanish ranch.

The park's name—which is Spanish for "new village"—comes from the nearby community of Villanueva. Settled in the 1790s at a time when Indian attacks were frequent, the village was built around a central plaza, with the

Bridge over the Pecos River at Villanueva State Park

backs of its buildings forming a high wall, parts of which can be seen today. Also remaining is a well-preserved mission church built in 1818. Originally called *Cuesta*—Spanish for "hillside"—villagers wanted a new name for the community when, as part of the United States, it was to get its first U.S. Post Office in 1890. Residents included two large families, the Aragons and the Villanuevas, and when they submitted their petition for a post office there were more signatures from members of the Villanueva family, so the village bears their name.

Fishing in the Pecos is best from fall through spring, when the river is stocked and anglers catch rainbow trout, German brown trout, and channel catfish. The river is open to canoeing whenever the water level is high enough, usually only from early May through mid-June. Swimming is also permitted for those hardy enough to brave the chilly water, which seldom gets warmer than the upper 40s.

The park has two maintained hiking trails. The Canyon Trail is a 2.5-mile loop from the river up to the top of the canyon and then back down to the river. From the main section of the park, near the showers, hikers cross a bridge over the Pecos River and turn right (south), heading gradually up the canyon wall. The trail gives good views down to the river, and also has two interpretive signs part way up the side of the canyon. One discusses ruins of a nineteenth-century Spanish colonial ranch and a threshing floor in which horses trampled sheaves of grain. The other describes a conflict in 1841 in which members of an invading Texas group were captured.

After the trail reaches the top of the canyon, there is an overlook that provides spectacular views of the river valley and surrounding mountains. The trail then heads north along a bluff before dropping back down into the canyon and following the river back to the bridge. Some shade is provided by piñon and juniper trees, with cottonwoods and mesquite along the river. Rated moderate, the trail is rocky and has some steep sections as it climbs the canyon wall but is relatively flat on top.

The El Cerro Trail starts from El Cerro Upper Campground and climbs to the top of the canyon, providing superb panoramic views of the river valley. The moderately difficult trail is rocky, with several steep sections, as it meanders through hillsides of piñon and juniper. There is also scrub oak and some ponderosa pine. The length out and back is about 1 mile.

Camping offers the option of sites along the river, shaded by tall cottonwoods, or sites on a hill above the river among piñon and juniper, with fine views of the river and down the valley and especially good sunsets. The electric hookup sites are along the river, near the park's only shower facility. Nearby is an historical marker that commemorates the route followed by the Spanish conquistadores, starting with Francisco Vasquez Coronado in 1540.

Among the animals likely to be seen in the park are mule deer, coyotes, fox, bobcats, cottontail rabbits, jackrabbits, skunks, and ground squirrels. Occasionally mountain lions are seen, and the park also has bullsnakes, water snakes, and diamondback rattlers. Golden eagles have been known to nest in the park or nearby, and roadrunners are frequently spotted. Other birds

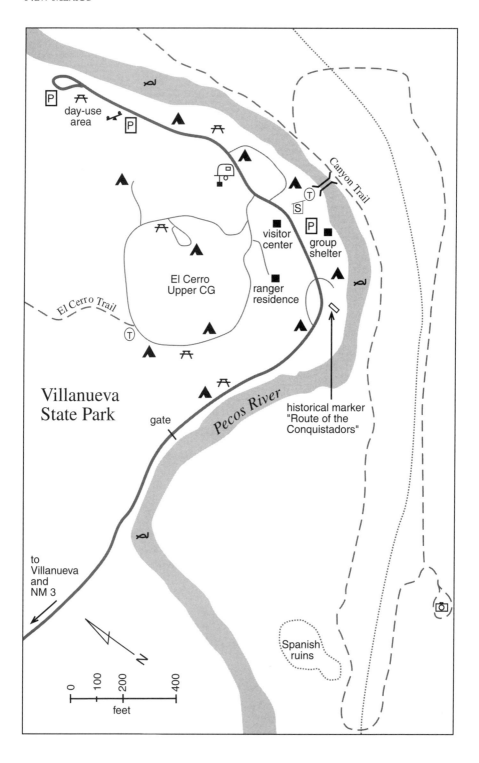

Villanueva
State Park

day-use
area

El Cerro
Upper CG

El Cerro Trail

visitor
center

ranger
residence

group
shelter

Canyon Trail

Pecos River

gate

historical marker
"Route of the
Conquistadors"

to
Villanueva
and
NM 3

Spanish
ruins

N

0   100   200   400

feet

that might be seen in the park include red-tailed hawks, yellow-breasted chats, cliff swallows, western kingbirds, mountain bluebirds, gray-headed juncos, northern flickers, mourning doves, chipping sparrows, western meadowlarks, black-billed magpies, summer tanagers, black-headed grosbeaks, blue grosbeaks, great horned owls, and rufous hummingbirds. Bird-watching is best in spring and summer, while larger mammals, such as mule deer, are more likely seen during fall and winter.

The park's visitor center has exhibits on the area's geology, human history, and plants and animals. Just outside the visitor center there is an interpretive garden, with signs identifying the plants of the area, including yucca, various species of cactus, and wildflowers.

Summer is the busiest season at the park, when its 12 electric hookup sites are often taken by midday, and even the non-hookup sites are 95 percent taken on weekends. High temperatures in summer are usually in the 80s and 90s, while lows are usually in the 50s. During the winter, days are in the 40s and 50s, with nights in the 20s. Spring and fall have daytime temperatures in the upper 60s and low 70s, while nights drop into the upper 30s and 40s. Although snow should be expected at any time in winter, it usually melts within a day, and there is almost never enough for cross-country skiing or other winter sports. Wildflowers and blooming cactus supply a variety of colors in late spring and early summer; and fall can be especially pretty with the contrast of red scrub oak against the bright yellow cottonwoods and deep greens of piñon and juniper. Mid-September through October may be the perfect time to visit, when temperatures are still relatively warm and the summer crowds have departed.

About 35 miles northeast of Villanueva State Park is the historic city of Las Vegas, with hundreds of buildings listed on the National Register of Historic Places, and Storrie Lake State Park, which are both discussed in this book's section on Storrie Lake State Park.

SOUTH-EASTERN NEW MEXICO

Dotted with oil rigs and cattle ranches, New Mexico's southeastern corner is mostly dry and flat, except for the Sacramento and Guadalupe Mountains, which rise from the desert floor and dominate the landscape for miles in all directions. Sparsely populated, the region's largest city is Roswell, known for the 1947 crash of what some believe was an alien spacecraft. Carlsbad Caverns National Park, one of the most spectacular caves in the world, attracts about 700,000 visitors each year, and nearby a unique state park combines a zoo and botanical garden specializing in the plants and animals of the Southwest. Several lake parks offer a variety of water recreation; and another park combines a rugged hike with an historical excursion from the area's Wild West days, when Apaches ambushed unsuspecting soldiers in a rocky canyon.

BOTTOMLESS LAKES STATE PARK

Hours/Season: Overnight; year-round
Area: 1,400 land acres, 45 lake surface acres
Elevation: 3,500 feet
Facilities: Visitor center, interpretive exhibits, swimming beach with lifeguards and paddle-board rentals (Memorial Day through Labor Day only), picnic tables, playground, restrooms with showers, group shelter, 32 RV campsites (6 with electric, water, and sewer hookups; 26 with electric and water hookups) and 12 designated tent sites and an overflow camping area, public telephone, RV dump station, phone: (505) 624-6058

Opposite: *Hiking Dog Canyon Interpretive Trail at Oliver Lee Memorial State Park*

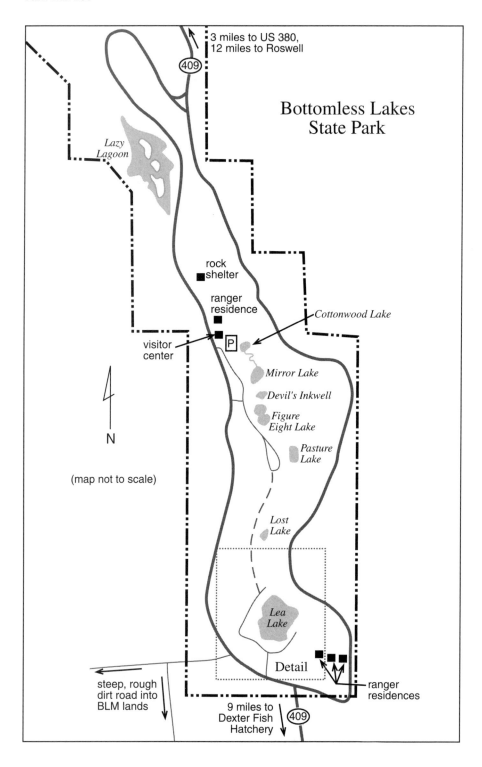

3 miles to US 380,
12 miles to Roswell

409

Bottomless Lakes
State Park

Lazy
Lagoon

rock
shelter

ranger
residence

Cottonwood Lake

visitor
center

P

Mirror Lake

Devil's Inkwell

Figure
Eight Lake

N

Pasture
Lake

(map not to scale)

Lost
Lake

Lea
Lake

Detail

ranger
residences

steep, rough
dirt road into
BLM lands

9 miles to
Dexter Fish
Hatchery

409

Attractions: Fishing, hiking, swimming, boating, scuba diving, wildlife viewing, bird-watching, nature talks

Nearby: Bitter Lake National Wildlife Refuge, Dexter National Fish Hatchery

Access: From Roswell head east on US 380 for 12 miles, and then south on NM 409 for 3 miles

Stunning red rock cliffs stand watch over a line of small, deep lakes at this desert park, New Mexico's first state park. Dedicated in 1933, the park's primary focus is its largest lake, Lea Lake, with a protected sandy beach, which is the only swimming area providing lifeguards in the New Mexico State Park System. In addition to swimming, the park offers a short hiking trail, camping, boating and paddle-boarding, fishing, and wildlife and bird viewing.

Named for its eight water-filled sinkholes, Bottomless Lakes was a favorite rest stop for nineteenth-century cowboys herding cattle along the Goodnight-Loving Trail, which ran between central Texas and southern Wyoming. The cowboys dubbed the lakes "bottomless" after their ropes failed to touch bottom. Park officials say the cowboys' ropes probably were simply not long enough, and that the lakes really do have bottoms, ranging in depth from 17 feet to 90 feet.

The sinkholes were created when gypsum deposits were dissolved by groundwater, forming underground caverns that eventually collapsed and filled with water. Most of the lakes have a greenish-blue color, resulting from algae and other plants that cover the lake bottoms.

Swimming is permitted only at Lea Lake, which has a surface area of 15 surface acres and a depth of 90 feet. The water here is clear, fed by an underground spring that delivers an average of 2.5 million gallons of water into the lake each day, making Lea Lake particularly popular with scuba divers. Water temperatures in summer rarely rise over 75 degrees F, even when air temperatures are over 100 degrees F. Along the beach is a handsome stone building, constructed in the mid-1930s by the Civilian Conservation Corps, which in summer houses a gift shop, boat rental station, and vending machines for refreshments.

Although lifeguards are on duty only during the summer, swimming is permitted year-round for those hardy enough, such as the students from New Mexico Military Institute in nearby Roswell, who usually start their swimming season in February.

Lea Lake is also the only one of the Bottomless Lakes where boating is permitted, and during the summer paddle-boards and pedal-boats are available for rent. Sailboards, inflatables, canoes, and other boats with motors up to three horsepower are also permitted but not available for rent at the park. There is no boat ramp.

Throughout the park are what are called Pecos Diamonds: quartz crystals that have formed inside clumps of gypsum, which then crumbles away to reveal the sparkling "diamonds." Although the crystals may not be removed from the state park, park rangers can direct visitors to areas on

Scarlet, a red-tailed hawk, at Bottomless Lakes State Park

nearby Bureau of Land Management property where the crystals can be collected legally. Plant life found in the park includes salt cedar—also called tamarisk—plus mesquite, saltbush, creosote, salt grasses, and other varieties that can tolerate a dry climate and saline soil.

A hiking trail of about 0.85 mile heads north from the Lea Lake day-use parking lot, with a cutoff to Lost Lake—the smallest of the eight lakes—before connecting with a paved park road that leads to five of the park's six other lakes and the visitor center. It is well worth the short hike to a vantage point above Devil's Inkwell, a small lake with steep banks and very dark water; and just north of Devil's Inkwell is Mirror Lake, named for its picture-perfect reflection of the surrounding red cliffs.

Because summers are hot, the best time to see wildlife is from late fall through early spring. Park residents include jackrabbits, rodents, roadrunners, turkey vultures, lizards, and rattlesnakes; and bobcats, mule deer, racoons, and coyotes are also occasionally seen.

During winter, visitors are apt to see coots—small black birds with white beaks that are members of the chicken family. There are also raptors, including an occasional peregrine falcon, red-tailed hawk, kestrel, prairie falcon, or Swainson's hawk. Watch for pelicans from early October through early November at Lazy Lagoon, at the north end of the park, where migrating snow geese, mallards, and sandhill cranes can sometimes be seen during winter.

For a close-up view of a red-tailed hawk, stop at the visitor center to meet Scarlet. She was injured and cannot fly well enough to survive in the wild, so she lives at the visitor center where she is fed tasty rodents and preens herself for her adoring public. The visitor center also has exhibits on the area's history, geology, flora, and fauna. During the summer, park rangers present a variety of nature talks and demonstrations each Saturday evening at Lea Lake beach.

Anglers will have the best luck from November through March, when several of the lakes are stocked with rainbow trout. Although the smaller lakes may freeze for brief periods during the winter, there is no ice fishing.

Campers will find roomy sites, RV hookups, and hot showers but little

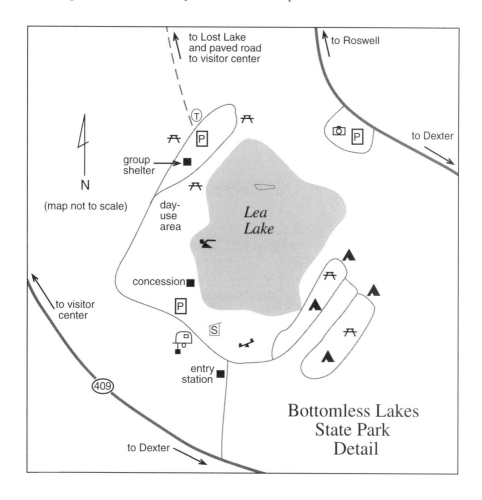

Bottomless Lakes
State Park
Detail

shade at Lea Lake. There are also less developed sites, with a bit more shade but no showers, along the rock bluffs near the other lakes. These offer pit toilets and centralized water. Those visiting during the summer months will find the best cooling breezes at Lea Lake.

Summers here are hot, sometimes unbearably so, with highs sometimes over 100 degrees F, and lows in the 60s, and the park is often crowded with area residents who come to swim and picnic, particularly on weekends. Winters are cool and sunny, with days reaching the mid-50s, while nights cool to the teens and 20s, and the park attracts numerous anglers, especially on weekends. April and May can be windy, but the park is fairly quiet, making this a good time for camping and hiking. The best time to visit, though, is September and October, when the weather is usually warm but not hot, there's little wind, and the park is practically empty. During fall and spring, high temperatures are in the 70s and 80s, and lows are usually in the 40s and 50s.

To see a variety of migrating waterfowl and sandhill cranes, visit their winter roosting site at nearby Bitter Lake National Wildlife Refuge. Up to 60,000 ducks and geese—some thirty species in all—stop at the refuge during their fall migrations each year, and many stay through February. Lesser sandhill cranes—sometimes as many as 70,000—also winter here. The best time to see the cranes is usually in mid-November. The wildlife refuge's headquarters is located about 9 miles northeast of Roswell. Take US 380 east from Roswell, turn left (north) onto Red Bridge Road, and then right (east) onto East Pine Lodge Road, which leads into the refuge. From the state

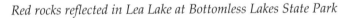

Red rocks reflected in Lea Lake at Bottomless Lakes State Park

park, return to US 380 and turn left (west) to Roswell, turn right (north) onto Red Bridge Road, and then follow the directions above.

Another easy side trip is to Dexter National Fish Hatchery, located on NM 190 just east of Dexter, about 16 miles southeast of Roswell via NM 2. From the state park, go south on a dirt road about 9 miles to NM 190 and go right (west) to the hatchery. A center for the study of threatened and endangered fish species, the hatchery has a visitor center, exhibits, and an aquarium containing endangered fish.

BRANTLEY LAKE STATE PARK

Hours/Season: Overnight; year-round
Area: 3,000 land acres, 2,800 lake surface acres
Elevation: 3,300 feet
Facilities: Visitor center, interpretive exhibits, picnic tables, group shelter, two playgrounds, restrooms with showers, 51 campsites with electric and water hookups and primitive camping for up to 50 units or tents, public telephone, boat ramps, RV dump station, phone: (505) 457-2384
Attractions: Boating, water-skiing, swimming, fishing, hiking, bird-watching, interpretive programs
Nearby: Carlsbad Caverns National Park, Living Desert Zoo and Gardens State Park
Access: 12 miles north of Carlsbad via US 285 and 4.5 miles northeast on Eddy County Road 30

An oasis in southern New Mexico's hot, desolate desert, Brantley Lake was created in 1988 by the completion of a 4-mile-long dam across the Pecos River that holds back some 42,000 acre-feet of water. Although its primary purpose is to protect downstream areas from floods while providing a reliable source of irrigation water for local farmers and ranchers, the lake also offers a variety of recreational uses, as well as fish and wildlife habitat. Terrain here is mostly flat and sandy, with creosote bush, desert grasses, mesquite, greasewood, cacti, and other Chihuahuan desert plants that can survive in the semiarid climate.

The Pecos River valley was first visited by prehistoric Indians some ten thousand years ago, and then in more recent centuries by Apaches, Spanish explorers, and Anglo-American ranchers. The site of one of the West's wildest towns, Seven Rivers, now lies under Brantley Lake. Founded in the late 1860s by settlers who traveled from Virginia by ox-wagon, it was originally called Dogtown, because of the area's large prairie dog population. The name was changed to Seven Rivers for the spot where seven arroyos entered the Pecos River, and this soon became a popular stop for cattle drives and a trade center for local ranchers.

During its heyday in the 1880s, the town had a population of about 300, a

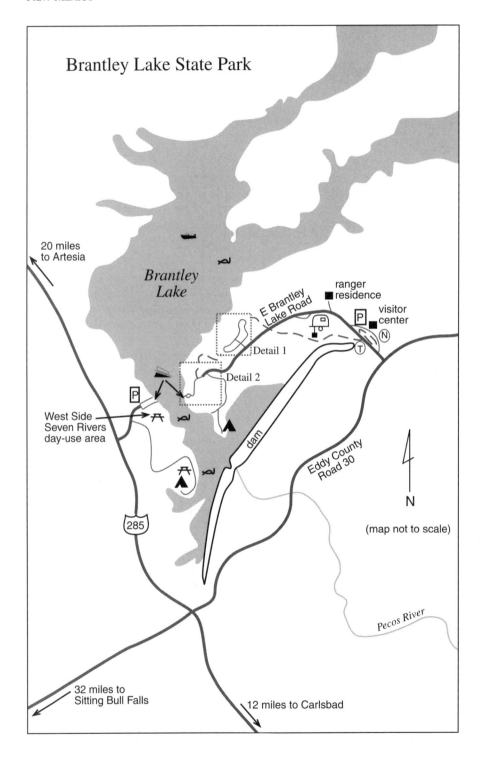

Brantley Lake State Park

Brantley Lake

20 miles to Artesia

ranger residence

visitor center

E Brantley Lake Road

Detail 1

Detail 2

West Side Seven Rivers day-use area

P

dam

Eddy County Road 30

285

N

(map not to scale)

Pecos River

32 miles to Sitting Bull Falls

12 miles to Carlsbad

post office, several stores, a hotel, a school, and two saloons—one that re-portedly had easily removable doors that served as stretchers for those who took second-place in its frequent gunfights. While many tales of the Wild West have been greatly exaggerated, historians have proof that Seven Rivers really was a wild place. When Brantley Dam was being built, graves in the old Seven Rivers cemetery were relocated to Artesia, about 24 miles north. Forensic scientists and anthropologists discovered that of the four-teen bodies of men between eighteen and forty-five years old, ten contained

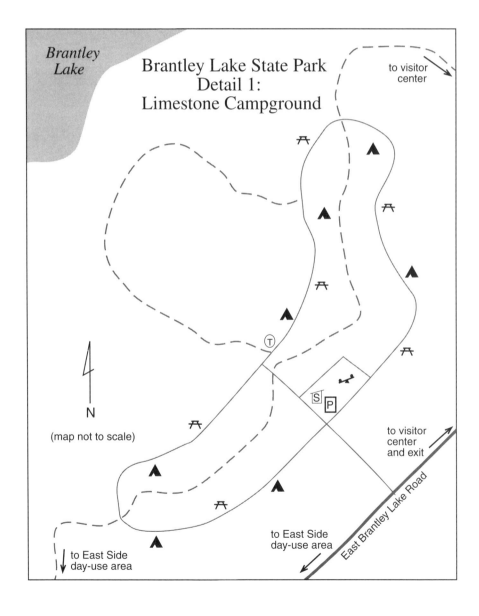

fragments of bullets or knives, including two with knives still in place.

Today, Brantley Lake attracts recreational boaters, particularly those who like speed, flying across the water on personal watercraft and water-skis. But the lake is large, and there is plenty of room for sailboats and even a few canoes and kayaks, and windsurfers have discovered that there is nothing out on the desert to block the spring winds. Swimming is permitted, but there are no designated swimming areas, and beaches are a bit rocky.

Although not really a destination park for hikers, Brantley Lake does have several trails, which are mostly packed sand, flat, and easy. One trail meanders for about 1.5 miles through the park, providing easy access to the lake, campground, and day-use areas. Another is a 0.6-mile loop through a grassy area between Limestone Campground and the lake; and a short nature trail near the visitor center has signs identifying the area's Chihuahuan desert plants.

Having the largest body of water in the area has made the park a prime location for bird-watching. October through the middle of February is a

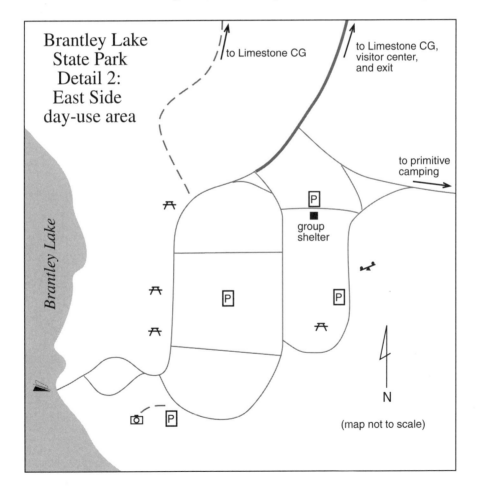

Brantley Lake
State Park
Detail 2:
East Side
day-use area

Brantley Lake

to Limestone CG

to Limestone CG,
visitor center,
and exit

to primitive
camping

P

group
shelter

P

P

N

(map not to scale)

particularly good time to see water birds, such as mallards, grebes, northern pintails, pelicans, common loons, teals, and Canada and snow geese. Other species likely to be seen in the park include red-tailed hawks, great horned owls, cactus wrens, western meadowlarks, white-crowned sparrows, barn swallows, scaled quail, rufous hummingbirds, belted kingfishers, and mourning doves.

Texas horned lizards also make their home in the park, and other animals include black-tailed jackrabbits, coyotes, racoons, and an occasional mule deer.

While summer brings out the water-skiers and other recreational boaters, spring and fall belong mostly to anglers, who catch crappie weighing a pound or more and largemouth bass that occasionally tip the scales at about nine pounds. Also caught are bluegills, white bass, channel catfish, and walleye. The lake is regularly stocked.

Limestone Campground is fairly close to the lake and within walking distance of the main day-use area. There are some trees. Camping the old-fashioned way is also available; just set up your tent or park your RV along the lakeshore. There are no designated sites in the primitive camping area, and availability varies with the amount of water in the lake. When the lake is at its highest level, there is room for fifteen to twenty tents or RVs, but when the lake is low, there is more beach area and space for about fifty.

The visitor center has exhibits and information on the park's plant and animal life. Campground programs take place most Saturday evenings from Memorial Day to Labor Day, with talks on various subjects, such as astronomy or the park's migratory birds. Taking full advantage of southern New Mexico's spring winds is the "Go Fly a Kite" rally, held in mid-March. Each May or June, a kid's fishing clinic takes place, with classes and contests.

Park use varies by season. Summer, with high temperatures often approaching or exceeding 100 degrees F, and lows in the 60s, is the time for boating and swimming, and the developed campground is full each weekend. Anglers particularly enjoy spring and fall. Spring is pretty, with wildflowers and cacti in bloom, but winds can get ferocious. Typical spring temperatures are highs in the 70s and low 80s, and lows in the 30s and 40s. Like most places, fall can be very pleasant, with daytime temperatures mostly in the 70s and low 80s, and nights dropping into the 40s and 50s. The quietest time at the park is in December and January, offering a prime opportunity for bird-watching. Daytime temperatures usually reach the upper 50s or low 60s, while nighttime lows are in the 20s.

Year-round, vacationers use the park as a base for visiting nearby attractions. Located 12 miles south in the city of Carlsbad is Living Desert Zoo and Gardens State Park, which is described in its own section of this book. About 20 miles farther is the spectacular Carlsbad Caverns National Park, one of the world's largest cave systems. Containing miles of caves, the park's stalagmites, stalactites, and other formations have created a wonderful fantasy land of shapes, rooms, and tunnels, producing sights that make the imagination run wild. There are easy-to-access sections, open to those in

Underground fantasy land at Carlsbad Caverns National Park near Brantley Lake State Park

wheelchairs, as well as remote areas of the caves that require strenuous hikes—what might be better described as crawls—through narrow, twisted tunnels miles beyond the reach of daylight.

LIVING DESERT ZOO AND GARDENS STATE PARK

Hours/Season: Memorial Day weekend to Labor Day, zoo and gardens open 8:00 A.M. to 8:00 P.M. (last entry 6:30 P.M.) and gift shop open 9:00 A.M. to 7:00 P.M.; Labor Day to Memorial Day weekend, zoo and gardens open 9:00 A.M. to 5:00 P.M. (last entry 3:30 P.M.) and gift shop open 9:00 A.M. to 4:00 P.M.; closed Christmas
Area: 1,100 land acres
Elevation: 3,200 feet
Facilities: Visitor center, nature trail, zoological and botanical exhibits, picnic tables, gift shop, restrooms, phone: (505) 887-5516
Attractions: Interpretive exhibits, wildlife viewing, bird-watching, photography, walking
Nearby: Carlsbad Caverns, Brantley Lake State Park
Access: On northwest edge of Carlsbad off US 285

▲ Living Desert offers a trip into the wilds of New Mexico, and particularly the Chihuahuan Desert, for a close-up view of the region's numerous animals and plants. Visitors walk a 1.3-mile trail that meanders through the various habitats that make up the Chihuahuan Desert, from the sand hills found along the nearby Pecos River to the gypsum rock formations of the desert uplands, and on through a dry desert stream bed to the mountainous piñon-juniper zone. Allow a minimum of 1.5 hours.

The Chihuahuan Desert covers over 200,000 square miles, from central Mexico into west Texas and southern New Mexico. Although the Chihuahuan Desert at first appears to be an arid wasteland—the average rainfall is 10 inches and temperatures exceed 100 degrees F in summer—the area actually is home to a myriad collection of animals, birds, and plants, which have all adapted to survive in this harsh and unforgiving environment.

Among the more than 200 animals in the park are mule deer, Rocky Mountain elk, pronghorn antelope, black bear, bison, badger, gray fox, kit fox, and porcupine. A prairie dog village is entertaining to observe, as the busy and curious little creatures cavort in the sun. There is a small herd of javelina, named for their short, javelin-sharp tusks, that enjoy a delicious meal of prickly pear cactus, spines and all. You can also see the endangered Mexican wolf, which was once common in the Southwest but has been virtually annihilated by what some consider a grossly misguided government program of "predator control." The park's resident bobcat and mountain lion will be found near the aviary, but you may need to look carefully, because they like to loll about on tree branches, often nearly hidden from view.

There are birds throughout the park, with many in the aviary, a screened-in oasis of trees and bushes. Visitors are asked to be as quiet as possible in the aviary, to not disturb the birds as they fly overhead or observe their human visitors from the safety of nearby tree limbs. Here you will find owls, broad-winged hawks, golden eagles, white-winged doves, and roadrunners, among others. There is also a waterfowl pond, which serves as a stopover for numerous migrating species of ducks and geese and is home to many fish and turtles.

Badger at Living Desert Zoo and Gardens State Park

The Reptile House provides a good opportunity to see snakes up close and learn which are poisonous and which are not, from behind a protective wall of glass. Among rattlesnakes on display are

Javelina at Living Desert Zoo and Gardens State Park

the black-tailed, prairie, and western diamondback. The Reptile House also includes the desert kingsnake, gopher snake, albino diamondback, coachwhip, and one of the few poisonous lizards, the Gila monster.

In addition to wildlife, the park is alive with plants of the Chihuahuan Desert, those hardy species that have evolved methods of enduring extreme heat and cold, sandy soil, and a decided lack of moisture. These include the tall, spindly ocotillo, mesquite, sotol, lechuguilla, and sagebrush. Living Desert has extensive well-labeled cactus gardens, and an indoor Succulents of the World exhibit that has more than 300 varieties of both Chihuahuan Desert and worldwide cacti and other water-hoarding species.

Along the trail is an overlook, offering distant views, including the Pecos Valley and the city of Carlsbad. The trail is paved, and, although it is a bit steeper in some sections than most handicapped-accessible paths, the entire park is accessible (with caution) to those in wheelchairs or with other mobility problems.

The large visitor center has a number of exhibits on the area's plants and animals, as well as geology and history, including a hands-on discovery area. There is also a gift shop and bookstore, and just outside the visitor center is a picnic area. A docent program presents guided tours, storytelling, and other activities.

The desert wildlife you see as you explore the park was not captured or even bred for their zoo careers; rather, they have been injured or orphaned and are brought to Living Desert because they cannot survive in the wild.

Each year, on the third weekend in May, the 4-day Mescal Roast takes place, which includes the Mescalero Apache traditional harvesting and preparation of spike-leaf agave, also known as the century plant. There are dances, a show and sale of American Indian art, and tasting of mescal, which is the cooked heart of the agave.

Summers here are hot, with high temperatures sometimes exceeding 100 degrees F, while nights cool into the 60s. Winters have warm days—usually in the upper 50s and low 60s—with nights in the 20s and occasional snow, although it usually melts quickly. Spring and fall are often the best times to see animals, with daytime highs mostly in the 70s, and nighttime lows in the 30s and 40s.

Living Desert Zoo and Gardens State Park has no camping facilities, but Brantley Lake State Park, 12 miles north, does have camping and is a good base for exploring this section of the state. In addition to a campground with RV hookups, it offers hiking, boating, fishing, and other activities. Brantley Lake is discussed in its own section of this book.

About 20 miles southwest of the city of Carlsbad is Carlsbad Caverns National Park, one of the world's largest cave systems. Containing miles of caves, the park's stalagmites, stalactites, and other formations have created a wonderful underground world of shapes, rooms, and tunnels, producing sights that cause the imagination to run amok. There are easy-to-access sections, open to those in wheelchairs, as well as remote areas of the caves that require strenuous hikes (actually, more like crawls) through narrow, twisted tunnels miles beyond the reach of daylight.

OASIS STATE PARK

Hours/Season: Overnight; year-round
Area: 197 land acres, 3.5 lake surface acres
Elevation: 4,000 feet
Facilities: Picnic tables, playground, playing fields, nature trail, restrooms with showers, 23 campsites (13 with electric and water hookups, 6 with water hookups only), group shelter, multipurpose playing field, RV dump station, phone: (505) 356-5331
Attractions: Fishing, hiking, bird-watching
Nearby: Blackwater Draw Archeological Site and Museum, Eastern New Mexico University Natural History Museum
Access: 6.5 miles north of Portales via NM 467

A true oasis in the barren desert of eastern New Mexico, this family-oriented park contains tall cottonwood trees, shifting sand dunes, and a bright blue-green 3.5-acre fishing pond. Although fishing is the park's main reason for being, it also has several hiking trails, a peaceful and shady campground, and an abundance of birds.

The park's cottonwood trees were planted by a homesteader in 1902, but the park and its pond—sealed with a bentonite clay liner—were not created

Relaxing by the pond at Oasis State Park

until 1962. In addition to being stocked with trout during the winter, the pond is stocked with channel catfish in the summer, and numerous area residents head to the park each weekend. The pond has several picnic tables, including two with shelters. Most anglers sit on the shore or bring lawn chairs. Swimming, wading, and boating are not permitted in the pond, and fires are not allowed on the shore.

Throughout the park, in addition to the cottonwoods, there are prairie grasses, yucca, desert wildflowers, and a variety of cacti. Unfortunately, there are also many sand and grass burrs, including a particularly vicious variety called goat heads, that you will want to be very careful to avoid.

The High Plains Trail runs along the base of the dunes, through prairie grasses, for about 1.5 miles. There is also a walking path of about 0.4 mile around the pond, and a nature trail, with markers describing the desert ecology, wanders through the sand for about 1 mile. Several other short trails connect camping areas to the pond and park facilities. A paved wheelchair-accessible trail runs from the parking area north of the pond to the pond. All other trails are sandy, fairly flat, and easy.

Sightings of more than eighty species of birds have been reported in the park. Although birds can be seen year-round, the greatest variety will be found in May, when visitors are likely to spot brown-headed cowbirds, western meadowlarks, Bullock's orioles, house sparrows, mourning doves,

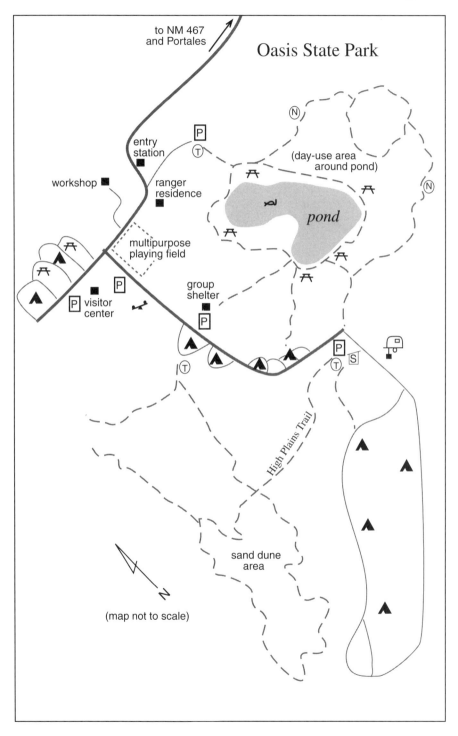

great blue herons, lesser yellowlegs, black-chinned hummingbirds, red-headed woodpeckers, scaled quail, scissor-tailed flycatchers, western blue-birds, and mockingbirds. Ducks and geese are often seen floating on the pond. April is the second-busiest month for bird-watchers. Coyotes, fox, deer, rattlesnakes, bullsnakes, and numerous lizards also call the park home.

The park is busiest from November through March, when the New Mexico Department of Game and Fish stocks the pond with rainbow trout every few weeks. Winter temperatures range from highs in the 50s and 60s to lows in the 20s and 30s, occasionally dropping into the teens. Some snow falls, but it seldom lasts long. In spring, days warm into the 70s and low 80s, while nights usually dip into the 40s. Summers are warm, with highs usu-ally in the upper 80s and low 90s, and lows in the low 60s. The cottonwood trees turn bright gold in fall—usually by mid-October—and fall tempera-tures are pleasant, with highs in the 70s and lows in the 40s.

Those interested in archeology will want to make a pilgrimage to the nearby Blackwater Draw Museum and Site. Just several miles north of the park via NM 467, evidence was found here in the early 1930s that humans had lived at the site more than eleven thousand years ago. Discovered were fluted spear points, which were named Clovis points, plus primitive hammers, scrapers, and other stone tools. Also found were the bones of the wooly mammoth, saber-toothed tiger, camel, and other animals of that period. Archeologists believe that at the time, there was a large pond near here that served as a water source for animals and a good hunting ground for hu-mans. The site is located several miles from the museum. The museum is open year-round, but the site is open from March through October only.

On the campus of Eastern New Mexico University in Portales is the university's Natural History Museum, which has exhibits, including aquariums and a bee colony, on the wildlife of eastern New Mexico.

OLIVER LEE MEMORIAL STATE PARK

Hours/Season: Overnight; year-round
Area: 180 land acres
Elevation: 4,300 feet
Facilities: Visitor center with interpretive exhibits, picnic tables, restrooms with showers, 44 campsites (18 with electric and water hookups), nature trail, public telephone, RV dump station, phone: (505) 437-8284
Attractions: Hiking, bird-watching, guided tours, historic sites
Nearby: Lincoln National Forest, town of Alamogordo, White Sands National Monument
Access: 12 miles south of Alamogordo via US 54

▲ A scenic park with an abundance of plant and animal life, Oliver Lee Memorial State Park offers rugged hiking and Old West history. Located along the western slope of the Sacramento Mountains, the park looks out across the arid Tularosa Basin to White Sands National Monument and missile range. Within feet of the barren desert are year-round springs that have created a lush forest of ash and cottonwood trees, maidenhair ferns, and wild orchids, where birds sing, and deer and fox stop for a drink.

Prehistoric Indians walked these trails more than four thousand years ago, hunting for rock that they chipped into knives, scrapers, drills, and hammers. Archeologists have found numerous pieces of these crude but effective tools in Dog Canyon, along with cylindrical holes in the rocks, created by the repeated grinding of seeds, such as those of the mesquite bush. These holes have come to be called "Indian wells," because they collect rain water, and there are a number of them in the park.

Although prehistoric Indians were here first, it was the Apaches that put Dog Canyon on the map and are given credit for inspiring the canyon's name. Historians believe the Apaches arrived in the area in the sixteenth

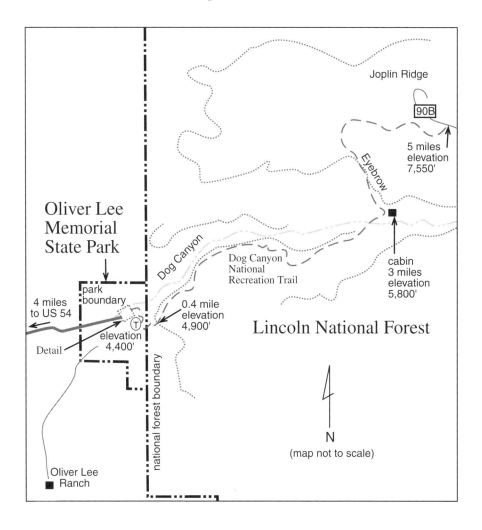

century and took advantage of the reliable water source and lush vegetation found in the box canyon.

When Europeans began moving into the region in the mid-1800s, the retaliating Apaches would raid their farms and ranches and then escape back into the canyon. Sometimes they would leave a trail for soldiers or settlers to follow, and then attack from above, sending rocks, arrows, and bullets down from atop a high bluff, scattering their pursuers. According to one story, in about 1850 a posse of European settlers followed a group of Apaches into the canyon but found only a dog that the Indians had left behind and thus gave the canyon its name. By the 1880s, the Apaches had been conquered—many killed or captured and forced onto reservations—and wide-scale European settlement of the area began.

In the mid-1880s, a Frenchman named Francois-Jean "Frenchy" Rochas started homesteading at the mouth of Dog Canyon. He built a rock cabin, raised cattle, and grew grapes, apples, cherries, plums, peaches, figs, and even olives. He also worked with a newcomer, Texas rancher Oliver Lee, to channel water from Dog Canyon to Lee's ranch, about a mile to the south. Frenchy mysteriously met his end just after Christmas in 1894, when he was found dead in his cabin, a bullet in the chest. Although the local authorities determined it was suicide, historians believe it is more likely that he was murdered by someone in a dispute over money or water.

This was not the only mysterious death in the area. In 1896, Lee and several other cattlemen were accused of the murder of a prominent New Mexico lawyer, Col. Albert Jennings Fountain, and his eight-year-old son

Frenchy's cabin, partially reconstructed, at Oliver Lee Memorial State Park

Henry. The bodies were never found, the case was circumstantial, and Lee and the others were acquitted. The mystery of the deaths, however, remains, and some of Fountain's descendants—convinced that Lee was somehow involved—expressed unhappiness when Oliver Lee Memorial State Park was established.

After Lee was acquitted, his ranching empire grew. In 1914, Lee and several other investors founded a cattle company that soon became the largest ranch in southern New Mexico, controlling almost 1 mililion acres. He also served in both houses of the New Mexico State Legislature. Lee died in 1941.

Visitors to Oliver Lee Memorial State Park today can learn about Lee, Frenchy Rochas, the Apaches and U.S. Cavalry soldiers who chased them, and the prehistoric Indians who lived here, in an extensive visitor center/museum, among the best in the New Mexico State Park System. In addition to historic artifacts, personal effects, photos, and other displays, there are exhibits on the archeological work done at the site of Frenchy's cabin in the late 1970s.

Photos identify the wildlife and plants that may be encountered in the park, and there is a collection of butterflies of Dog Canyon. Another exhibit shows the area's native plants and how they were used by Apaches for food and drink, medicines, clothing, and religious ceremonies. For instance, Apaches used the pods and seeds of mesquite to create an alcoholic drink similar to beer and the leaf buds of cottonwood trees as an ointment for burns and skin irritations. The various parts of the yucca had the most uses, ranging from food to clothing to shampoo.

West of the visitor center is Frenchy's two-room cabin, which has been partially reconstructed, and nearby is a grouping of "Indian wells." Oliver Lee's ranch headquarters have been rebuilt and authentically furnished as they would have been when Lee and his family lived there from 1893 to 1907. Some of the Lee family's personal belongings are also on display. The ranch house is located about 1 mile south of the visitor center and can be seen only on guided tours, which usually take place Saturday and Sunday afternoons.

The campground, just southwest of the mouth of Dog Canyon, is in typical Chihuahuan Desert terrain: dry and rocky, with desert grasses, mesquite, ocotillo, saltbush, yucca, and various species of cacti. Campsites have little shade but provide good views across the desert into the Tularosa Basin, with Dog Canyon and the Sacramento Mountains at your back.

There are two main trails—the easy one and the hard one. The easy 0.25-mile (one-way) Dog Canyon Interpretive Trail starts east of the visitor center and follows a spring-fed stream, with signs along the way that discuss the plants and other aspects of a riparian area. Bird- and butterfly-watching opportunities abound. The trail is partly dirt, with some sections of boardwalk and some wooden steps. Off this trail to the west, another short trail leads along the river to Frenchy's Cabin and several "Indian wells."

The Dog Canyon National Recreation Trail is for serious hikers. Fairly strenuous, it climbs about 3,500 feet from behind the visitor center at the mouth of Dog Canyon to an elevation of 7,500 feet at Joplin Ridge, leaving the park for the rugged terrain of the Lincoln National Forest. The trail is 5 miles (one-way) through mostly desert environment, rocky and steep in some sections. Sturdy hiking boots and drinking water are strongly recommended, and spring and fall are the best times to avoid the extreme summer heat and unpredictable winter weather. Allow a full day round-trip, or plan to camp on one of the rock benches along the way.

This trail is essentially the same one trod for over four thousand years—first by prehistoric Indians seeking a route into the mountains, and then by Apaches who used it as a hideout after raids on area ranches. The trail climbs the canyon's south slope for the first 3 miles, gaining about 1,400 feet, before arriving at a grassy oasis of cottonwoods and willows, the river, and nearby the remains of a small rock cabin built by ranchers in about 1900. Along the way, the views of the Tularosa Basin and the glistening white gypsum of White Sands National Monument get progressively better.

For those who want a shortened hike, this is a good spot to turn around. Hikers continuing will soon reach the Eyebrow, a steep, winding section of the trail across a 2,000-foot bluff, that in 1880 was the scene of a classic western battle. A detachment of the Ninth U.S. Cavalry had tracked an Apache raiding party to Dog Canyon, intending to capture them and send them back to the reservation. The Indians led the way up the trail, and when the soldiers were halfway up the steep slope the Apaches bombarded them with rocks, boulders, and gunfire from above, ending the chase. Next stop is Joplin Ridge, the end of the trail, with spectacular panoramic views.

A reliable water source in the desert always attracts wildlife. Here you are likely to see mule deer in winter, plus black-tailed jackrabbits, racoons, and skunks. Also present but not as frequently seen are coyotes, ringtails, kit foxes, and kangaroo rats. Bats also live at the park, including the California myotis, hoary bat, and big brown bat.

Numerous birds are heard and spotted, particularly along the river but also in the arid sections of the park. Frequently seen are black-throated and black-chinned sparrows, solitary vireos, cactus and canyon wrens, Gambel's quail, blue-gray gnatcatchers, ladder-backed woodpeckers, mourning doves, and roadrunners. Also seen, although not quite as commonly, are rufous and broad-tailed hummingbirds, northern orioles, mockingbirds, and great horned owls. The greatest number of birds will usually be seen from March through July.

The busiest time at the park is from February through April. The cacti, yucca, and wildflowers—including desert marigold, Indian paintbrush, yellow columbine, and firewheel—usually bloom from late March through midsummer. Cottonwoods turn golden yellow in the fall, usually in late October or November.

Summers here are hot, with days often in the mid- to upper 90s and sometimes exceeding 100 degrees F. Summer nights cool into the 60s. Winters usually have pleasantly warm days with highs in the 50s, and nights in the upper 20s. Spring is windy, with highs in the 70s, and lows in the 40s; and fall—particularly September and October—brings the best weather, with

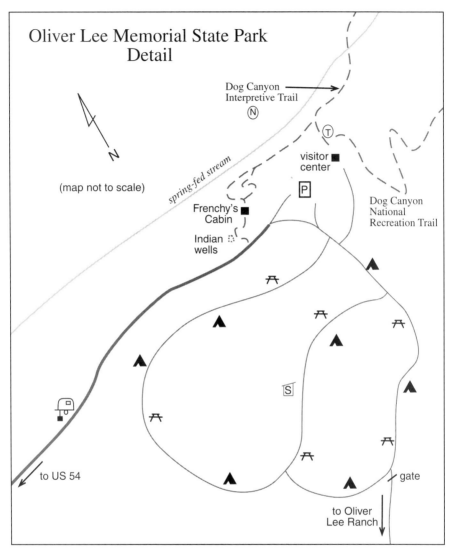

Oliver Lee Memorial State Park
Detail

Dog Canyon
Interpretive Trail

(N)

(map not to scale)

spring-fed stream

(T)

visitor
center

P

Dog Canyon
National
Recreation Trail

Frenchy's
Cabin

Indian
wells

N

S

to US 54

gate

to Oliver
Lee Ranch

highs in the upper 70s and 80s, and lows in the upper 40s and 50s.

Oliver Lee Memorial State Park often serves as a base camp for visiting the town of Alamogordo, 12 miles north via US 54. Anyone interested in space exploration will want to visit the Space Center, containing the International Space Hall of Fame, Clyde W. Tombaugh Space Theater, and several other facilities related to the history of space research. Also in town is a small zoo; and for fans of electric trains, there is the Toy Train Depot, with hundreds of electric trains. Most were made from the 1930s to the 1950s, but there are some toy trains from the 1800s. From Alamogordo, it is

White Sands National Monument is an easy day trip from Oliver Lee Memorial State Park.

15 miles southwest on US 70/82 to White Sands National Monument, an awe-inspiring expanse of pure white gypsum sand dunes. There is a 16-mile dunes loop drive and a visitor center with exhibits.

SANTA ROSA LAKE STATE PARK

Hours/Season: Overnight; year-round
Area: 1,500 land acres, 3,800 lake surface acres
Elevation: 3,900 feet
Facilities: Picnic tables, restrooms with showers, group shelter, 74 campsites (22 with electric hookups and 8 with electric and water hookups) and primitive camping, public telephone, boat ramp, RV dump station, phone: (505) 472-3110
Attractions: Boating, water-skiing, canoeing, fishing, swimming, hiking, wildlife viewing
Nearby: Blue Hole
Access: 7 miles north of Santa Rosa via NM 91

▲ Surrounded by low, rocky hills dotted with piñon and juniper, this pretty lake is not only popular with boaters and anglers but also attracts water-skiers, canoeists, and wildlife enthusiasts. The panoramic views seem to go forever. Created to provide irrigation water and flood control along the Pecos River, the level of the large lake varies considerably depending on irrigation needs. The dam, constructed in 1981, stands 212 feet high and is

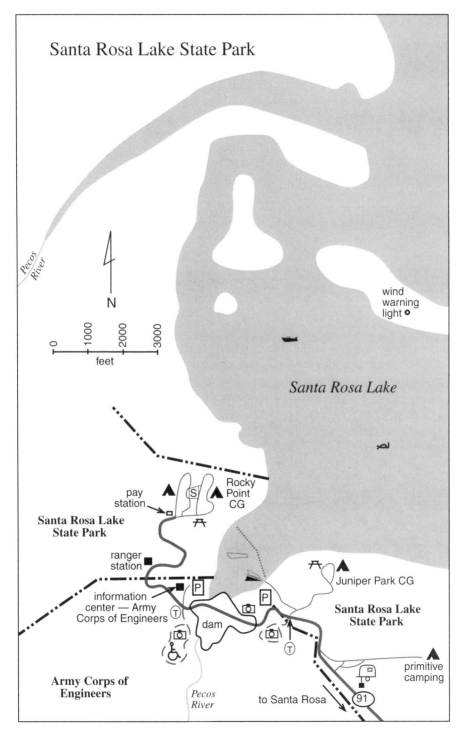

Santa Rosa Lake State Park

Pecos River

N

0 — 1000 — 2000 — 3000

feet

wind warning light ⊙

Santa Rosa Lake

Rocky Point CG

pay station →

S

Santa Rosa Lake State Park

ranger station

information center — Army Corps of Engineers

P

P

dam

Juniper Park CG

Santa Rosa Lake State Park

Army Corps of Engineers

Pecos River

to Santa Rosa

91

primitive camping

1,950 feet long. Facilities are managed jointly by the New Mexico State Parks System and the U.S. Army Corps of Engineers.

Anglers usually have excellent luck fishing for channel catfish, large-mouth and smallmouth bass, walleye, and crappie. There are also sunfish, yellow perch, and a few trout. The lake has no marinas. Most of the boats are of the fishing and skiing variety, 20 to 25 feet long, and are hauled over to the park's paved four-lane boat ramp. Those with canoes enjoy circling the lake's several islands and exploring its secluded coves, and occasionally a sailboat glides across the water. Although swimming is permitted, there are no designated swimming areas, and most of the beaches are rocky or covered with brush and other vegetation. Water temperatures in summer usually hit the mid-70s.

There are two short, easy trails, both paved and wheelchair-accessible, that are maintained by the U.S. Army Corps of Engineers. The Scenic Trail is a loop of about 0.5 mile that offers good panoramic views of the lake and picturesque rock outcroppings at its beginning and end, and in between meanders through a low forest of piñon, juniper, prairie grasses, and cholla and prickly pear cacti. The Handicap Trail is a loop of about 0.75 mile through similar terrain. It has one fairly long incline and offers views of the

Pronghorn antelope are sometimes seen near the entrance to Santa Rosa Lake State Park. (photo by Don MacCarter, courtesy New Mexico Dept. of Game and Fish)

Tarantula at Santa Rosa Lake State Park

rocky lakeshore through the trees. Both trails have wildflowers in spring and early summer.

There are also trails leading from Rocky Point Campground down a rocky slope to the lake, a distance of about 0.25 mile, although the distance varies depending on the lake level. This is a good area in which to catch a glimpse of mule deer, racoons, skunks, squirrels, foxes, or coyotes as they come in for water. There are also rare sightings of bobcats and mountain lions in the park, and pronghorn antelope are occasionally spotted along the road near the park entrance.

The lake attracts Canada geese, pelicans, ring-billed gulls, and a variety of ducks; and in recent years, bald eagles have had winter roosts on snags on the islands and along the lakeshore. Other birds observed in the park include barn swallows, mourning doves, scaled quail, and ospreys. Visitors climbing around the rocks should watch where they put their hands and feet to avoid disturbing rattlesnakes. There are also nonpoisonous bullsnakes and racers, and tarantulas are often seen in late summer and fall.

The park has two campgrounds, in rocky terrain of piñon, juniper, and cactus. Rocky Point Campground has showers and is open year-round, but Juniper Park Campground does not have showers and closes in winter. There is also a primitive camping area that is used primarily as an overflow. Both the state park and U.S. Army Corps of Engineers have offices at the lake. The Corps of Engineers office contains an information center, with exhibits on the lake's plants, animals, and recreational opportunities. It also has displays on the dam's construction, including archeological artifacts discovered during the work.

Summer is the busiest time at the park, when it is often packed with boaters and anglers on weekends. Wildlife viewing is best from fall through spring. Summer temperatures range from days in the 80s and 90s to nights in the 50s; and winter highs are usually in the 40s and 50s, with lows in the teens and 20s.

Although scuba diving is permitted in Santa Rosa Lake, most divers go into the town of Santa Rosa to the Blue Hole, an 81-foot-deep natural artesian spring. Averaging 80 feet across at the top, the bell-shaped pool expands to as much as 130 feet across at the bottom. The water is 64 degrees F year-round and has good visibility—some 80 feet when not disturbed.

SUMNER LAKE STATE PARK

Hours/Season: Overnight; year-round
Area: 6,700 land acres, 4,500 lake surface acres
Elevation: 4,300 feet
Facilities: Picnic tables, group shelters, restrooms with showers, 41 campsites (18 with electric and water hookups and a few also with sewer hookups) and primitive camping for up to 400 units, boat ramps, courtesy dock, public telephone, RV dump station, phone: (505) 355-2541
Attractions: Boating, water-skiing, swimming, fishing, wildlife viewing
Nearby: Fort Sumner State Monument, grave of outlaw Billy the Kid
Access: From Fort Sumner take US 84 northwest 10 miles, and then head west on NM 203 for 6 miles

This sparkling blue lake, with a rocky shoreline and gently rolling hillsides of juniper, provides a refreshing change from the flat grasslands of New Mexico's eastern plains. The lake attracts boaters and anglers, and the park serves as a base for visiting the historic sites of the area, particularly the grave of notorious outlaw Billy the Kid.

Created by damming the Pecos River, Sumner Lake provides irrigation water for a large area, causing the lake level to fluctuate greatly. Nevertheless, boaters flock to Sumner Lake from May through September. Both powerboats and sailboats use the lake, and windsurfers take advantage of the spring winds. There are no horsepower restrictions. The lake does not have a marina, and no boat rentals are available.

Swimming is permitted, although there are no designated swimming beaches. One of the best spots for a swim is just north of the boat ramp near the main campground. As the lake level changes, sandy beaches appear, and those with boats can often find secluded little coves with protected swimming areas.

While swimmers, water-skiers, operators of personal watercraft, and sailboaters use the lake in the warmer months, anglers are here year-round. The most frequently caught fish are walleye, crappie, and white bass; but there are also channel catfish, black bass, and bluegill in the lake.

Camping runs the gamut from full RV hookups to primitive lakeshore camping. The developed campsites are mostly well-spaced, with good lake views and easy walking access to the lake. Although not exactly a forest, there are trees, including junipers and cottonwoods, plus prairie grasses and several varieties of cactus. Unfortunately, there are also unpleasant little sand burrs. Campers seeking developed sites can choose from among four separate campgrounds. The two on the lake, just above the dam, have RV hookups; the two along the Pecos River just below the dam do not. The East Side Campground, on the east side of the lake, offers especially good views of sunset over the lake. There are practically unlimited possibilities for primitive camping along the river and lakeshore.

All this water attracts migrating waterfowl each winter, including geese,

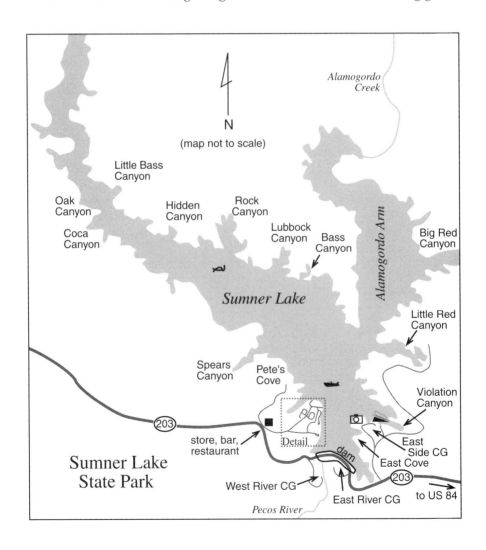

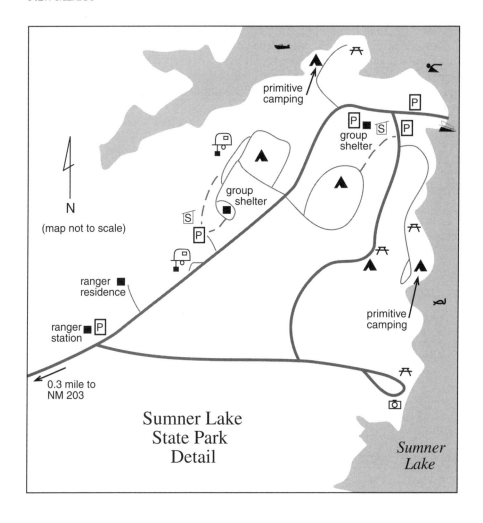

primitive
camping

group
shelter

group
shelter

ranger
residence

ranger
station

0.3 mile to
NM 203

primitive
camping

N

(map not to scale)

Sumner Lake
State Park
Detail

Sumner
Lake

pelicans, and various ducks. Watch for raptors, such as osprey, a variety of hawks, and both golden and bald eagles. Also seen in the park are racoons, squirrels, porcupines, skunks, rabbits, fox, and lizards. Almost everyone visiting in the fall will see deer.

The park has no hiking trails, just a few paths to get from the campgrounds to the lake or restrooms. There is a restaurant/bar/store just outside the park's western boundary, 0.3 mile from the park office.

Sumner Lake is busiest from Memorial Day to Labor Day. Although the campsites with RV hookups are first to fill, campers can always find someplace to stake a claim. Those visiting in spring will see wildflowers and a few cactus in bloom. One of the best times for camping is fall, when the summer crowds have gone, days are still warm, and wildlife is abundant. Summer temperatures range from the upper 80s and 90s during the day to the low 60s at night. During winter, highs are usually in the 50s, while lows drop into the 20s. Both spring and fall bring highs in the 70s and lows in the upper 30s and 40s.

Those interested in the history of the West will want to visit Fort Sumner State Monument, located 2 miles east of the town of Fort Sumner on Billy the Kid Road. This fort housed troops that guarded thousands of Navajos who were captured and forced onto a reservation near here. Although the buildings are gone, a museum at the site tells the story of this rather sad chapter of American history. About 0.25 mile east of the state monument is Old Fort Sumner Museum, which has exhibits on the fort and the area. Behind the museum is the grave of Billy the Kid and his original tombstone, which is held securely in place with metal straps after being stolen and recovered several times.

Tombstone of outlaw Billy the Kid is held down with metal straps near Sumner Lake State Park

SOUTH-WESTERN NEW MEXICO

This land of desert and mountains was likely the first part of New Mexico to be seen by Europeans, when Spanish conquistadores arrived in 1540 seeking gold and other riches of the New World. Gold also was responsible for the appearance of numerous boomtowns in the nineteenth century, some of which remain today as ghost towns. The rugged San Mateo and Mogollon Mountains and the Black Range soar above the desert, where temperatures also soar, often to over 100 degrees F during the long summers. Rocks dominate the landscape and several state parks as well, including one that encourages visitors to take home what they find. The Rio Grande, which cuts through the eastern third of this quadrant, has helped create four recreation parks, including one that contains the state's largest lake and becomes New Mexico's second-biggest population center on Memorial Day and Fourth of July weekends. In the northern reaches of this region is a quiet mountain park, and along the state's southern boundary is a park dedicated to the last invasion of the continental United States by foreign troops, when Mexican revolutionary Pancho Villa attacked the tiny New Mexico town of Columbus. A number of the region's parks have elaborate cactus gardens that burst with color each spring. The state's second largest city, Las Cruces, is the region's biggest population and trade center.

CABALLO LAKE STATE PARK

Hours/Season: Overnight; year-round
Area: 5,300 land acres, 11,500 lake surface acres

Opposite: *Park volunteer Harold Melton shows visitors rocks found at Rockhound State Park.*

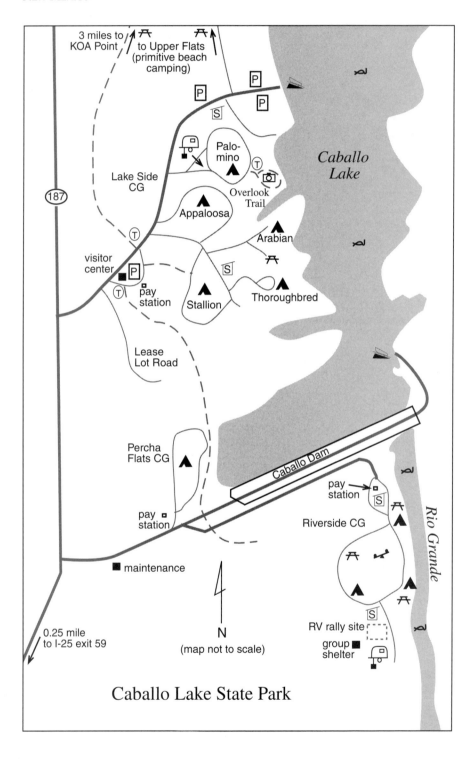

3 miles to
KOA Point

to Upper Flats
(primitive beach
camping)

P

P

P

S

Palo-
mino

T

Lake Side
CG

Appaloosa

Overlook
Trail

Arabian

Caballo
Lake

(187)

T

visitor
center

P

T

pay
station

S

Stallion

Thoroughbred

Lease
Lot Road

Percha
Flats CG

Caballo Dam

pay
station

S

pay
station

Riverside CG

pay
station

maintenance

N

(map not to scale)

Rio Grande

RV rally site

group
shelter

0.25 mile
to I-25 exit 59

Caballo Lake State Park

Elevation: 4,100 feet

Facilities: Visitor center, interpretive exhibits, picnic tables, group shelter, RV rally site, two boat ramps, playground, restrooms with showers, 170 campsites (64 with electric and water hookups) and unlimited beach camping along the lakeshore, public telephone, RV dump station, phone: (505) 743-3942

Attractions: Fishing, boating, water-skiing, swimming, bird-watching, hiking

Nearby: Town of Truth or Consequences, Elephant Butte Lake State Park, and Percha Dam State Park

Access: 16 miles south of Truth or Consequences via I-25 exit 59 and NM 187

In the shadow of the rugged Caballo Mountains, this long, skinny lake surrounded by Chihuahuan Desert provides ample opportunities for fishing and water sports. Relatively quiet and family-oriented, the park also has several hiking trails and good bird-watching possibilities.

Another in a series of lake parks created by the damming of the Rio Grande, Caballo Lake has a surface area of more than 11,500 acres, making it New Mexico's third largest state park. Created in the late 1930s with the construction of an earth-filled dam 96 feet high by 4,558 feet long, the lake's main purpose is to catch and store water released by Elephant Butte Dam (25 miles upstream) during electric generation. The water is released in the summer for irrigation. When full, the lake is 18 miles long.

Primitive camping on a peninsula at Caballo Lake State Park

The main activity here is fishing, primarily for white bass and walleye, although anglers also catch black bass, crappie, catfish, northern pike, and sunfish. Outside the main section of the park but close by are several fishing supply stores.

Although most boating here is for getting to the best fishing spot, the lake also attracts small sailboats and windsurfers, especially in spring. Canoeists often put into the Rio Grande just south of Elephant Butte Dam near the town of Williamsburg and paddle down to Caballo Lake, a distance of about 10 miles. There is no designated swimming beach, but the best swimming is usually just west of the dam and in the Upper Flats, which is on the north edge of the main park campgrounds.

There are developed campsites on a bluff overlooking the lake, with all the usual amenities, and even a few trees. There is also a lesser-developed beach camping area to the north of the main section, which has picnic tables, grills, and chemical toilets, and where campers can set up their tents or park their RVs wherever they want.

The bulk of the park's facilities are in this main section, on the west side of the lake, just north of the dam. Another campground is located along the Rio Grande just south of the dam. It has more trees—cottonwoods, black willow, green ash, and Arizona sycamore—and is more secluded than the lake section of the park. It is also here that the park's RV rally site is located—the only one in the New Mexico State Park System—with a large group shelter, huge barbecue grills, and a gated campground that can accommodate over 200 recreational vehicles.

Trails at Caballo Lake are more for walking from place to place than serious hiking, and all of the park's 5.5 miles of sandy trails are considered easy. The 0.25-mile Overlook Trail is a loop over a grassy and cactus-studded knoll that offers good views out across the lake. Another trail heads north from the campgrounds about 3 miles to an area called KOA Point, which, not coincidentally, is near a KOA campground. A branch of this trail also goes south of the visitor center to the lake. The park also has several well-tended cactus gardens, with yucca, agave, ocotillo, prickly pear, mesquite, and other desert plants.

Bird-watching is most successful mid-week when there are fewer boats on the lake, although it is generally not quite as good as at nearby Percha Dam State Park. In recent years, a breeding pair of bald eagles have made Caballo Lake their winter home. Also seen are golden eagles, northern goshawks, double-crested cormorants, common loons, snowy egrets, scaled quail, sandhill cranes, American white pelicans, and roadrunners. There are dozens of songbirds, several species of hummingbirds, and numerous geese and ducks.

Mammals include a seemingly endless parade of rock squirrels and cottontail rabbits, plus the park is home to coyotes, wolves, foxes, racoons, mule deer, and an occasional black bear. There are also rattlesnakes, lizards, frogs, and turtles.

The small visitor center has displays on archeology of the area and historic photos from the construction of Caballo Dam. There are color photos

Sandhill cranes are among the birds sometimes seen at Caballo Lake State Park. (photo by Don MacCarter, courtesy New Mexico Dept. of Game and Fish)

of the birds, fish, and plants of the park to help with identification, and there is a sandbox with stamps to create footprints of the park's wildlife, including deer, bald eagles, frogs, and snapping turtles. Annual events at the park include several fishing tournaments, including a father-and-child fishing tournament on Father's Day and a youth's fishing derby in late September. Each April, Earth Day is celebrated with tree plantings.

The busiest season at the park is summer, when campsites with electric hookups fill quickly, especially on weekends. Summer temperatures usually hit the 90s and sometimes exceed 100 degrees F during the day, but drop into the 60s at night. Fall is pretty, and the park is less busy. The water is still warm enough for swimming in October, and air temperatures are usually in the mid-70s during the day and the upper 40s and low 50s at night. Winters are quiet in the park, making this a particularly good time for bird watching, with daytime temperatures in the 50s, and nights in the 20s and 30s. Spring can be windy, with high temperatures ranging from the 60s to low 80s, and lows from the upper 30s to low 50s. The cactus often produce their best flower display in late March or early April.

Percha Dam State Park, which is discussed in its own section of this book, is located 2 miles south of Caballo Lake via NM 187. About 20 miles north of Caballo Lake State Park's visitor center, via I-25, is the town of Truth or Consequences and Elephant Butte Lake State Park, which are both discussed in this book in the section on Elephant Butte Lake State Park.

CITY OF ROCKS STATE PARK

Hours/Season: Overnight; year-round
Area: 680 land acres
Elevation: 5,200 feet
Facilities: Visitor center, botanical garden, picnic tables, nature trail, restrooms with showers, 62 campsites (10 with electric and water hookups), group barbecue area, public telephone, RV dump station, phone: (505) 536-2800
Attractions: Photography, hiking, rock climbing, bird-watching, interpretive programs, historic exhibits
Access: From Deming take US 180 northwest 24 miles, and then go northeast on NM 61 for 4 miles to the park access road

A fantasy land of huge boulders, this geological wonder looks out of place in the southern New Mexico desert, as if these stone skyscrapers were abandoned by some ancient race of giants, or perhaps created by the special effects wizards in Hollywood for some other-worldly adventure. But no, these are the real thing—ash spewed from volcanos some thirty-three million years ago hardened into rock and sculpted by the forces of wind, water, and blowing desert sand into the fanciful and bizarre shapes we see today.

Most park visitors come primarily for the rocks—to climb over them, photograph them, camp among them, or just sit and gaze at them while listening to the wind whistling through. Some let their imaginations run wild, seeing this rock pile as so many bowling pins, or, as those who named it, a silent city. To those with active imaginations, individual boulders become bears, turtles, camels, rockets, temples, ice cream cones, or people, and the illusions change as the sun moves across the sky, producing constantly changing shadows.

Although Hollywood may not have had anything to do with the creation of this other-worldly place, producers did know a good thing when they saw it. *The Tall Texan,* starring Lloyd Bridges and Lee J. Cobb, was filmed here in 1953, three years before City of Rocks was given state park status.

The first humans to gaze upon this odd landscape are believed to have been the Mimbres Indians, who lived in what is now southwestern New Mexico from about 950 to 1200. Because there was little water here even then, it is unlikely that the Mimbres had a permanent home at this particular site, but pieces of pottery, arrowheads, and holes in the rock where crops were ground prove that they spent time here and were not just passing through. Artifacts, including a rusted buckle, show that Spanish conquistadores were also here, probably in the sixteenth or seventeenth century. There are also curious crosses carved on rocks that some say must point the way to buried treasure.

Today's visitors may not find any treasure, but they will be comfortable

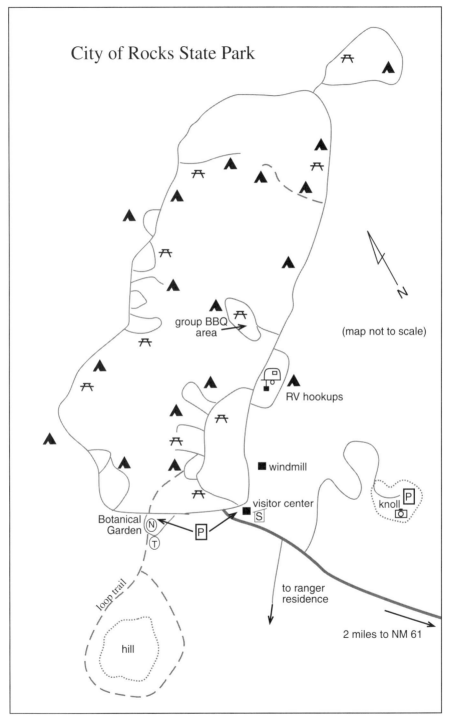

City of Rocks State Park

(map not to scale)

group BBQ area

RV hookups

windmill

visitor center

knoll

Botanical Garden

loop trail

hill

to ranger residence

2 miles to NM 61

N

in the park's campgrounds, either tucked among the boulders and juniper trees of the "city," or in the new RV section, which is more open but has electric and water hookups. Sites in the RV section are spacious, fairly level, and more suited to large RVs than the campground among the rocks, where finding a level site can be a challenge.

The well-tended Botanical Garden has neatly labeled cacti, ocotillo, yucca, and other desert plants, and just off the back of the garden is the beginning of a 0.75-mile loop trail. Easy, with almost no elevation change, the trail circles a low knoll just to the southwest of the main grouping of boulders, offering good views of the rocks and surrounding desert, with its grasses, mesquite, and prickly pear cactus. Although this is the park's only officially designated trail, hikers can travel for several miles, walking around and over the boulders, or along the 1.5-mile dirt road that circles the park's clustered namesake "city of rocks."

More than seventy-five species of birds have been spotted in the park, including golden eagles, common ravens, Swainson's hawks, greater roadrunners, red-tailed hawks, prairie falcons, scaled quail, cactus wrens, yellow warblers, Scott's orioles, black-throated sparrows, yellow-rumped warblers, eastern meadowlarks, western tanagers, black-chinned hummingbirds, and great horned owls. Mammals you are likely to see include cottontail rabbits, black-tailed jackrabbits, rock squirrels, kangaroo rats, porcupines, and coyotes. Also in the park are numerous lizards—mostly whiptails but some collared—and desert box turtles, plus bullsnakes and western diamondback and prairie rattlesnakes, which are seen mostly during the summer.

Desert plants among the boulders at City of Rocks State Park

A new visitor center has exhibits on geology, focusing on how these rocks were formed, as well as the archeology, plants, and animals of the park. Monthly campfire programs are planned, usually the Saturday evening before the full moon, with music, storytelling, and other activities. Each year, usually in mid-May, the park celebrates Heritage Preservation Day with guided tours, demonstrations, and other activities.

For a distant view of the rock formations, seen in contrast to the surrounding desert, drive the 0.25-mile (one-way) dirt road up to Observation Point, in the southeast corner of the park. From this perspective, the formations look almost surreal.

Spring and fall are the most popular times at the park, with moderate temperatures, although spring can be windy. During spring, which is the busiest time, high temperatures are usually in the 60s and 70s, with lows dropping into the 30s; while fall temperatures are a bit warmer. Wildflowers and cactus are often in bloom in April and May. Summers are hot, often reaching the upper 90s and sometimes exceeding 100 degrees F, with nights dropping into the 50s. Winters have pleasant daytime temperatures, with highs usually in the 50s, and nights in the 20s and occasionally the teens.

ELEPHANT BUTTE LAKE STATE PARK

Hours/Season: Overnight; year-round
Area: 24,500 land acres, 36,500 lake surface acres
Elevation: 4,500 feet
Facilities: Visitor center, interpretive exhibits, boat ramps, courtesy docks, marinas, store, restaurants, bar, cabin rentals, picnic tables, group shelter, playground, restrooms with showers, 127 campsites (85 with electric and water hookups) and unlimited primitive camping along shoreline, nature trails, public telephone, RV dump stations, phone: (505) 744-5421
Attractions: Boating, water-skiing, sailing, canoeing, kayaking, fishing, swimming, hiking, bird-watching
Nearby: Truth or Consequences, Caballo Lake State Park, and Percha Dam State Park
Access: Park headquarters are 5 miles north of Truth or Consequences via I-25 exit 83

New Mexico's largest and most popular state park, Elephant Butte is a huge reservoir that serves as the state's main water sports destination, offering opportunities for just about every form of water-based recreation, from water-skiing to scuba diving to canoeing. It has sandy beaches, quiet little coves, full-service marinas, and enough open water for cabin cruisers and houseboats.

Efforts to dam the Rio Grande to provide a reliable source of water for area farms began in the 1890s but were stopped by the United States Supreme

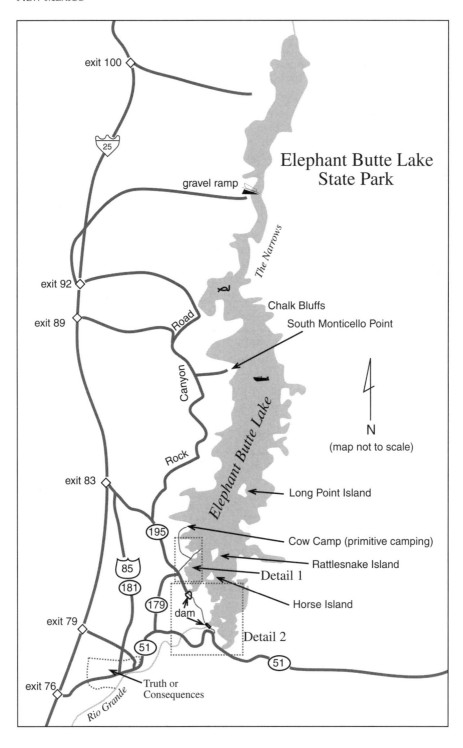

Elephant Butte Lake
State Park

exit 100

25

gravel ramp

The Narrows

Chalk Bluffs

South Monticello Point

Road

Canyon

Rock

exit 92

exit 89

Elephant Butte Lake

N
(map not to scale)

Long Point Island

exit 83

195

85

181

179

dam

51

51

exit 79

exit 76

Rio Grande

Truth or
Consequences

Cow Camp (primitive camping)

Rattlesnake Island

Detail 1

Horse Island

Detail 2

This island gave Elephant Butte Lake State Park its name. Some can see an elephant facing left in the formation.

Court after protests from residents of El Paso, Texas, and Mexico, who insisted that they also had a right to use of the Rio Grande's water. However, agreements on water sharing were reached, and the dam was finally completed in 1916, at a cost of $5 million. It was 306 feet high and 1,674 feet long and created a reservoir that covered about 40,000 acres with 250 miles of shoreline. At the time, it was the largest humanmade lake in the world. A hydroelectric power plant was added in 1940, and Elephant Butte Lake became a state park in 1965.

The lake is named for a rock formation that resembles an elephant, at least to some observers who see the left side of its head, with a prominent ear, and its trunk curled by a foot. The formation, which is actually the eroded core of an ancient volcano, is an island in the lake, just northeast of the dam. One of the best places to see the "elephant" is from the parking lot of the Damsite Restaurant.

Although not known when the rock formation and lake were named, this area once had real elephants. Fossils of a primitive ancestor of today's elephants, the stegomastodon, have been found just west of the lake. The animal was about 7 feet tall and stocky, with long upper tusks.

Boating is the primary activity here, and with a lake some 38 to 42 miles long and up to 4 miles wide, there is plenty of room for every imaginable type of watercraft, from the tiniest inflatable to the largest and most luxurious cabin cruiser. A number of no-wake areas make canoeing and kayaking

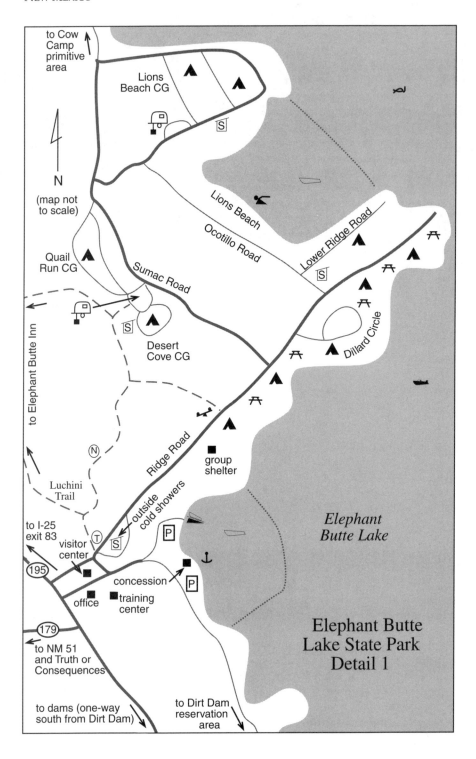

to Cow Camp primitive area

Lions Beach CG

N

(map not to scale)

Quail Run CG

Sumac Road

Lions Beach

Ocotillo Road

Lower Ridge Road

S

S

Desert Cove CG

Dillard Circle

to Elephant Butte Inn

N

Luchini Trail

Ridge Road

outside cold showers

group shelter

to I-25 exit 83

visitor center

T

S

P

195

concession

P

office

training center

179

to NM 51 and Truth or Consequences

Elephant Butte Lake

Elephant Butte Lake

Elephant Butte Lake State Park Detail 1

to dams (one-way south from Dirt Dam)

to Dirt Dam reservation area

fun and safe, and canoes are also put into the Rio Grande just south of Elephant Butte Dam and paddled down to Caballo Lake, a distance of about 10 miles. Personal watercraft and ski boats are popular, and colorful sailboats and sailboards are often seen on the lake. Rentals are available for those who neglected to bring a boat of their own. The lake has good sandy beaches for swimming within easy walking distance of the campgrounds, as well as secluded boat-in only coves.

Anglers catch big bass—largemouth, smallmouth, striped, and white. The state record bass—a fifty-four-pound, eight-ounce striped bass—was caught on April Fool's Day, 1992. Record catfish and sunfish have been taken, and anglers also catch walleye, crappie, and bluegill. In all, close to two dozen fish species have been found in the lake, which was first stocked in 1919, just three years after completion of the dam. Trout fishing is good in the Rio Grande south of the dam.

Quieter times at the park—winter and mid-week in summer—are best for seeing wildlife, and those with boats have the advantage of being able to seek out the undeveloped and lesser-used areas. Bald eagles are often seen in the winter, particularly in January. Also seen in winter are numerous species of ducks, ring-billed gulls, and an occasional American white pelican. Bird-watchers also have a good chance of seeing red-tailed hawks, great horned owls, black-chinned hummingbirds, great blue herons, scaled and Gambel's quail, mourning doves, lesser yellowlegs, killdeer, western grebes, rufous-crowned sparrows, barn swallows, western bluebirds, and double-crested cormorants. The park is also home to cottontail rabbits, black-tailed jackrabbits, an occasional deer, rattlesnakes, and numerous lizards.

Camping here can take several forms. There are paved sites with electricity and water hookups and shelters with picnic tables. There are also developed sites without hookups, and many of these are on a bluff overlooking the lake. Those who want to rough it can camp along the beach but should be careful to avoid getting their vehicles stuck in the soft sand. Plans call for construction of a new campground with 180 sites, all with electric and water hookups, at South Monticello Point.

Although most of the park is desert terrain, carpeted with grasses, cactus, yucca, mesquite, and similar desert plants, the Winding Road Day-Use Area has an abundance of tall trees shading the picnic tables that provide views out over the lake. There are numerous massive stone walkways, retaining walls, and other structures that were built in the 1930s.

The park has two nature trails and a short hiking trail, plus miles of beach to stroll along. The Luchini Trail is a triangular 1.6-mile loop that connects the visitor center/park entrance to Quail Run Campground and Elephant Butte Inn, one of several lodgings and restaurants serving the park. The sandy trail is flat and easy as it winds through desert grasses and cactus.

One 0.5-mile leg of the Luchini trail is an interpretive nature trail, with signs identifying plants, such as honey mesquite, prickly pear cactus, soaptree yucca, Mormon tea, desert sage, desert willow, and desert Christmas cactus. A brochure, available at the visitor center, describes the plants and discusses their uses. The Old Butte Nature Trail is located at the southern end of the lake, near the Damsite Restaurant. A 0.5-mile loop, it is steep and rocky, with signs identifying a variety of desert plants. It leads to a high overlook that provides wonderful panoramic views of the lake and its namesake island rock formation.

The park's visitor center has exhibits on the geology, fish, and birds of the area, plus historic photos of the dam construction and local towns and military posts that preceded the lake's creation. Also on display is a relief map of the park and a cast of the jawbone of a tyrannosaurus dinosaur that was discovered in the park in 1983.

Several hundred special events take place at the park each year, including more than a dozen sailing regattas and over forty fishing tournaments. The Balloon Regatta, which takes place in late April, has fifty hot air balloonists flying over the lake, and then touching down (called splash and dash) to pick up a baton from teammates in a boat. The balloonists then fly off to drop the baton on a target before landing. The park also hosts a spectacular fireworks display, reflected in the lake for a double show, over the July

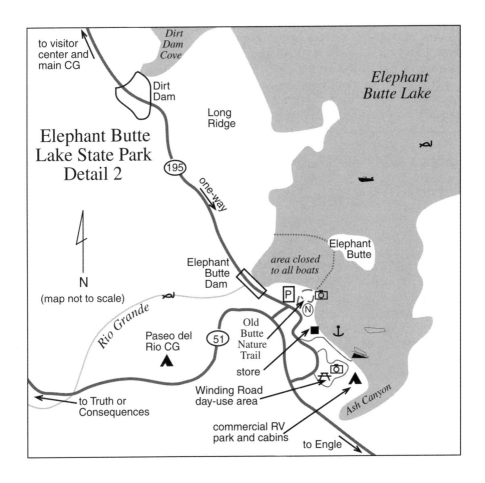

Elephant Butte Lake State Park
Detail 2

to visitor center and main CG

Dirt Dam Cove

Dirt Dam

Long Ridge

Elephant Butte Lake

195

one-way

N
(map not to scale)

Rio Grande

Elephant Butte Dam

area closed to all boats

Elephant Butte

P

Paseo del Rio CG

51

Old Butte Nature Trail

store

Winding Road day-use area

to Truth or Consequences

commercial RV park and cabins

Ash Canyon

to Engle

Fourth weekend, and drag boat races during July, August, and September.

Although popular year-round, the park's peak season is from April through Labor Day, with the period from Memorial Day through July the busiest. Memorial Day and Fourth of July weekends are jammed with up to 120,000 people, which, if Elephant Butte State Park were a city, would make it the state's second largest. Weekdays are the best times to avoid crowds, and September and October can be wonderful, with clear skies, warm air and water temperatures, and relatively few people.

June and July are the hottest months, with highs usually in the 90s and lows in the 60s. By fall, days are still in the 70s and low 80s, while nights are dropping into the upper 40s and 50s. Winters see daytime temperatures in the 50s and low 60s, with nights dropping to just above or just below freezing. Spring days are generally windy, with highs in the upper 60s and 70s, and lows mostly in the 40s. Although the area receives an average of only 9 inches of precipitation each year, over two inches of that falls in August. Each winter sees a dusting of snow, but it usually melts quickly.

Several miles south of the park is the town of Truth or Consequences, or T or C as it is known locally, which was named for the radio and television game show of the 1940s and 1950s. The community holds a fiesta each spring to celebrate the changing of the town's name from Hot Springs to Truth or Consequences in 1950. There are mineral baths fed by the area's hot springs and two small museums—one devoted to the history of the area from prehistoric times to the present, and the other dedicated to antique and classic automobiles. South of Truth or Consequences are two more state parks, Caballo Lake and Percha Dam, which are discussed in their own sections of this book.

LEASBURG DAM STATE PARK

Hours/Season: Overnight; year-round
Area: 140 land acres
Elevation: 4,200 feet
Facilities: Picnic tables, group shelter, playground, restrooms with showers, 27 campsites (18 with electric and water hookups) and primitive camping for about 10 tents or RVs, botanical garden, public telephone, RV dump station, phone: (505) 524-4068
Attractions: Fishing, canoeing, hiking, bird-watching
Nearby: Fort Selden State Monument, White Sands National Monument
Access: Go 15 miles north of Las Cruces on I-25; get off at exit 19 and take NM 157 west to the park entrance

▲ A quiet desert oasis, this state park provides peace and relaxation, beautiful cactus gardens, several short trails, and opportunities for fishing and canoeing in the Rio Grande. Built in 1908, the Leasburg Diversion Dam diverts water from the Rio Grande to irrigate farmland in the upper Mesilla

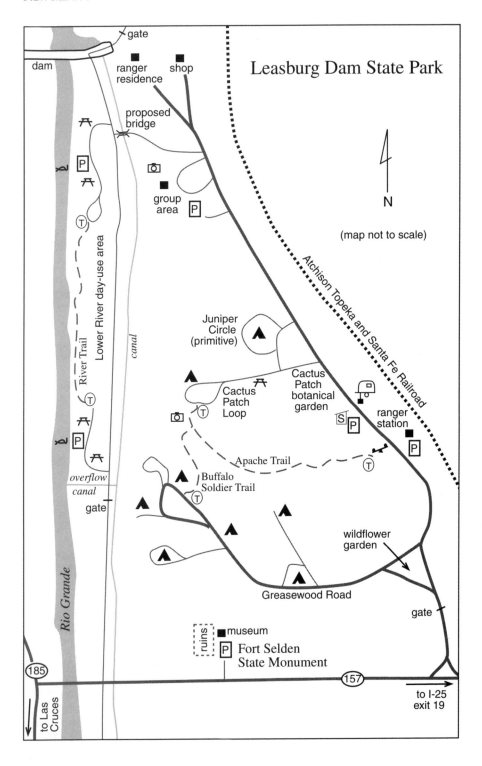

Leasburg Dam State Park

Valley. The name Leasburg comes from a trading center, located about 3.5 miles southeast of the dam, that was established in the 1860s and named for its first postmaster, Adolphe Lea.

The trails here are used mostly for after-dinner or early-morning walks, or as shortcuts to various sections of the park. The Apache Trail runs 0.33 mile (one-way) from the west end of Cactus Patch Campground to the playground, meandering through a sandy desert of creosote bush, prickly pear, desert Christmas cactus, cholla, and ocotillo. There are two benches along the way, with views out over an arroyo toward the Rio Grande and out toward the Sierra de Las Uras mountains. The trail is fairly easy, with several steep but short sections.

Buffalo Soldier Trail branches off of Apache Trail, near its west end, and goes through an arroyo for about 0.2 mile (one-way) to connect Cactus Patch Campground with Greasewood Road Campground. The 0.25-mile (one-way) River Trail connects the two river day-use areas, following the Rio Grande through a riparian area of willows, tamarisk, and mesquite.

The large, well-tended Cactus Patch botanical garden contains numerous species of cactus and other desert plants, with identifying labels. These include huge yucca and agave, cholla, cow's tongue, prickly pear, mesquite, creosote bush, and ocotillo. In addition to the Cactus Patch, there are a number of smaller cactus gardens throughout the park, which look spectacular in spring when the cactus are in bloom.

The park makes a good put-in or take-out point for canoeing the Rio Grande, coming downriver about 45 miles from Percha Dam State Park, or going downriver from Leasburg Dam about 10 miles to Las Cruces. The river is mostly calm, with little white water. Fishing is best in spring and summer, when the river is at its highest, and anglers catch channel catfish, white bass, and some walleye.

Among animals seen in the park are cottontail rabbits, black-tailed jackrabbits, rock squirrels, and coyotes. Deer are spotted occasionally along the river, and in recent years there has been one reported sighting of a black bear. Birds known to frequent the park include sandhill cranes, roadrunners, Gambel's quail, ladder-backed woodpeckers, and pyrrhuloxias (also called desert cardinals).

Yucca in bloom at Leasburg Dam State Park

Special events at the park include Sky Safaris, which occur two or three times each year, with local astronomers leading sky-watching sessions. Each October, petroglyph tours to area archeological sites are based in the park; and during Historic Preservation Week in mid-May, the park, in conjunction with Fort Selden State Monument, presents programs on the area's pioneer days, including black powder and other living history demonstrations. A convention of off-road-vehicle enthusiasts each February brings some 200 four-wheel-drive vehicles to the park as a home base for explorations of nearby Bureau of Land Management (BLM) property.

Summers here are busy on weekends, with anglers and picnickers from Las Cruces, but quiet during the week. Summer temperatures range from highs in the 90s or above to lows in the 60s. There are usually more campers from fall through spring. Fall is especially pretty along the river, and in spring the desert comes alive with blooming cactus and wildflowers. High temperatures in fall are usually in the 70s, while lows are in the 40s. Winters are pleasantly warm, with highs mostly in the 50s, although at night it usually drops into the 20s. In spring, days warm into the 60s and 70s, while nights are in the 30s and 40s.

The state park makes a good base for visiting area attractions, including Fort Selden State Monument, 0.5 mile west of the park. Established in 1865 to protect settlers from Apaches and outlaws, it served that purpose until 1891.

Reenactment at Fort Selden State Monument near Leasburg Dam State Park

Today, the adobe ruins of the fort can be toured, and a visitor center/museum has exhibits on frontier military life in the late nineteenth century. Living history demonstrations are scheduled on most summer weekends.

About 60 miles to the east, via I-25 and US 70, is White Sands National Monument, a spectacularly beautiful expanse of pure white gypsum sand dunes. There is a visitor center with exhibits on how the dunes were formed and continue to change, and a 16-mile loop drive that takes you into the dunes. You are also invited to get personal with the dunes, by climbing them, running your fingers through the sand, or taking off your shoes and wiggling your toes in the cool, white grains of gypsum.

MANZANO MOUNTAINS STATE PARK

Hours/Season: Overnight; May through October
Area: 168 land acres
Elevation: 7,600 feet
Facilities: Picnic tables, group shelter, restrooms (no showers), 18 campsites (6 sites with electric hookups), nature trail, RV dump station, phone: (505) 847-2820
Attractions: Hiking, photography, wildlife viewing, bird-watching
Nearby: Salinas Pueblo Missions National Monument
Access: 16 miles northwest of Mountainair via NM highways 55 and 131

At the foot of the Manzano Mountains, in a forest of ponderosa pine, piñon, and alligator juniper, this small, peaceful park offers an escape from civilization, as well as a lush, green change from the state's many desert parks. There is hiking and wildlife viewing, but this is such a pretty little park you may want to just sit in the campground and put your feet up, listening to the wind blowing through the tall pines.

Manzano is Spanish for "apple tree," and the mountains as well as a nearby village were named for apple trees that were growing here when the village was established by Spanish colonizers in 1829. Local legend had held that the trees were planted by Spanish missionaries in the seventeenth century, when Manzano was still the site of an Indian pueblo, and were the oldest apple orchards in North America. Tree-ring studies, however, have found no evidence of trees planted before 1800.

Campsites are well-spaced, shaded by a thick forest of pines and junipers. There are relatively level sites for RVs, and several attractive tent sites among the trees. There is one designated wheelchair-accessible site. There are also horseshoe pits near the group shelter—bring your own horseshoes. The nearest public telephone is in the village of Torreon, about 9 miles north.

The park has about 3 miles of interconnecting hiking trails and a marked nature trail, and it offers easy access into the Cibola National Forest. Trails wind through the forest, circling the main section of the park, where

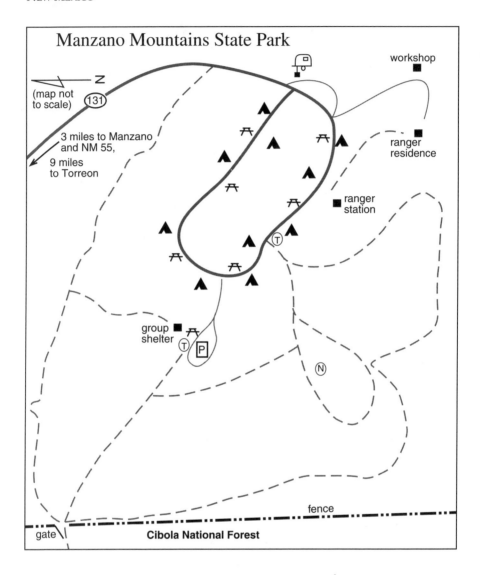

Manzano Mountains State Park

N
(map not to scale) 131

3 miles to Manzano and NM 55,

9 miles to Torreon

workshop

ranger residence

ranger station

ranger residence

group shelter

T P

N

fence

gate

Cibola National Forest

the campground, office, and other facilities are located. Easy-to-moderate, the trails are fairly flat and bordered with shrub oak. Three trail sections lead to a gate into the national forest, where hikers, mountain bikers, and horseback riders can access miles of forest trails into the Manzano Mountains.

The park's easy 0.5-mile nature trail makes a loop into the forest, with a spur connecting to the rest of the park's trail system. A trail guide, available at the park office, discusses the trees and other plants. Watch for the alligator juniper, named for the checkered pattern on the bark of old trees. Also along the nature trail is evidence of a forest fire in 1978 that devastated this area, which is now being healed with new growth.

Quari Mission ruins, part of Salinas Pueblo Missions National Monument near Manzano Mountains State Park

Most park visitors will see wildlife of some sort, such as squirrels, gophers, and racoons. Mule deer are often observed from the trails or the campground. More elusive, although you may notice their tracks along the trails, are elk, bears, and mountain lions. Everyone sees and hears a wide variety of birds, and close to 200 species have been observed in the park. These include mountain bluebirds, warbling vireos, rock wrens, violet-green swallows, mountain chickadees, yellow-bellied sapsuckers, downy woodpeckers, western kingbirds, black-chinned sparrows, song sparrows, dark-eyed juncos, black-chinned hummingbirds, red-tailed hawks, and both golden and bald eagles.

Open only from May through October, the park seldom gets very crowded, although the small campground can fill, especially on summer weekends. Summer high temperatures are usually in the low 80s, with nighttime lows in the upper 40s. Small amounts of snow should be expected in early May and late October.

Nearby, in the town of Mountainair (18 miles southeast of the park), is the visitor center for Salinas Pueblo Missions National Monument. The monument's sites, which range from 8 to 26 miles from Mountainair, contain the ruins of old American Indian pueblos and Spanish missions from the seventeenth century.

PANCHO VILLA STATE PARK

Hours/Season: Overnight; year-round
Area: 60 land acres
Elevation: 4,000 feet
Facilities: Visitor center, interpretive exhibits, recreation hall, nature trail, botanical garden, picnic tables, group shelters, playground, restrooms with showers, 61 campsites (56 with electric and water hookups and some with multiple sets of hookups), public telephone, RV dump station, phone: (505) 531-2711
Attractions: Hiking, desert botanical garden, bird-watching, historic exhibits
Nearby: Columbus Historical Museum; Las Palomas, Mexico; Rockhound State Park
Access: In the village of Columbus, 35 miles south of Deming via NM 11

▲ Named for the famed Mexican bandit-revolutionary Francisco "Pancho" Villa, this park commemorates the day in 1916 that Villa's troops attacked the border town of Columbus, New Mexico, killing eighteen Americans and wounding another twelve, and the U.S. military incursion into Mexico that followed. In addition, the park has extensive cactus gardens, a pleasant campground, and good bird-watching possibilities.

There was no moon during the early morning hours of March 9, 1916, when guerilla revolutionaries under General Pancho Villa crossed the border from Mexico. They attacked, looted, and set fire to Columbus, in what is generally recognized as the last armed invasion of the continental United States. A small garrison of U.S. troops at Camp Furlong, on the south edge of town, mounted a defense, and by dawn the Mexicans were back across the border. Initial reports said there were 2,000 attackers, but later estimates put that closer to 500. Estimates of Mexican guerillas killed ranged from about 100 to more than 200.

As to why Villa's troops attacked Columbus, a likely reason is that Villa wanted to punish the United States, and particularly President Woodrow Wilson, for recognizing and helping his political rival, Mexican president Venustiano Carranza. Villa also needed the supplies he expected to get from looting the town and Camp Furlong.

If nothing else, the raid did get the attention of President Wilson, who sent General John "Black Jack" Pershing on what was called a "punitive expedition," in which thousands of U.S. troops chased Villa for eleven months, traveling some 400 miles into Mexico. Although there were a number of skirmishes with Villa's men, in which 75 to 100 Mexican guerillas were killed, Villa avoided capture.

However, documents unearthed in the National Archives in Washington, D.C., in 1991 indicate that the U.S. tried to assassinate Villa—and came very close to doing so—in 1916. According to the reports, written by an Army

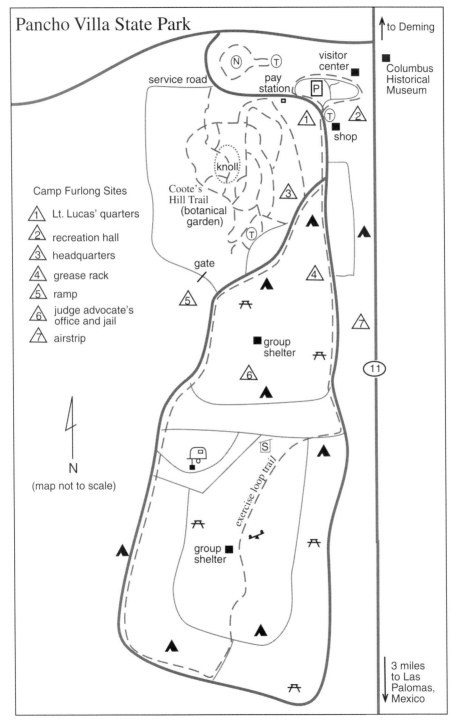

Pancho Villa State Park

to Deming

visitor center

pay station

service road

N T

P

Columbus Historical Museum

1 T 2

shop

knoll

Coote's Hill Trail (botanical garden)

3

T

Camp Furlong Sites

1 Lt. Lucas' quarters

2 recreation hall

3 headquarters

4 grease rack

5 ramp

6 judge advocate's office and jail

7 airstrip

gate

5

4

7

group shelter

6

11

S

N

(map not to scale)

exercise loop trail

group shelter

3 miles to Las Palomas, Mexico

Historical marker at Pancho Villa State Park

intelligence officer, the Army hired two Japanese, who made their way to Villa's camp and went to work as cooks. They had been given a poison, supposedly odorless and tasteless and that would kill in 3 days, and after a few days in the camp put some in Villa's coffee. Always cautious, Villa poured half of it into another man's cup, watched him drink it, and then drank the rest himself. The Japanese then quickly and quietly left. While it is not known if Villa and the other coffee-drinker suffered any ill effects, it is known that Villa did not die at that time. He was finally killed in 1923, reportedly by Mexican enemies with no connection to the U.S. Army.

Although Pershing's trek through Mexico in search of Villa did not attain its goal, it proved successful training for World War I, which the United States was about to enter. Industrialization had brought changes to the world, and to war. Pershing's punitive expedition was the last time the U.S. would use mounted cavalry and was also the first time that a U.S. military operation would use motorized trucks and planes. Ironically, fuel for the new internal combustion engines was carried by mules.

Park visitors today can see the ruins of the camp, including the adobe shells of the judge advocate's office and jail and the first grease rack installed to service military vehicles. Also remaining is the camp's airstrip, used by the Army's First Aero Squadron, which consisted of eight biplanes. The old U.S. Customs Service building, constructed in 1902, serves as the park's visitor center and contains artifacts, historic photos, and exhibits describing Villa, the attack on Columbus, and the U.S. military's incursion into Mexico. There is also a 25-minute movie on the raid, in which a number of survivors describe their experiences when the shooting started.

Each year on March 9, the park hosts "Raid Day," which is sponsored by the Columbus Historical Society. It includes a commemorative program to remember those Americans who were killed in the raid, usually with a guest speaker and a barbecue. Other activities are scheduled at the Columbus Historical Museum and throughout the town.

Despite this park's name, it has another side that has absolutely nothing to do with Villa and his attack. The park is home to extensive botanical gardens, filled with more than thirty varieties of cacti and their drought-resistant brethren, including cow tongue and beavertail prickly pear, tree and cane cholla, claret cup, horse crippler, long mama, yucca, agave, ocotillo, sotol, and Joshua trees. The campground does not have an abundance of shade, although there are a few trees. Some large campsites have multiple RV hookups, and there is a small tenting area.

Trails here are short and easy. A 130-yard nature trail has identifying signs on cactus and other desert plants. The Coote's Hill Trail—about 0.5 mile total—is a series of interconnecting trails that winds through a botanical garden and up to the top of Coote's Hill, providing a good view of the campground and surrounding countryside, all the way to Mexico. The park's only paved trail, it was named for a soldier who was stationed here. There is also a 1-mile exercise loop trail that is convenient for getting to and from the campground and other park facilities.

Bird-watchers have catalogued more than fifty species in the park, including American kestrels, red-shafted flickers, Inca doves, mourning doves, starlings, western meadowlarks, scaled quail, Brewer's blackbirds, brown-headed cowbirds, cactus wrens, roadrunners, red-tailed hawks, ravens, and an occasional sandhill crane. The park also has jackrabbits, coyotes, javelina, rattlesnakes, and bullsnakes. Every once in a while, a bobcat is seen.

The busiest time at the park is from October through March. During that period slide presentations and talks are presented occasionally in the restored Camp Furlong Recreation Hall, and potluck suppers for campers take place most Thursday evenings. Winter, with high temperatures typically in the 60s and lows in the 30s, is the best time for bird-watching. Summers are hot, with high temperatures often exceeding 100 degrees F, while lows are in the 60s. May, when the park comes alive with blooming cactus and wildflowers, also has pleasant weather, with highs usually in the 80s, and lows in the 50s. Fall temperatures are similar to those in May.

Those who want to find out more about Villa's raid on Columbus, or other aspects of the village's history, can walk across the street from the park to the Columbus Historical Museum, housed in an old Southern Pacific Railroad depot. It contains exhibits and artifacts from Villa's raid, plus exhibits from the community's early railroad days. Also nearby—about 3 miles south—is the Mexican border town of Las Palomas, with a variety of shops and restaurants. Because special Mexican auto insurance is required for those taking vehicles across the border, many people park on the U.S. side and walk. Most of the businesses in Las Palomas accept U.S. currency. Rock collectors will want to visit another nearby site, Rockhound State Park, which is discussed in its own section of this book.

PERCHA DAM STATE PARK

Hours/Season: Overnight; year-round
Area: 84 land acres
Elevation: 4,100 feet
Facilities: Picnic tables, group shelter, playground, playing field, restrooms with showers, 75 campsites (6 with electric hookups) and abundant less-developed camping, phone: (505) 743-3942
Attractions: Fishing, bird-watching, canoeing, hiking
Nearby: Caballo Lake State Park
Access: 21 miles south of Truth or Consequences via I-25 exit 59

If the New Mexico State Park System has a hidden treasure, this delightful little park might be it. Virtually unknown—although the word is getting out—Percha Dam State Park is a quiet and serene getaway, with excellent fishing and bird-watching. Under the shade of tall cottonwoods, Russian olives, green ash, and salt cedars, and with a carpet of grasses, the park hugs the Rio Grande in a rich riparian area that seems a bit out of place in the southern New Mexico desert.

Among the state's smallest and less-used parks, its name comes from Percha Creek, which enters the Rio Grande above the dam. The word *percha* is Spanish for "roost"—usually a chicken roost—or a snare for birds. The small dam was built in 1917 to provide irrigation water for local farms; the park was established in 1970.

Today's visitors enter the park near the low Percha Dam, crossing a wooden vehicle bridge over an irrigation canal that runs perpendicular to the river near the park entrance. Fishing for walleye is very good, especially just below the dam, and anglers also catch white bass and catfish. The shady river is also a prime spot for canoeing.

Swimming is permitted in the river but not recommended, and it is prohibited in the irrigation canal. There are no designated swimming areas. Much of the riverbank is rocky or marshy, but there are abundant dry, grassy areas close by for sunbathing and lounging.

Among the area's best bird-watching locales, Percha Dam State Park has most of the same species that are seen at nearby Caballo Lake State Park, but often in greater numbers, and it is easier to see them because Percha Dam is usually less crowded. Migratory species include ducks and geese, American white pelicans, trumpeter swans, sandhill cranes, both great blue and little blue herons, golden eagles, bald eagles, northern goshawks, scaled quail, yellow-rumped warblers, song sparrows, red-winged blackbirds, great-tailed grackles, western meadowlarks, western bluebirds, willow flycatchers, dark-eyed juncos, and yellow-breasted chats. Also seen scurrying through the underbrush and in the grassy fields are rock squirrels and cottontail rabbits, and although somewhat more elusive, there are also coyotes, foxes, racoons, and mule deer, plus lizards, frogs, and turtles.

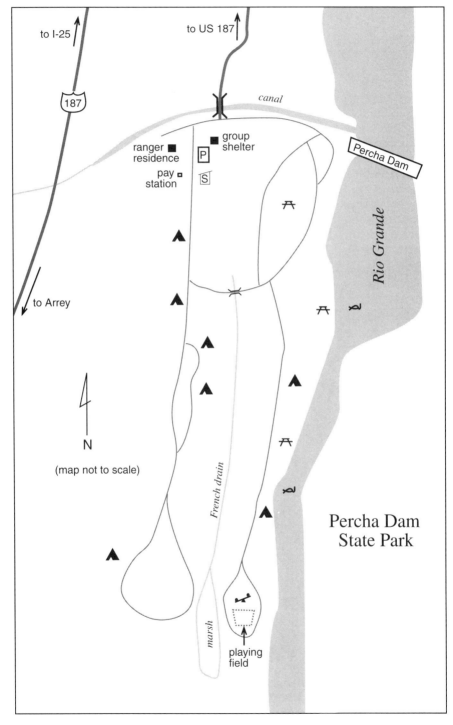

to I-25

to US 187

187

canal

Percha Dam

ranger residence

group shelter

P

pay station

S

Rio Grande

N

(map not to scale)

French drain

Percha Dam State Park

marsh

playing field

to Arrey

The park has no designated hiking trails—just paths leading to favorite fishing and bird-watching spots—but a very pleasant walk of a mile or so can be had along the park's dirt roads.

The developed campsites are spacious, shady, and serene, and most are close enough to hear the river, even when its view is blocked by trees. There is also an open, grassy area at the south end of the park that is available for less-developed camping. Nearby is a playground, and next to it is a playing field with a volleyball net.

Although the park is usually under-used, it can get busy on holidays and summer weekends. Weekdays are usually the best for those seeking solitude, and bird-watching is always more productive when there are fewer people. Summer temperatures are warm and sometimes hot, usually in the 90s or above during the day, but dropping into the 60s at night. Fall is spectacular when the cottonwoods turn golden yellow, with temperatures usually in the mid-70s during the day and the upper 40s and low 50s at

Mule deer are often seen at Percha Dam State Park. (photo by Don MacCarter, courtesy New Mexico Dept. of Game and Fish)

night. Winters are very quiet, with daytime temperatures in the 50s, and nights in the 20s and 30s. During spring, high temperatures range from the 60s to low 80s, and lows are from the upper 30s to low 50s.

Nearby attractions include Caballo Lake State Park, located 2 miles north via NM 187, which is discussed in its own section of this book. About 20 miles north of Caballo Lake is the town of Truth or Consequences and Elephant Butte Lake State Park, both of which are discussed in the section in this book on Elephant Butte Lake State Park.

ROCKHOUND STATE PARK

Hours/Season: Overnight; year-round
Area: 1,100 land acres
Elevation: 4,500 feet
Facilities: Visitor center, interpretive exhibits, botanical garden, picnic tables, group shelter, playground, restrooms with showers, 32 campsites (29 with electric and water hookups), public telephone, RV dump station, phone: (505) 546-6182
Attractions: Hiking, rockhounding, wildlife viewing, interpretive programs
Nearby: City of Rocks State Park and Pancho Villa State Park
Access: From Deming take NM 11 south 5 miles, and then head east on NM 141 for about 9 miles

This is one of the few public parks in the United States where visitors are permitted—no, encouraged—to attack the land with shovels and haul off the fruits of their labors. Established in 1966, Rockhound State Park sits on the rugged western slope of the Little Florida Mountains, in an area of volcanic origins that is rich in colorful agates, quartz crystals, and other rocks and minerals. For those who can take their eyes off the ground, the scenery is fine too, and there are opportunities for hiking and bird-watching.

Each visitor is permitted to take up to fifteen pounds of rock from most areas of the park. Rock hounds can use rock hammers and small shovels—no power equipment—and usually find that the farther one gets from the campground and visitor center, the more interesting the specimens.

A 1.2-mile loop trail provides access to rock-collecting areas, plus adjacent state and federal lands that are also open to the public. The trail, rated moderate, has a few steep sections as it climbs into the Little Florida Mountains, passing through several gullies and wandering through a rugged and rocky terrain of cactus, yucca, mesquite, scrub oak, juniper, and hackberry. From this trail, hikers can follow gullies and paths higher into the mountains. Although half of the park's visitors are searching for rocks, others come just for the hike, with its panoramic views of the surrounding mountains. These include the Sierra Madre Mountains of Mexico to the southwest and the Victorio Mountains, named for the famous Apache chief, to the west.

Sunsets can be spellbinding from the southwest-facing campground, especially from the higher-elevation sites. Juniper, mesquite, and other low bushes and trees produce little shade, but sites are spacious. A botanical garden contains numerous species of cacti and other desert plants that are identified with signs. The Little Florida Mountains were named by early Spanish explorers for the large number of flowering plants in the foothills, especially for the wildflowers and cactus that bloom in spring.

A visitor center has exhibits of rocks and minerals that are found in the park, showing what they look like in the ground and then after they have been cut and polished. These include silica, quartz crystals, blue agate, white-pink common opal, and chalcedony. Jasper is among the park's most common semi-precious stones, and variegated nodules—called

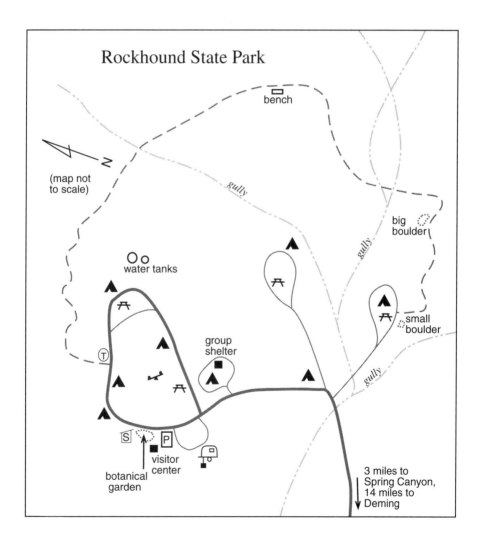

thundereggs and geodes—often contain intriguing patterns of agate, common opal, manganese oxide minerals, or quartz crystals.

Spring Canyon is a seasonal day-use area about 3 miles south of Rockhound. With elevations that range up to 7,800 feet, it is far more rugged than the Rockhound section of the park. Open from Easter through November, it offers good possibilities of seeing wildlife, particularly Persian ibex, a type of wild goat that was imported into this area in 1976. Also at home in Spring Canyon are rock squirrels, gray foxes, and mule deer. Mountain lions are present but are seldom seen. There are no designated hiking trails, but there are miles of trails left by cattle and other animals. In addition, the area has picnic tables, a group shelter, and solar energy-powered vault toilets. Primitive camping—for tents and small truck campers only—may be available in the future.

Most of the animals likely to be seen at Spring Canyon—except the Persian ibex—are also present at Rockhound but in smaller numbers. Birds frequently spotted in both areas of the park include Gambel's and scaled quail, mourning doves, roadrunners, raptors, and a variety of songbirds and hummingbirds. Migratory birds, such as ducks, geese, and sandhill cranes, often stop by in spring. Both sections also have rattlesnakes and numerous lizards.

During the park's busiest times—from October through March—there are several geology talks and rock-hounding tours each week; about one per month is offered the rest of the year. A great number of rock hounders use the park as their headquarters during the annual Rock Hound Roundup in early to mid-March in Deming. Summers here are hot, with daytime highs in the 90s and sometimes exceeding 100 degrees F, and lows in the 60s. Winters are pleasant, with occasional dustings of snow, daytime temperatures in the 50s and 60s, and nights dropping to the mid-20s. Fall and spring high temperatures are in the 70s and 80s, while lows are usually in the 40s; and spring is usually windy.

Those who have not had their fill of rocks should head to nearby City of Rocks State Park, about 28 miles northwest of Deming, which does not offer rock-hounding but instead provides an almost surrealistic landscape of huge boulders. For a spot of exciting western history and magnificent cactus gardens, go to Pancho Villa State Park, on the Mexican border 35 miles south of Deming. Both parks are discussed in their own sections of this book.

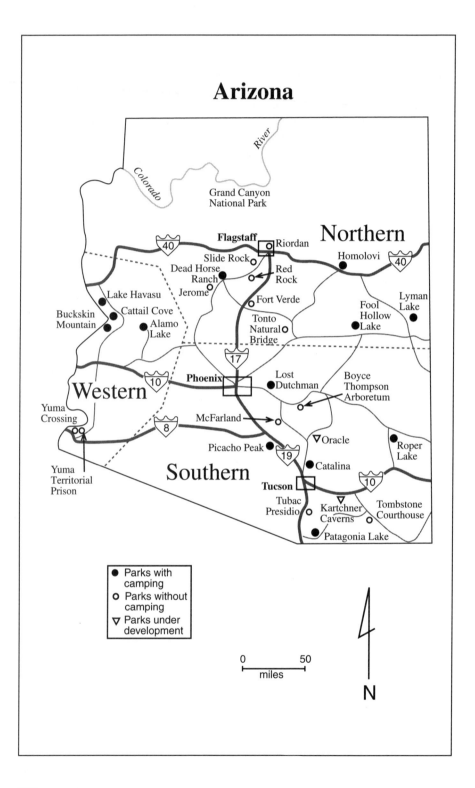

Arizona

Colorado River

Grand Canyon
National Park

Northern

Flagstaff ◉ Riordan

Slide Rock ○   Homolovi
Dead Horse   Red
Ranch ●   Rock ○
Jerome ○   Fort Verde ○   Lyman
Lake Havasu ●   Fool   Lake ●
Buckskin   Cattail Cove ●   Tonto   Hollow
Mountain ●   Alamo   Natural ○   Lake ●
     Lake ●   Bridge

Western

Phoenix   Lost   Boyce
Dutchman ●   Thompson
          Arboretum

Yuma   McFarland →○
Crossing ○○

Yuma   Picacho Peak ●   ▽ Oracle   Roper
Territorial   Lake ●
Prison   **Southern**   ● Catalina

Tucson ▢
Tubac   ▽
Presidio ○   Kartchner   Tombstone
          Caverns   Courthouse ○
          Patagonia Lake ●

- ● Parks with camping
- ○ Parks without camping
- ▽ Parks under development

0   50
miles

N

ARIZONA PARKS

A physically large state—sixth in the nation in terms of square miles—Arizona is far from its Hollywood image of being one big barren desert, flat and hot, with nothing in sight in any direction but cactus. Certainly Arizona has its deserts, and unquestionably parts of the state are hot, but Arizona also has tall, snow-capped mountains, forests of fir and pine, oak-shaded river canyons, and vast grasslands. About 40 percent of the state is technically desert, 25 percent is grasslands, and the rest is forest or woods.

The climate varies considerably, depending mostly on elevation. The coldest temperatures will likely be found in the mountains above Flagstaff, where you will find Humphrey's Peak, the state's highest point at 12,643 feet; but you will have to look far before finding any place as hot and dry as Yuma, at 70 feet the state's lowest point and often the hottest spot in the nation.

Nomadic peoples roamed this area more than 10,000 years ago, and by the first few centuries A.D. began creating communities—first of pit houses and then multi-story pueblos. Spanish explorers arrived in the mid-1500s, and although they did not find the cities of gold they sought, they were the first to record their impressions of the Grand Canyon. By the mid-1700s the Spanish established missions at Tubac and nearby Tumacacori, which are considered the first permanent European settlements in Arizona. Most of Arizona became part of the United States in 1848 with the Treaty of Guadalupe Hidalgo, although Tucson and points south waited five years until their purchase from Mexico. The second half of the nineteenth century saw an influx of white settlers, resulting in numerous conflicts with the Navajos and Apaches, until U.S. forces defeated them in the late 1880s. Also during this period mining boom towns such as Tombstone sprang up, and Arizona began to acquire its Wild West image. Arizona became the United States' 48th state on February 14, 1912.

For the purposes of this book, Arizona is divided into three main regions: northern, southern, and western.

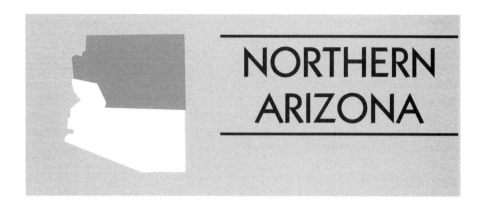

NORTHERN ARIZONA

Dominated by the Grand Canyon, a masterpiece of erosional beauty carved by the Colorado River over millions of years, northern Arizona has the state's highest mountain peaks, most snow, and greatest variety of terrain. Flagstaff, once a rough lumber town, is the region's largest city and home to a unique historic park. The San Francisco Peaks, north of Flagstaff, stand majestically on the landscape and are considered sacred by the Hopi Indians. South of Flagstaff is Oak Creek Canyon, known for its beautiful red sandstone rock formations, where several spectacularly scenic state parks are located. To the northeast are the high windswept plains that are home to the Hopi and Navajo Indians, plus the colorful Painted Desert. Ancient Indian ruins can be explored at a state park in this area. Along the state's eastern border are the deep forests of the Mogollon Rim—a 1,000-foot escarpment—and the White Mountains, home to several scenic lake parks. While not as high as the San Francisco Peaks, this area gets the most precipitation in the state—some 25 inches each year.

DEAD HORSE RANCH STATE PARK

Hours/Season: Overnight; year-round
Area: 725 land acres
Elevation: 3,300 feet
Facilities: Visitor center, picnic tables, restrooms with showers, canoe-launching area, playground, public telephone, 127 campsites (45 with electric and water hookups), group shelters, RV dump station, corral, phone: (520) 634-5283

Opposite: *Slide Rock State Park in scenic Oak Creek Canyon*

Attractions: Hiking, bird-watching, fishing, canoeing, photography, mountain biking, horseback riding, swimming

Nearby: Slide Rock State Park, Red Rock State Park, Jerome and Fort Verde State Historic Parks, Tuzigoot National Monument, Coconino National Forest

Access: In Cottonwood, from US 89A West, turn north on Main Street, go several blocks, turn north again onto North 10th Street, and follow that to the park entrance; from US 89A East, turn east on Mingus Avenue, follow it to North 10th Street, and go north to the park entrance

▲ Hiking, bird-watching, and fishing are among the top attractions at Dead Horse Ranch State Park, where a rich riparian area along the Verde River, shaded with tall cottonwoods and willows, offers a refreshing change from the surrounding desert. However, desert lovers are also accommodated here, with hillsides covered by mesquite, prickly pear cactus, sotol, and other typical desert vegetation.

The park's name dates to the early 1950s, when the ranch was purchased by a California family by the name of Ireys. It seems that the family had visited several ranches in the valley, and when the father asked the children which ranch they wanted to move to, they said "the one with the dead horse," referring to a skeleton they had seen in a pasture. The name stuck, and when the family sold the ranch to the Arizona State Parks System in 1973 a condition of the sale was that the name be retained.

Today, there are no dead horses lying about, but horseback riding is popular on the park's multiuse trails and in the adjacent Coconino National Forest. The trails are also used by a growing number of mountain bikers.

Within and immediately outside the park in the national forest are approximately 15 miles of trails, with connections to additional national forest trails. Most park trails are interconnected, with a major intersection just south of the main campground. There are also a number of short paths that have been created by anglers heading to the river.

The Verde River Greenway Trail is a tree-shaded 1.5-mile loop that follows a section of the Verde River, passes by the fishing lagoon, and connects with several day-use and picnic areas. Although sandy along the shore, the trail is an easy hike. It is also particularly scenic and provides excellent opportunities to see wildlife.

The park's toughest hiking or biking is on the Lime Kiln Trail, which runs 2 miles (one-way) from the group-use area due east into the Coconino National Forest. Although it is a bit steep at the beginning, the trail soon levels out and is rated moderate overall. Mostly in the desert section of the park, it provides good views of the river valley, as well as access to the national forest.

The park also has several short trails, ranging from 0.25 mile to 0.5 mile (one-way), that connect the various sections of the park; and it is a fairly easy 2-mile walk (one-way) out of the park to Tuzigoot National Monument, although the route may include fording a shallow stream.

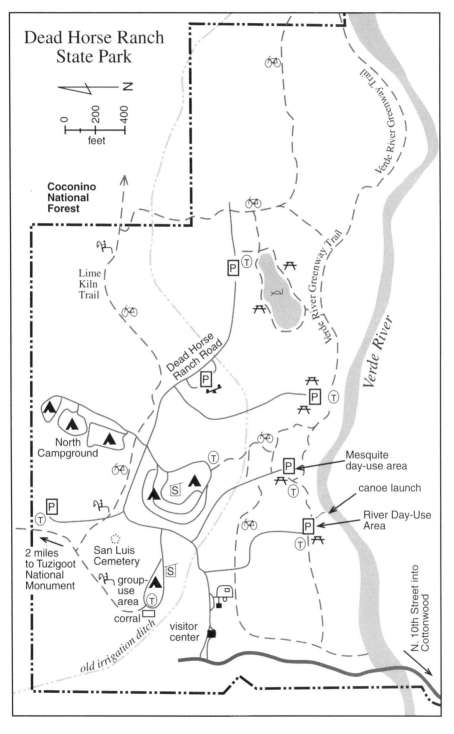

Dead Horse Ranch State Park

N

0 200 400
feet

Coconino National Forest

Lime Kiln Trail

Verde River Greenway Trail

Verde River Greenway Trail

Dead Horse Ranch Road

Verde River

North Campground

San Luis Cemetery

2 miles to Tuzigoot National Monument

group-use area

corral

visitor center

old irrigation ditch

Mesquite day-use area

canoe launch

River Day-Use Area

N. 10th Street into Cottonwood

Great blue heron at Dead Horse Ranch State Park

The Main Campground is among the nicest in central Arizona, well-designed, with RV hookups, shade, and some degree of privacy provided by a variety of deciduous and evergreen trees. The new North Campground has three loops on a mesa of open desert, with good panoramic views of the Verde River and nearby mountains, and plans for RV hookups. There is also a group-use area that is available for overflow camping when not reserved for a group.

Well over 100 species of birds are seen in the park, including two that are listed as endangered species: the common black hawk and the willow flycatcher. Both are spotted occasionally in summer. Seen at various times are Gambel's quail, osprey, numerous ducks and geese, great blue herons, American coots, red-tailed hawks, Gila woodpeckers, and both bald and golden eagles.

The wetlands also attract racoons, squirrels, skunks, and mule deer. There are coyotes, and occasionally a javelina or mountain lion will be spotted. During summer, rattlesnakes are sometimes seen in the desert sections of the park.

The park is also home to at least one endangered plant, the Arizona cliff rose, which grows in the northern section of the park at higher elevations, off the Lime Kiln Trail. Those who want to find the plant should ask a park ranger for specific directions.

Fishing is good year-round, in both the Verde River and the 4-acre stocked fishing lagoon. Anglers catch catfish, largemouth bass, bluegill, sunfish, and rainbow trout.

Swimming is prohibited in the lagoon but permitted in the river. However, the river is shallow and really more suitable for wading. The best spot to get your feet wet is at the River Day-Use Area, southwest of the Main Campground. Canoes and small inflatable boats are permitted in the river, but motors are prohibited. A canoe-launch site is located along the river at the east end of the River Day-Use Area. Boating is prohibited in the lagoon, but future plans call for creation of two more lagoons that will connect with the river and be open to canoes and other non-motorized boats.

Verde River Days, held the last Saturday in September, feature activities dealing with river ecology that often include canoe rides and sandcastle building contests. Free fishing clinics for both children and adults are held mid-month in March and June. Fishing licenses are not required on those two days, and use of fishing equipment is provided free. Throughout the year, there are occasional evening activities, such as discussions of the park's flora and fauna, or a program with a local astronomer.

A small in-holding, surrounded by the state park, includes the historic San Luis Cemetery, which is open to the public and contains graves of farmers and miners who lived in the area in the 1920s and 1930s.

Summers here are hot, with temperatures frequently exceeding 100 degrees F in the daytime but dropping into the 60s at night. Winters are known for warm daytime temperatures, often in the 50s and 60s, and cold nights, usually below freezing. October may be the ideal time to visit, when the park is less crowded than in summer, and the cottonwoods, alders, and sycamores turn magnificent shades of yellow, red, and orange. October temperatures usually range from the mid-80s during the day to the upper 40s at night. During spring, nights are usually in the 40s, while daytime highs reach the upper 60s and 70s.

Ancient stone village at Tuzigoot National Monument, near Dead Horse Ranch State Park

Dead Horse Ranch State Park is located close to a number of other attractions, and many park visitors camp here and head out on day trips. The closest is Tuzigoot National Monument, an ancient American Indian stone village that sits on the summit of a ridge and can be seen from the north side of the state park. Within easy driving distance are Slide Rock State Park, Red Rock State Park, Jerome State Historic Park, and Fort Verde State Historic Park, which are each discussed in their own sections of this book.

FOOL HOLLOW LAKE RECREATION AREA

Hours/Season: Overnight; year-round
Area: 800 land acres, 149 lake surface acres
Elevation: 6,300 feet
Facilities: Picnic tables, playgrounds, group shelters, restrooms with showers, public telephone, 123 campsites (60 with electric, water, and sewer hookups; 32 with electric and water hookups), RV dump station, boat ramp, courtesy dock, wheelchair-accessible fishing piers, fish-cleaning stations, amphitheater, phone: (520) 537-3680
Attractions: Fishing, boating, hiking, wildlife viewing, bird-watching, cross-country skiing, snowshoeing
Nearby: Apache/Sitgreaves National Forest hiking trails, Petrified Forest National Park
Access: 2 miles northwest of Show Low, just off AZ 260, on Old Linden Road

One of the few true mountain escapes in the Arizona State Parks System, Fool Hollow offers a picturesque lake set in a forest of tall ponderosa pine, piñon, juniper, and even a few maple trees. At the base of the White Mountains, and with spacious, shady campgrounds, this is a popular spot for Phoenix residents trying to beat the heat.

The area acquired its name after Wesley Adair and his son Aaron began farming here in the mid-1870s, and locals remarked that "Only a fool would try to farm that area." The Mormon settlement of Adair was established in 1878, and a post office opened in 1899. The town site slipped beneath the surface of the lake when the dam was completed in 1957.

The park is a cooperative effort by Arizona State Parks, the U.S. Forest Service, Arizona Game and Fish, and the city of Show Low. The main activities here are fishing, canoeing, hiking, wildlife viewing, birding, and lounging along the lakeshore. This also makes a good base camp for hiking in the surrounding national forest.

The well-planned campgrounds have paved roads and sites. Sites are well-shaded, with an abundance of ponderosa pine trees, and many campsites provide good views of the lake. Campground loops are named for species of birds that live in the park. A separate tent area is open to RVs as well, although no generator use is permitted. The park's group-use shelters are popular for wedding receptions, family reunions, and similar events.

The lake is stocked with rainbow trout in the summer and catfish in the fall. Anglers also catch crappie, walleye, and both largemouth and smallmouth bass, with the best fishing in early summer and fall.

Most boats on the lake are 12- to 14-foot fishing boats, with small trolling motors—there is an eight-horsepower maximum-size limit. It is also a good lake for canoes and even attracts a few sailboats. Windsurfers are not attracted to it, though, because the lake is protected from the wind. Although

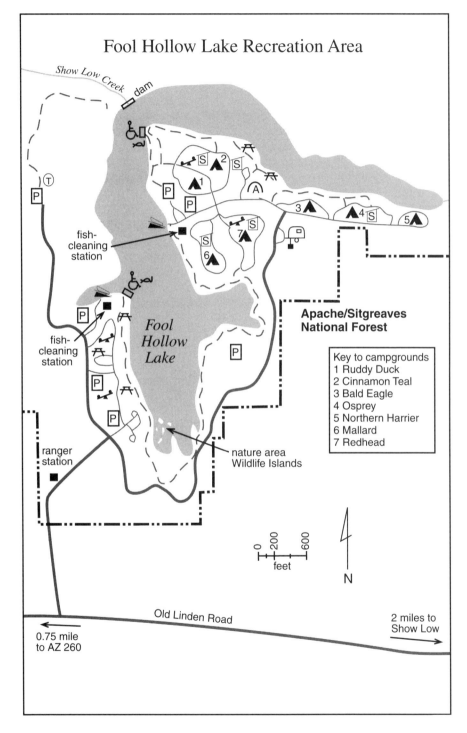

Fool Hollow Lake Recreation Area

Show Low Creek

dam

fish-cleaning station

fish-cleaning station

Fool Hollow Lake

ranger station

Apache/Sitgreaves National Forest

nature area
Wildlife Islands

Key to campgrounds
1 Ruddy Duck
2 Cinnamon Teal
3 Bald Eagle
4 Osprey
5 Northern Harrier
6 Mallard
7 Redhead

0 200 600
feet

N

Old Linden Road

0.75 mile
to AZ 260

2 miles to
Show Low

swimming is permitted, it is not recommended, since the lake is 65 feet deep at the dam and cold year-round.

Hikers and mountain bikers will find a maintained trail along the shore for about 1.25 miles, offering a generally easy trek with picture-perfect views. Although the trail is graveled with crushed red granite, one spot at its southern edge is sometimes flooded, requiring a detour along a nearby road. There are also short maintained paths throughout the park, providing lake and restroom access, and a number of old dirt roads that offer good hiking opportunities when they are dry but should be avoided when wet.

Outside the park, the White Mountains Trail System is composed of about 180 miles of connected hiking, mountain biking, and horseback riding trails that stretch across the Lakeside Ranger District of the Apache/ Sitgreaves National Forest, plus urban trails in the nearby towns of Show Low and Pinetop/Lakeside. Maps and additional information are available from park rangers.

As this is among the best spots for bird-watching in this part of Arizona, visitors are quite likely to see and hear a variety of songbirds in summer, hawks year-round, and numerous migratory species in spring and fall. Great blue herons roost in the trees year-round, and campsites along the northern edge of the park are closed each winter to avoid disturbing the bald eagles, osprey, and hawks that winter here. Other birds that are often seen in the park, depending on season, include mallards, ruddy ducks, northern pintails, common mergansers, American coots, mourning doves, great horned owls, rufous hummingbirds, violet-green swallows, Steller's jays, canyon wrens, orange-crowned warblers, and red-winged blackbirds.

Mammals that frequent the park include fox, racoon, beaver, and porcupine. Elk are sometimes seen late in the day during fall and winter, and bear have been spotted in the area although not inside the park boundaries.

The Wildlife Islands, near the southern edge of the lake, are an excellent locale for spotting birds; and there are beaver ponds in many places just below the dam. There is also good wildlife viewing in an undeveloped woodlands area maintained by Arizona Game and Fish, just east of the park boundary.

The park has a ranger station with a small lobby, and plans are underway for construction of a nature center with an interpretive center, a wildlife viewing area, and an amphitheater. On summer weekends, rangers lead guided nature walks and present campfire programs on various subjects, such as the area's geology, wildlife, and plant life. The park also has a few petroglyphs dating from the thirteenth century; rangers can help direct you to them.

During winter, the trails and dirt roads are open to cross-country skiers and snowshoers, although the snow does not usually last very long. Although the lake occasionally ices over, the ice is not thick enough to support anglers or other winter recreationists. Winter temperatures usually range from the teens at night to the 40s during the day.

June, July, and August are the busiest times at Fool Hollow, and the campground usually fills on summer weekends, with Friday evening the worst possible time to arrive. Summer days usually warm to the mid-80s and low 90s, while nighttime temperatures drop into the 50s. The park is particularly pleasant in fall, when the air is cool and crisp, with daytime temperatures in the 70s, and nights in the 40s, and visitation is cut in half from summer. It is possible to see a dusting of snow by late October. Spring temperatures vary greatly, with highs from the 60s to the 80s, and lows ranging from the 20s to the upper 40s. Those looking for wildflowers will find them in bloom in April and May and again in late August and September.

From Fool Hollow Lake, it is less than an hour's drive to Petrified Forest National Park, located north and east of the state park via AZ 77 and either US 180 or I-40. Well worth a visit, this national park preserves a vast quantity of petrified wood and a painted desert. Both are particularly colorful under early morning or late afternoon light and especially attractive just after a rainstorm has washed away the dust. A 27-mile scenic drive provides access to about two dozen scenic overlooks and a number of short walks. Most of the petrified wood is in the southern part of the park, while the best views of the painted desert are in the park's northern section.

FORT VERDE STATE HISTORIC PARK

Hours/Season: 8:00 A.M. to 4:30 P.M. daily; closed Christmas
Area: 11 land acres
Elevation: 3,100 feet
Facilities: Visitor center/museum, picnic tables, restrooms, phone: (520) 567-3275
Attractions: Historical exhibits, interpretive programs
Nearby: Jerome State Historic Park, Dead Horse Ranch State Park, Montezuma Castle National Monument
Access: In Camp Verde on Holloman Street; go 3 miles east of I-17 exit 287 on AZ 260, and then follow signs 1.5 blocks east to the fort; also accessible from Montezuma Castle via Montezuma Lane

A visit to Fort Verde State Historic Park is a trip back in time, when the Wild West was really wild, and life on the frontier could be hard. Considered the best surviving example of an Arizona military post from the Indian Wars period, Fort Verde shows not only the buildings, clothes, weapons, and utensils used by soldiers of that era, but also delves into the soldiers' lives, showing the human side of the military.

Although Indians had inhabited the Verde Valley for centuries, it was not until 1583 that the first Europeans saw the area, and these Spanish conquistadores did little more than look around, stake a few claims, and keep going. Mountain men and trappers, including a young Kit Carson, explored the area in the early nineteenth century, but it was not until 1865 that whites started settling the area.

The Verde Valley's long growing season and fertile land made it an ideal location for farming, and the food would fetch a good price in the new territorial capital of Prescott, about 60 miles to the west, and its nearby mining camps.

This European invasion was upsetting to the Apache and Yavapai peoples, who had been hunting and gathering in the Verde Valley for generations. The first recorded Indian attack was in May 1865, and although no one was killed, there were injuries, and the settlers lost valuable crops and livestock. Within two months, the settlers asked the U.S. Army for help.

A small military unit arrived that summer, and by winter a permanent military post was established. First called Camp Lincoln, the name was changed to Camp Verde in 1868, because there were too many other military posts named in honor of President Lincoln after his assassination.

The post was abandoned and reestablished, and then moved—construction of the present fort began in April of 1871. In 1879, the camp officially became Fort Verde, and it remained active on and off until the last soldiers left in the spring of 1891.

Fort Verde was typical of the frontier military posts of the day, which means that it was not really a fort at all. Contrary to what we have learned from the movies and television, the so-called forts of this era—including Fort Verde—had no walls around them because there was no need; they were seldom or, as in the case of Fort Verde, never attacked. The Indians found it easier to raid individual farms and ranches and battle the military away from the fort.

During its busiest period, in the 1870s, Fort Verde included twenty-two buildings—fourteen frame and eight adobe—neatly lined up around a parade ground. There was a hospital, storehouse, magazine, guard house, bathhouse, laundry, and offices, plus four barracks for soldiers and quarters for officers, a post doctor, and a hospital matron. Remaining today are four adobe buildings—the wooden ones were torn down by settlers for their lumber. Now a museum, these were the fort's administration building, commanding officer's quarters, bachelor officers' quarters, and post doctor's quarters. There are also foundations from several other buildings and part of the parade ground.

The post's primary function was to serve as a staging area for military operations, generally against the Yavapai and Apache. The most successful foray was during the winter of 1872/1873, when General George Crook and his troops chased the Indians throughout the region, until many were worn down and essentially starved into surrender. Those who gave up—mostly Yavapai—were placed on a reservation, where they built an irrigation system and began to cultivate crops. However, local settlers who wanted the land insisted that the Indians be moved, and in 1875, against the wishes of the Army, the U.S. Indian Bureau ordered the entire Yavapai reservation population—some 1,500 people in all—to be moved to a new reservation to the southeast, where productive farming was almost impossible.

It then became the Army's job to hunt down the remaining bands of Apaches and to keep the Indians on the reservations. In many cases, the Army hired Indian scouts to help. One of the last major battles between the Army and Indians in Arizona occurred in July 1882, at Big Dry Wash, about 35 miles east of the fort. The Army won.

Today, exhibits in the Fort Verde museum describe not only the battles fought and the post's military history; they also present a picture of the day-to-day life of the soldiers stationed at the fort, many of whom did not really want to be there. This is shown primarily through individual soldiers' life stories, in letters, photographs, and personal effects. The exhibits do not take sides but simply try to present the soldiers, local civilians, and Indians objectively, as human beings that were products of their times and cultures. Perhaps the one message that does come through is that neither side seriously tried to understand the other.

The best place to start your visit is at the museum in the fort's administration building, and then explore the three other buildings—all furnished—that show how Army officers lived on the Arizona frontier in the 1870s. You will want to allow at least 45 minutes, and those particularly interested in Old West history can easily spend several hours.

The park celebrates Fort Verde Days each year on the second weekend of October, with a parade and historical reenactments. Special events, often with reenactors, are also scheduled during the park system's observation of Arizona's historic preservation, held each spring. Living history programs are presented occasionally at other times; check at the museum for information.

Doctor's quarters at Fort Verde State Historic Park

January and February are the quietest months at the park, and visitation is fairly steady the rest of the year although very busy during reenactments. Summers are hot, with temperatures sometimes exceeding 100 degrees F. Pets and smoking are prohibited in the park.

For a different view of the Old West, go about 22 miles northwest to Jerome State Historic Park. Dead Horse Ranch State Park, which offers camping, is located close to Jerome. Both of these state parks are discussed in their own sections of this book. Also nearby, about 5 miles north, is Montezuma Castle National Monument, a five-story, twenty-room cliff dwelling built by Sinaguan farmers in the twelfth century.

HOMOLOVI RUINS STATE PARK

Hours/Season: Campground overnight, year-round; ruins 6:30 A.M. to 7:00 P.M. daily; visitor center 8:00 A.M. to 5:00 P.M. daily except Christmas
Area: 4,500 land acres
Elevation: 4,850 feet
Facilities: Visitor center, picnic tables, restrooms with showers (showers closed in winter), 53 campsites (all with electric and water hookups, although water is shut off in winter), RV dump station, phone: (520) 289-4106
Attractions: Historical exhibits, interpretive programs, hiking, bird-watching
Nearby: Petrified Forest National Park
Access: Two miles east of Winslow; from I-40 exit 257 take AZ 87 for 1.3 miles north to the park access road

Ruins left by the ancestors of today's Hopi Indians are being preserved, studied, interpreted, and offered to public view at this state park, which also includes a cemetery from a nineteenth-century Mormon settlement, a surprising amount of birds and animals, and a pleasant campground.

Homolovi (pronounced Hoe mole' oh vee) is a Hopi word meaning "place of the little hills," and it was a busy place indeed, with seven separate pueblos, when the area was occupied between 1260 and 1400. Archeologists believe that the pueblos were built by various prehistoric peoples, including the ancestors of the present-day residents of the Hopi Mesas to the north. They were attracted by the fertile soil and water of the floodplain of the Little Colorado River and grew cotton, corn, beans, and squash.

Most archeologists refer to the people who lived here as Anasazi, because that is what they were called by the Navajo guides who were hired by the nineteenth-century anthropologists and archeologists who explored these sites. However, the word Anasazi is the Navajo word for "ancient ones" or "enemies of our ancestors." The Hopi prefer to call them "Hisat'sinom," which can be translated as "long-ago people."

The visitor center offers a good introduction to the human history of the area, with displays of pottery sherds, baskets, and other artifacts, as well

Examining the ruins at Homolovi Ruins State Park

as information on the flora and fauna of the park, plus books and brochures for sale. There is also an interactive computer display on the various aspects of the park.

Three of the seven Homolovi sites at the park are accessible, including the biggest and most extensively excavated, Homolovi II, which has a walkway leading through it and interpretive signs describing the structures and life of the residents.

Occupied between 1330 and 1400, Homolovi II has about 1,200 rooms, three large rectangular plazas, and about forty rectangular kivas (underground ceremonial chambers). A kiva and several rooms have been reconstructed and can be seen from the path that leads through the ruin. Archeologists say that, based on pottery and other artifacts found here, it appears that the inhabitants were trading with those on the Hopi Mesas to the north. It is believed that much of this involved the exchange of Homolovi cotton for Hopi pottery.

The path through Homolovi II is wheelchair-accessible but a bit long, and those with mobility impairments can make arrangements at the visitor center to have a gate opened to give closer vehicle access.

Additional sites at the park include seven small clusters of pit houses, occupied before A.D. 1260, although to the untrained eye these appear simply as depressions in the earth. A short path leads from the visitor center to the site of one pit house village.

There are also a number of petroglyphs that can be seen along a short trail; because they are somewhat hard to find, it is best to ask for specific directions at the visitor center.

The cemetery from the 1870s settlement of Sunset can also be visited. Sunset was one of a series of farming communities along the Little Colorado River that was established by Mormon missionaries in the late 1870s. Led by Lot Smith, the pioneers dammed the river and tried to irrigate the flood-plain. However, the river frequently flooded, destroying their dams and crops, and the settlement was abandoned in the early 1880s. Although the rest of the community was washed away, the cemetery survived, as it was perched on a rise overlooking the river. Among the gravestones are those of three of Lot Smith's children.

There are about 6 miles of dirt roads in the park that are open to hikers, mountain bikers, and horseback riders, in addition to the established trails leading to archeological sites. These old roads are open and often dusty, with little shade, but offer good close-up and panoramic views of the desert terrain.

In addition to attracting humans for over one thousand years, the Little Colorado River also attracts a wide variety of birds and animals. Hawks and golden eagles are often spotted soaring high above, and other commonly seen species include Gambel's quail, great blue herons, killdeer, several types of sparrows, and red-shafted flickers. A bird checklist of more than 100 species is available at the visitor center. Among mammals that frequent the park are prairie dogs, mice, desert cottontails, jackrabbits, antelope ground squirrels, porcupines, badgers, bobcats, gray foxes, and several species of bats. Elk are sometimes seen in winter, and coyotes are heard but seldom seen. Reptiles include the Hopi rattlesnake, western king rattler, bull snakes, collared lizards, desert spiny lizards, and horned lizards.

The campground is set on a bluff of high desert grassland, with little shade but nicely spaced sites. Both the campground roads and site parking areas are paved.

Although hot, June and July are considered by many to be the best months to visit, because that is when you can see archeologists at work. Archeological digs are conducted weekdays from 7:00 A.M. to 3:00 P.M. during June and July, and visitors can watch the archeologists and sometimes have the opportunity to talk with them. The last Saturday in July is Archeology Day, with guided tours of that summer's dig before it is back-filled to protect it from the elements. Other annual events include Storytelling Day, featuring American Indian storytellers, which is presented on the first Saturday in March.

Daytime temperatures in summer often hit the upper 90s, although nights are cool, with temperatures in the 50s and 60s. Winters are cold, dropping into the teens at night, although sunny skies and daytime temperatures in the 40s and low 50s make outdoor activities pleasurable. Spring is often windy and dusty, with low temperatures in the 20s and 30s and highs in the 60s and 70s. A very pleasant time to visit is late September and October, when the park is quiet, and temperatures are warm but not nearly as hot as summer, with highs in the 70s and low 80s, and lows mostly in the 40s.

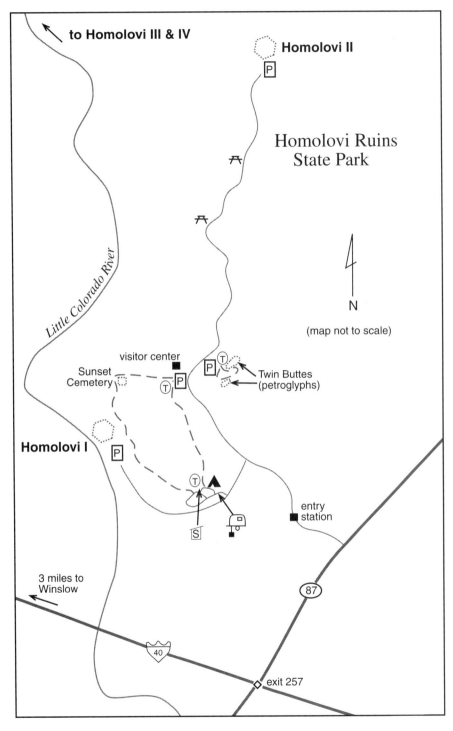

to Homolovi III & IV

Homolovi II

P

Homolovi Ruins
State Park

Little Colorado River

N

(map not to scale)

visitor center

Sunset
Cemetery

T P

P T

Twin Buttes
(petroglyphs)

Homolovi I

P

T

S

entry
station

3 miles to
Winslow

87

40

exit 257

Visitors to Homolovi Ruins State Park are reminded that although they will almost certainly see pot sherds and arrowheads on the ground, these are protected by both state and federal law and should not be moved. While this is true in every state and federal park with cultural sites, an added reason to leave Homolovi Ruins artifacts where they are found lies in the Hopi religion. According to Hopi teachings, the Homolovi sites are not only a sacred part of their heritage, to which they continue to make pilgrimages, but the broken pottery, pieces of stone tools, and arrowheads have become one with the land and must be left to provide a trail of their ancestors' migrations.

Petrified Forest National Park, located about 54 miles east of the state park via I-40, preserves a vast quantity of petrified wood and a painted desert. Both are particularly colorful under early morning or late afternoon light and especially attractive just after a rainstorm has washed away the dust. A 27-mile scenic drive provides access to about two dozen scenic overlooks and a number of short walks. Most of the petrified wood is in the southern part of the park, while the best views of the painted desert are in the park's northern section.

JEROME STATE HISTORIC PARK

Hours/Season: 8:00 A.M. to 5:00 P.M. daily; closed Christmas
Area: 3 land acres
Elevation: 5,000 feet
Facilities: Museum, picnic tables, public telephone, restrooms, phone: (520) 634-5381
Attractions: Historical exhibits, interpretive programs
Nearby: Town of Jerome (a national historic landmark), Red Rock State Park, Slide Rock State Park, Dead Horse Ranch State Park, Fort Verde State Historic Park
Access: In Jerome, off US 89A, on Douglas Road

▲ Housed in a mansion that was built by one of the wealthiest and most prominent citizens of the copper mining boomtown of Jerome, this state park takes a peek into the wild side of the Wild West, as well as the refinements imported by those with money. Through a video presentation, carefully restored rooms, numerous exhibits, mining equipment, and hundreds of historic photos, you can step back in time and learn a bit about mining, minerals, and the history of the town of Jerome and the Douglas family, who built this imposing hillside landmark.

Although prehistoric Indians had spent time here a thousand years ago, and Spanish explorers passed through in the sixteenth century, no one took a serious interest in settling down here until 1876, when miners discovered rich deposits of copper. By 1883, the United Verde Copper Company was formed, and the town was named for one of its financial backers, Eugene Jerome, a wealthy New York City lawyer who never visited his namesake. The mining operation got off to a good start; however, the price of copper soon took a nosedive, and the mine was shut the following year.

But that was not the end. Senator William A. Clark of Montana bought the idle mine and reopened it in 1888. The price of copper began to rise, and by 1894 the mining company built a narrow-gauge railroad to connect to a spur of the Santa Fe Railroad. By the early twentieth century, the United Verde was the largest producing copper mine in Arizona.

Also at this time, Jerome evolved from a wild mining camp of tents, shacks, and saloons—with catastrophic fires between 1897 and 1899—to an almost civilized community of brick-and-frame homes, several churches, a school, and even an opera house.

In 1912, a newcomer arrived on the scene, when James "Rawhide Jimmy" Douglas bought an existing mine, the Little Daisy, and discovered a particularly rich vein of copper just in time for a steep hike in copper prices during the first World War. Douglas, who had followed his father's footsteps as a mining engineer, acquired his nickname not for some Wild West bravado but for a somewhat boring but very useful method he developed for utilizing rawhide to reduce roller wear on cable cars.

It was Douglas who in 1916 built the mansion that houses the state park today. Costing $150,000, the elegant 8,000-square-foot structure was designed not only as his family home but as a hotel to house and entertain visiting mining officials, investors, politicians, and other prominent people of the day. Built of adobe, it was the grandest home in the area, with steam heat, an unheard-of central vacuum cleaner system, a marble shower, a wine cellar, and a billiards room.

When the mine closed in 1938, Douglas returned to his native Canada. In 1962, his two sons, James and Lewis, donated the mansion to the state park system. Jerome's last mine closed in 1953, and the entire town was designated a national historic landmark in 1967.

Most visitors to the state park today are combining their trip to the park with a look at the other historic attractions in Jerome. A good introduction to the town is the state park's 25-minute video, which is well-documented, informative, and entertaining. Then wander through the rooms, checking out the exhibits on minerals and mining, the town's history, and the Douglas family. Several rooms are furnished as they would have been in the early twentieth century; among the most popular exhibits is a three-dimensional model of the town and mines below, including all the mine workings, as it looked in 1937.

Outside the stately white mansion is a carriage house with Douglas family wagons and carriages, plus ore cars and mining and milling equipment. There is a picnic area that provides splendid views out over the Verde Valley. Those walking through the neatly landscaped lawns and gardens may see an occasional mule deer or javelina, or possibly a spiny lizard or rattlesnake. Most visitors will see a variety of birds, including evening

Douglas mansion at Jerome State Historic Park

grosbeaks, rufous-sided towhees, scrub jays, hummingbirds, finches, sparrows, orioles, quail, red-tailed hawks, and great horned owls.

On the third weekend in May, the state park participates with about a half-dozen other historic buildings in the Jerome Home Tour. Special activities are also usually planned during the Arizona State Park System's observation of historic preservation, held each spring.

The weather is pleasant in Jerome most of the year, with the busiest months at the park being March, April, May, and October. Most visitors spend at least an hour in the museum, and many spend from 2 to 4 hours before heading out to see Jerome's other historic buildings. Guides to the dozens of historic structures remaining in Jerome can be obtained at the state park and at downtown shops. No mine tours were available in Jerome as of this writing.

Among the other nearby attractions are Fort Verde State Historic Park, as well as Dead Horse Ranch State Park, Slide Rock State Park, and Red Rock State Park, which are all discussed in their own sections of this book.

LYMAN LAKE STATE PARK

Hours/Season: Overnight; year-round
Area: 1,200 land acres, 1,500 lake surface acres
Elevation: 6,000 feet
Facilities: Visitor center, nature trails, store (open April through September only), picnic tables, restrooms with showers, boat ramps, docks, 61 campsites (38 with electric and water hookups), a large beach-camping area, boat camping, a group-camping area (with 11 water, sewer, and electric hookups), group shelters, recreation hall, public telephone, RV dump station, phone: (520) 337-4441
Attractions: Boating, swimming, water-skiing, windsurfing, fishing, hiking, mountain biking, bird-watching, wildlife viewing, interpretive exhibits, archeological sites, environmental education
Nearby: Casa Malpais Archeological Park, Raven Site Ruin, Petrified Forest National Park
Access: 11 miles south of St. Johns off US 180/191

A true multi-purpose park, Lyman Lake, established in 1961, is the oldest recreational park in the Arizona State Park System. A popular family getaway, it offers excellent fishing, some of the state's best water-skiing, several hiking trails, impressive archeological sites, and even a herd of bison.

Named for local Mormon bishop Francis M. Lyman in the early 1900s, the lake was created by damming the Little Colorado River to provide irrigation water for the community of St. Johns. Because it is a large lake (the largest in northeastern Arizona), it has no size or speed restrictions on boats, although the western end has a no-wake requirement to make life easier for anglers. The lake is stocked with rainbow trout, channel catfish, and largemouth bass. Anglers also catch walleye, carp, and bluegills. Local fishing legend tells of one lone northern pike, "Ike the Pike," that has been eluding anglers for years. The park store rents fishing boats and fishing equipment during the summer.

Approximately 1 mile wide by 3 miles long, the lake is exceptionally smooth. A slalom water-skiing course is set up each summer, and two tournaments are held annually in June and August. In addition to water-skiers and anglers, windsurfers come to the lake, mostly in spring and fall. Lyman Lake also draws those with canoes, paddle boats, and small inflatables. Occasionally a sailboat will be seen. The lake does not usually freeze.

There is a swim beach in a protected cove, and, even though the lake is fed by snowmelt from the nearby mountains, water temperatures during summer often rise into the 70s. At high water, the deepest part of the lake is about 45 feet.

The park has several short maintained trails, plus a dirt road that runs along the lake. Mountain bikes are permitted on trails 1 and 2 and the dirt

A petroglyph at Lyman Lake State Park

road, but bikers must stay on the trails. Bike racks are provided in several areas of the park, including the visitor center, in the center of the main campground, and at the trailhead for Trail Number 1.

Trail Number 1, also called the Peninsula Petroglyph Trail, is about 1 mile round-trip, beginning at the day-use area near the campground and climbing onto a rocky peninsula, where it passes several groups of petroglyphs. Most of the petroglyphs were made by ancestors of the Hopi, who lived in the area from 700 to 1400, although some petroglyphs appear to be from the Basketmaker period, from 300 to 700. As it climbs to the top of the peninsula, this trail provides panoramic views across the lake. Generally easy, it has a 200-foot elevation change.

Trail Number 2, about 1.2 miles round-trip, is also rated easy, with a 200-foot elevation change. Starting and ending near the park's picnic area, it includes two loops. The lower loop provides access to the lake, primarily for anglers, while the upper loop offers hikers a good view across the lake. The park's unnamed dirt road is a 3-mile (one-way) walk or bike ride through typical high desert terrain, with some good views of the park and lake. An unnamed trail, more of a path, leaves the campground and meanders through desert terrain of low hills for about 1 mile, ending near the intersection of US 180/191 and the park access road.

The Ultimate Petroglyph Trail is located on the east side of the lake and is accessible only by boat on ranger-led tours, offered in summer. The tours are scheduled Saturdays and Sundays at 10:00 A.M. from Memorial Day to Labor Day. Participants take the park's pontoon boat across the lake, and then have a moderately difficult 1-mile round-trip hike to a large boulder covered with rock art, some created by hunter-gatherers who lived in this area from about 6000 B.C. to about A.D. 300 but most from later periods, up to about 1400.

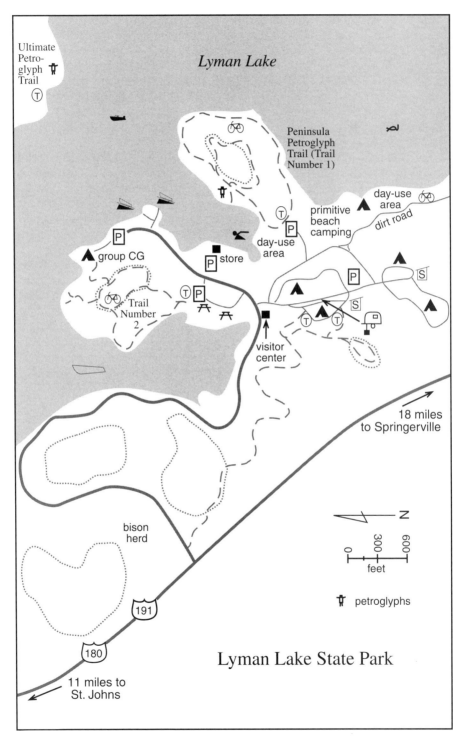

Ultimate Petro-glyph Trail

Lyman Lake

Peninsula Petroglyph Trail (Trail Number 1)

day-use area

primitive beach camping

dirt road

day-use area

P store

group CG

P

Trail Number 2

P

visitor center

S

S

18 miles to Springerville

N

300

600

0

feet

bison herd

191

180

ⵟ petroglyphs

Lyman Lake State Park

11 miles to St. Johns

Also accessible only in summer is Rattlesnake Point Pueblo, which can be visited on a ranger-led tour that starts with a boat ride across the lake or by private vehicle, with directions available at the visitor center. Tours are scheduled Saturdays and Sundays at 2:00 P.M. Believed to have been inhabited between 1325 and 1390, the pueblo was one story tall and had eighty to ninety rooms. Perched on a ledge overlooking the Little Colorado, it is believed to have been home to the ancestors of the Hopi and possibly other pueblo tribes. Some of the walls and several rooms, including a kiva, have been completely excavated.

With a large and reliable source of water, and terrain that includes piñon and juniper trees, Lyman Lake attracts many waterfowl and other birds, especially from fall through spring. Species that are commonly seen in the park include great blue herons, Canada geese, mallards, northern pintails, American kestrels, rufous hummingbirds, violet-green swallows, northern mockingbirds, Wilson's warblers, and brown-headed cowbirds. Bald eagles and osprey are also seen occasionally.

A herd of about a half-dozen plains bison, owned and cared for by the Lyman Lake Buffalo Club, graze on a pasture adjacent to the state park and can often be seen, especially in the morning, near the park entrance. Bison can be unpredictable and should be observed from a distance and not approached. Other wildlife you may see in the park includes desert cottontail

Bison at Lyman Lake State Park

rabbits, prairie dogs, white-tailed deer, coyotes, beaver, and an occasional pronghorn antelope. There are also a few western diamondback rattlesnakes, although visitors will more likely see western bull snakes, which are not poisonous. The park is also home to a few painted turtles and Texas horned lizards.

The developed campground has some trees, although not a lot, with fairly well-spaced sites for both recreational vehicles and tents. This park also permits beach camping, offering practically unlimited camping for RVs, tents, station wagons, or whatever else you might have.

A small visitor center/ranger station has exhibits on the park's archeological sites, flora, and fauna, plus information on scheduled activities.

Summer is the busiest season here, attracting boaters, swimmers, and archeology buffs. July and August temperatures can reach the mid-90s, but at the park's 6,000-foot elevation, nights remain pleasantly cool and comfortable. July and August are also the wettest months at the park, with rains often coming in the form of afternoon thunderstorms. June has slightly cooler daytime temperatures and usually is much drier than July and August. Fall is also a beautiful time to visit, with fewer visitors and color provided by nearby cottonwoods. Fall daytime temperatures are usually in the 70s, with nights dropping into the 30s. Winters have cold nights, with temperatures in the teens, but comfortable days, often in the 50s. Spring tends to be windy, with daytime temperatures in the 60s and 70s and nights often dropping into the 20s; snow remains a possibility into April and May.

Those particularly interested in the prehistoric people who lived in this area will want to visit several other nearby sites. These include Raven Site Ruin at the White Mountain Archeological Center, about 6 miles south of the park on US 180/191, and Casa Malpais Archeological Park in the town of Springerville, about 18 miles south of the park on US 180/191.

Another worthwhile side trip is to Petrified Forest National Park, about 55 miles northwest of the park via US 180, where you can see a vast quantity of petrified wood and a "painted" desert. A 27-mile scenic drive provides access to about two dozen scenic overlooks and a number of short walks. Most of the petrified wood is in the southern part of the park, while the best views of the painted desert are in the park's northern section.

RED ROCK STATE PARK

Hours/Season: 8:00 A.M. to 5:00 P.M. daily October through March; 8:00 A.M. to 6:00 P.M. daily April through September; closed Christmas
Area: 286 land acres
Elevation: 3,990 feet
Facilities: Visitor center, nature trails, picnic tables, restrooms, phone: (520) 282-6907
Attractions: Nature education programs, hiking, mountain biking, horseback riding, bird-watching, wildlife viewing

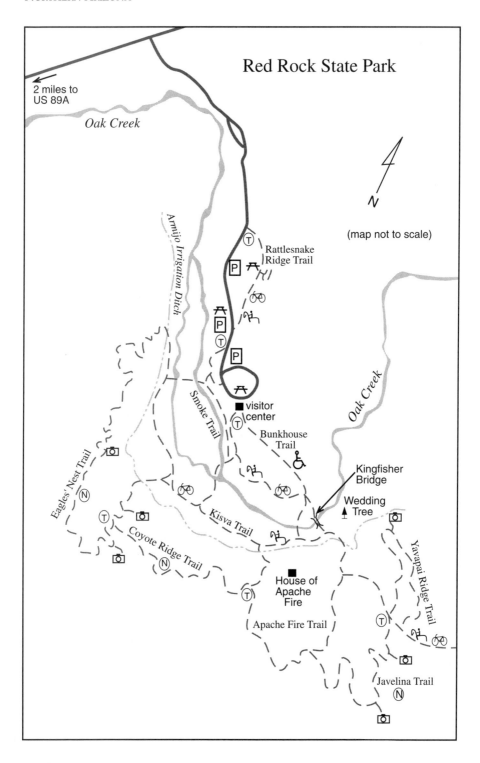

Red Rock State Park

2 miles to
US 89A

Oak Creek

N

(map not to scale)

Armijo Irrigation Ditch

T
Rattlesnake
Ridge Trail
P

P
T

P

visitor
center
T
Bunkhouse
Trail

Smoke Trail

Oak Creek

Kingfisher
Bridge

Wedding
Tree

Eagles' Nest Trail

N

T

Kisva Trail

Coyote Ridge Trail

N

House of
Apache
Fire

T

Apache Fire Trail

T

Yavapai Ridge Trail

Javelina Trail

N

Nearby: Dead Horse Ranch State Park, Slide Rock State Park, Jerome State
  Historic Park, Fort Verde State Historic Park
Access: 5 miles southwest of Sedona on Lower Red Rock Loop Road

A bit different than what one usually thinks of as a state park, Red Rock
is primarily a nature center, with numerous guided hikes, talks, and
bird-watching opportunities. With the picturesque Oak Creek meandering
through the park, shaded by cottonwood, willow, and sycamore trees, there
is an abundance of plants and wildlife, plus splendid views not only along
the creek but spectacular panoramas of the park's namesake red rock cliffs.

Your first stop should be the visitor center, which has exhibits describing
a riparian area—a land-based ecosystem associated with a body of water,
such as a stream, pond, or lake. There are also exhibits on the park's
aquatic life, including a fish tank that contains some of Oak Creek's native
fish species. Interactive exhibits include animal-track identification, a nature
question-and-answer display, and a children's activity center. A small
theater in the visitor center shows videos and slide presentations on a
variety of subjects.

Because of its environmental education bent, Red Rock has more
planned activities than other state parks, and although you can see almost
all of the park on your own, the best way to get the maximum enjoyment
from your park visit is to participate in one or more of its programs and especially to join a guided walk or hike.

Guided nature walks are given year-round, usually twice daily; and
guided bird walks, which often include areas of the park not usually open
to the public, are given three mornings a week year-round. There are also
moonlight walks several evenings each month from April through October—an excellent chance to see the park's larger animals—and guided
hikes are offered several days a week from September through May.

There is usually a special program on the first Sunday of each month,
year-round, covering various subjects, such as the park's wildflowers, a
particular park animal, or the area's human history. Annual events include
Earth Day in April, with free admission and numerous activities, and an
astronomy festival in June, featuring programs with Arizona astronomers.
The park has also become popular for weddings, and those wanting an outdoor ceremony under a towering cottonwood "wedding" tree should contact
the park office.

A prime hikers' and walkers' destination, Red Rock State Park has about
5 miles of trails, all interconnecting and most rated easy. Individual trails
range in length from less than 0.5 mile to almost 2 miles round-trip from the
visitor center, but most hikers combine sections of different trails.

The 1.7-mile Kisva Trail and the 0.4-mile Smoke Trail meander through
the riparian area along Oak Creek, beneath tall cottonwoods and umbrella-
like willows, and provide close-up views of the wetlands. Flat and well-
maintained, these shady trails are particularly popular on hot summer
days. The Bunkhouse Trail is a short, paved, handicapped-accessible loop
that departs from the visitor center.

Sections of the Kisva and Bunkhouse Trails have numbered signs identifying plants and discussing other natural aspects of the park, with informative booklets, keyed to the signs, available at the visitor center.

The park's most challenging trail, rated moderate, is Eagles' Nest Trail, a 1.9-mile loop that climbs about 200 feet to the park's highest point, providing splendid panoramic views of the red rock cliffs from several overlooks. The rock gets its color from hematite—iron oxide—so essentially what you are looking at is rusty rocks. The trail is a bit rocky, and with less shade than trails along Oak Creek, so hikers will want to wear hats and carry plenty of drinking water.

Hiking a nature trail at Red Rock State Park

Apache Fire (1.7 miles), Javelina (1.75 miles), Yavapai Ridge (1.5 miles), and Rattlesnake Ridge (1.3 miles) Trails also lead away from the creek, providing a combination of riparian and desert terrain. Distances are round-trip from the visitor center.

Mountain bikes and horses are permitted on Kisva and Rattlesnake Ridge Trails, but not on other park trails. Mountain bikers also have access to the 6.5 mile round-trip Cathedral Bike Loop, which starts and ends in the park but is mostly outside the park. It changes terrain from lush riparian to stark desert, following trails that range from sandy to rocky and a paved road. At one point, it is necessary to ford Oak Creek. A detailed map is available at the visitor center.

Bird-watchers have plenty of opportunities here, particularly along the Kisva Trail and other trails in the wetlands. There is also a bird-feeding station just behind the visitor center, which can be seen from a trail or from an observation deck on the visitor center roof.

Among the 150 or so species that frequent the park and surrounding areas, forty to fifty are permanent residents. Frequently spotted year-round in the park are great blue herons, common mergansers, Cooper's hawks, greater roadrunners, great horned owls, Anna's hummingbirds, belted kingfishers, red-naped sapsuckers, black phoebes, bushtits, canyon wrens, northern cardinals, and lesser goldfinches. Summer visitors are also likely to see common black-hawks, which may be nesting in the park in spring as well, plus turkey vultures, white-throated swifts, violet-green swallows, northern mockingbirds, and hooded orioles. There are also a number of species that spend winters here, such as the bald eagle, and migratory birds that stop off for a while in spring and fall.

The park also has a resident herd of mule deer. Other animals seen include rock squirrels, pocket gophers, cottontail rabbits, beaver, coyotes, and javelina. Racoons and ringtail cats also live in the park but are nocturnal and rarely seen. Occasionally, a bear or mountain lion wanders through the park.

Spring and fall are considered the best times to visit Red Rock State Park. There are numerous migratory birds, and the weather is perfect for hiking, with highs mostly in the 70s and low 80s, and lows generally in the 40s. April and May, which get the most visitors, are usually best for wildflowers, and the fall colors can also be pretty, usually peaking in late October. Summers are pleasantly temperate by Arizona standards, with highs usually in the 90s and lows in the 60s. Afternoon rains are common in summer, so morning visits are often best. During winter, nights are often in the 20s, but daytime temperatures usually rise into the 50s.

Swimming or wading in Oak Creek is prohibited, and pets are not permitted anywhere in the park. Although there is no camping in the park, Dead Horse Ranch State Park, about 15 miles southwest of Red Rock, offers camping and makes a good overnight base for exploring the area. Also nearby are Slide Rock State Park, Jerome State Historic Park, and Fort Verde State Historic Park, all discussed in their own sections of this book.

RIORDAN MANSION STATE HISTORIC PARK

Hours/Season: 8:00 A.M. to 5:00 P.M. daily May to September; 11:00 A.M. to 5:00 P.M. daily October to April; closed Christmas
Area: 6 land acres
Elevation: 6,900 feet
Facilities: Visitor center/museum, picnic tables, restrooms, phone: (520) 779-4395
Attractions: Historical exhibits, interpretive programs
Access: In Flagstaff at 1300 Riordan Ranch Street; from the junction of I-40 (exit 195B) and I-17 (exit 340), head north on Milton Road (US 89A) for 1.3 miles, turn right (east) onto Riordan Road for 1 block, and then right (south) on Riordan Ranch Road and follow signs to the park

Roughing it in an Arizona Territory frontier town in the early years of the twentieth century was not too bad, as long as you had plenty of money. Riordan State Historic Park shows how two brothers and their wives and children lived a luxurious life in what was then the rough-and-tumble timber town of Flagstaff.

Tim and Mike Riordan were prominent Flagstaff businessmen who developed a very successful logging operation, the Arizona Lumber and Timber Company. The brothers, originally from Chicago, married two sisters—Caroline and Elizabeth Metz of Cincinnati—and in 1904 built a unique duplex mansion. Essentially two beautiful homes connected by a large common room, the mansion has forty rooms covering over 13,000 square feet of living space.

Politically and socially prominent in early Flagstaff, the Riordan brothers were instrumental in the construction of an electric power plant for the city. Tim built a dam to impound water for use in the timber industry, which later provided municipal water for Flagstaff and was named Lake Mary after Tim's eldest daughter. Both men served on various government boards and committees, were involved with local financial institutions, and had other business interests. In short, the Riordans were VIPs.

The two homes are practically mirror images of each other, although each was adapted somewhat for that family's preferences. For instance, Tim enjoyed telling stories at the dinner table, so the dining room in his side of the mansion was designed around a long, pointed, oval dining table that gave him the best position for weaving his yarns.

Constructed of log-slab siding, hand-split wooden shingles, and stone arches, the building looks more like a huge log cabin than the mansion of two of the wealthiest families in town. Once one steps inside, however, it becomes obvious that these people were cultured, well-traveled, and financially able to buy the best. The home was constructed and then furnished in American Arts and Crafts style, also called Craftsman, which was popular from the late 1890s through the mid-1920s. Craftsman furniture was simple, well-made, and durable. This style was quite different from common,

Riordan brothers' home at Riordan Mansion State Historic Park

turn-of-the-century, Victorian-style furnishings that were mass-produced in a cheap and overly decorated fashion.

What makes the mansion especially unique is that, unlike almost all other historic homes, it contains practically all of its original furnishings—the very pieces that the Riordans purchased to furnish it in 1904. Perhaps that is why you do not feel that you are viewing an exhibit, but rather that you are actually an invited guest in the Riordans' home, and they will step through the door at any moment.

Guided tours are given of Tim's side of the house and the common room, which is sometimes called the billiard room. What you see is a very comfortable home, furnished beautifully but not ostentatiously, with neatly painted and papered walls, hardwood floors, and handcrafted furniture. There are many built-in cabinets and bookcases, Tiffany-style stained glass windows, a Steinway piano, and a wicker swing in front of the living room fireplace that can be turned around to face an open window in summer. The home contains many personal items, including family photos, memorabilia, and clothing, such as Caroline Riordan's evening dress from 1915.

The common room, which both Riordan families used for entertaining, is the only room in the mansion that has log interior walls. It contains a billiards table, various types of seating, and a stone fireplace topped with a bison head. This is also where the families set up their Christmas trees. The kitchen has its original furnishings, where Caroline Riordan occasionally enjoyed cooking for the family, although she had a full-time cook and other servants.

Outside, you can examine the massive stone arches, made of volcanic rock from the Flagstaff area, look for two totem faces carved into the ends of log beams, and see the gatekeeper's cottage and the six-car garage, which now serves as the visitor center. Also on the grounds are what remains of Tim Riordan's tennis court, but several trees block any possible play. The estate also had its own golf course, which is now gone.

The visitor center has displays on the Riordan families and Flagstaff in the late nineteenth and early twentieth centuries, and a children's "Please Touch" table of historic artifacts. A short slide program discusses the house and the Riordans, and publications on early Flagstaff and the Riordan family can be purchased.

Each year during the Christmas season, the mansion is decorated as it would have been for Christmas, 1904, and several evenings in January or February are set aside for "Timber Tales" storytelling. In addition, Riordan offers several nights of special tours with interpretive programs immediately prior to Halloween. These are geared for adult audiences and not recommended for children. A variety of special events are also scheduled during the Arizona State Park System's observation of historic preservation, held each spring.

The only way to see the inside of the house is on a guided tour, which lasts about 45 minutes. Summer weekends are the busiest times, although the house never seems crowded, because tours are limited. Reservations are strongly recommended at all times, especially during the summer months.

SLIDE ROCK STATE PARK

Hours/Season: 8:00 A.M. to 7:00 P.M. summer; 8:00 A.M. to 5:00 P.M. winter; 8:00 A.M. to 6:00 P.M. spring and fall; closed Christmas
Area: 43 land acres
Elevation: 4,930 feet
Facilities: Ranger station, picnic tables, store, public telephone, nature trail, volleyball court, restrooms, phone: (520) 282-3034
Attractions: Swimming, sunbathing, hiking, fishing, bird-watching, historic exhibits, interpretive programs
Nearby: Red Rock State Park, Dead Horse Ranch State Park, Jerome State Historic Park, Fort Verde State Historic Park, city of Sedona, Coconino National Forest
Access: 7 miles north of Sedona on US 89A

Beautiful scenery and a natural red-rock water slide are the big draws at this very popular day-use park, which also has picnicking, fishing, historic buildings and farm equipment, and an apple orchard. Located in Oak Creek Canyon, considered among Arizona's most scenic areas, Slide Rock State Park combines spectacular red rock formations, the rich green of piñon and juniper, and the churning, bubbling Oak Creek.

Slide Rock State Park is on the site of an early twentieth-century farm, homesteaded by Frank Pendley, a Texan who had moved to Arizona and worked as a stone driller miner. He moved to the canyon in 1908 and filed for ownership of the property in 1910 under the Homestead Act. Pendley created a unique irrigation system—a portion is still in use today—and in 1912 planted his first apple orchard. During winters, he trapped bobcats, selling the skins for $5 apiece. When the road through the canyon was paved in 1932 it not only helped Pendley get his crops to market but provided outsiders with easy access to Oak Creek Canyon's beauty. Pendley saw the potential for tourism, and the next year he built a series of rustic vacation cabins, three of which still remain.

The Pendley family operated the farm until the mid-1980s, planting additional crops, and then sold the homestead to the state of Arizona, which opened Slide Rock State Park in 1987. The state continues to operate the farm as an historic agricultural property, growing about a dozen varieties of cooking and eating apples, plus other crops. Visitors today can see the orchards—apple blossoms usually bloom in mid-April—plus antique farm equipment. You can also see the exteriors of the Pendley family home, built in 1927; an apple packing barn, which was built in 1932 and resembles the Alamo, recalling Pendley's Texas roots; and the three tourist cabins built in 1933. Apples are harvested each fall and sold at the park's store, the Slide Rock Market.

While apples and history may be important aspects of the park, the great majority of warm-weather visitors are more interested in lying about or cavorting on the smooth red rocks and slipping down the natural rock water

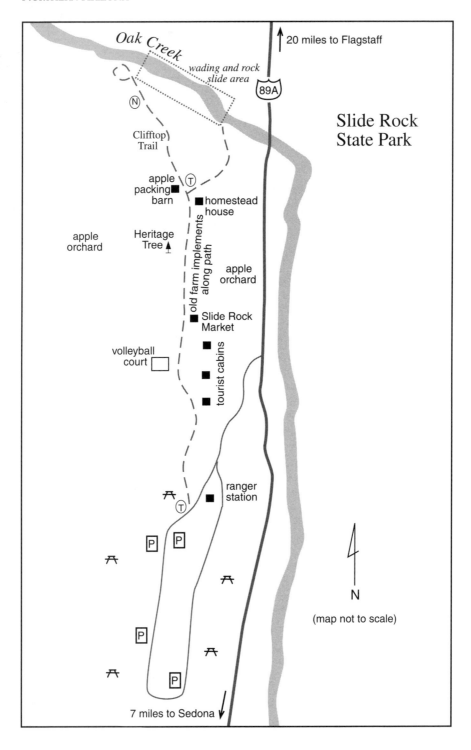

Playing on the rocks and in the water at Slide Rock State Park

slide. Summer water temperatures are usually in the mid-60s, while air temperatures often reach the mid- to upper 90s. Summer nights usually dip into the 60s. Climbing among the rocks is more comfortable with water shoes of some kind, and those planning to experience the water slide can save wear and tear of expensive swimming suits as well as tender flesh by slipping on a pair of sturdy shorts or cut-off jeans. Pets and glass containers are prohibited in the swimming area.

Fishing is best when the weather is too cool for swimmers. The creek is stocked with rainbow trout and occasionally with brown trout. White-water boating and canoeing are not permitted.

Park trails total about 1 mile—mostly just to get from parking and picnic areas to the creek, Slide Rock Market, and so forth. The 0.25-mile (round-trip) Clifftop Trail—part of which is wheelchair-accessible—leads up along the red rocks above Oak Creek to a series of scenic overlooks, with four sitting areas looking down on Slide Rock. The trail is relatively easy.

Birding in the park is best early in the day, before the swimmers, sun-bathers, and picnickers take over. The park's various vegetative zones provide habitat for over 100 species. Among year-round park residents are song sparrows, rufous-sided towhees, European starlings, American dippers, American robins, canyon wrens, black phoebes, red-naped sapsuckers, western screech owls, red-tailed hawks, and common mergansers. In winter, bald eagles are occasionally spotted on the cliffs above the creek.

Also sometimes seen in the park, usually late in the day, are deer, javelina, bobcats, and coyotes. Mountain lions and black bears have also been known to frequent the park, but are seldom seen. There are also rattlesnakes and a variety of lizards.

The ranger station, housed in a farm workers' building constructed in 1926, contains information on park activities. Guided tours of the historic Pendley Homestead, lasting about 45 minutes, are offered Saturdays from April through September and concentrate on the history of agriculture in Oak Creek Canyon. From April through November, ranger-led bird walks are scheduled Sunday mornings, and a variety of natural history walks are scheduled Friday mornings during summer months. Fall-color walks are often offered in October.

While summers are particularly busy and the best time to visit for those who want to get wet, the park has much to offer year-round. The red rock scenery is always beautiful, and fall colors can be particularly attractive. Temperatures in the fall range from the upper 60s to low 80s during the day to the 40s and low 50s at night. Spring temperatures are much the same, and winter days can be very pleasant in the protected canyon, with daytime temperatures reaching the 50s and low 60s, while nights drop into the 20s and 30s.

If this area looks familiar, it could be because you have been to the movies. Oak Creek Canyon was a popular spot for movie makers in the 1940s and 1950s and is prominently featured in a number of westerns, including the 1946 John Wayne hit *Angel and the Badman;* the 1950s' film *Broken Arrow,* with James Stewart; and *Drum Beat,* filmed in 1954 and starring Alan Ladd and Charles Bronson.

Just 7 miles south of the state park, the picturesque town of Sedona, with its dozens of art galleries and boutiques, provides a base camp for off-road, helicopter, and hot-air-balloon tours of Oak Creek Canyon's red rock country. There are also a number of other swimming, picnicking, and camping sites along the creek in the Coconino National Forest. About 4 miles south of Sedona is Red Rock State Park, which is discussed in its own section of this book. Also nearby, and discussed in their own sections of this book, are Dead Horse Ranch State Park (with camping), plus Jerome and Fort Verde State Historic Parks.

TONTO NATURAL BRIDGE STATE PARK

Hours/Season: 8:00 A.M. to 7:00 P.M. June through August; 8:00 A.M. to 6:00 P.M. September, October, April, and May; 9:00 A.M. to 5:00 P.M. November through March; closed Christmas

Area: 160 land acres

Elevation: 4,600 feet

Facilities: Visitor center, gift shop, picnic tables, nature trail (under development), restrooms, phone: (520) 476-4202

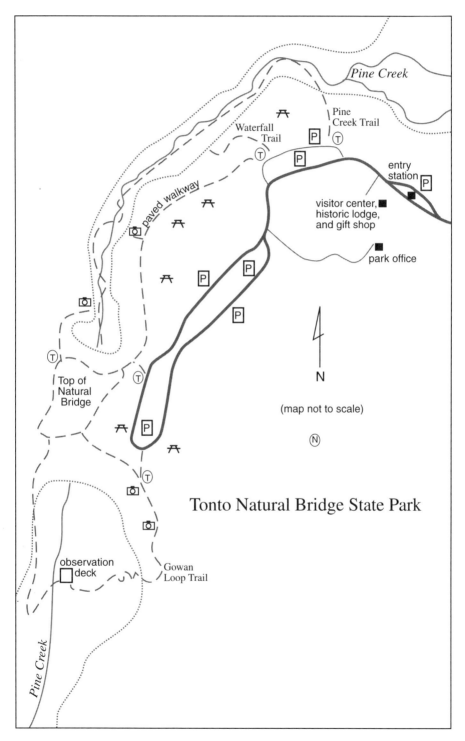

A large hole through solid stone forms Tonto Natural Bridge

Attractions: Natural bridge, hiking, passive water play, historic lodge and exhibits, interpretive programs
Nearby: Tonto National Forest
Access: 10 miles north of Payson on AZ 87

⊥ This huge stone bridge, formed by eroded deposits of limestone, is believed to be the largest natural travertine bridge in the world, and Tonto Natural Bridge State Park protects the bridge and an historic hotel, while providing hiking, swimming, and picnicking opportunities in a forest of piñon, juniper, Arizona cypress, and oak.

The bridge is 183 feet high, creating a tunnel 150 feet wide and 400 feet long. Geologists say that a series of volcanic eruptions, erosion, and uplifts created the narrow Pine Creek Canyon. Springs then carried deposited carbonate to form a natural dam, and water from Pine Creek eventually made its way through the dam to form Tonto Natural Bridge.

Apaches had hunted and farmed in the valley for hundreds of years when the bridge was first seen by Army troops in 1870. The troops had stopped to water their horses in the creek while trailing a group of Apaches. Then in 1877, a Scottish gold prospector named David Gowan was running from Apaches when he discovered the natural bridge, where he remained hidden for three days. After the danger passed, Gowan looked around, decided he liked the area, and filed a squatter's claim.

By the early 1880s, Gowan had built a cabin on the bridge and planted walnut, apricot, peach, cherry, and pear trees. He continued looking for gold and worked a small gold mine in the area for about ten years. Gowan's nephew, David Gowan Goodfellow, brought his wife Lillias and their three young children from Scotland to Arizona in 1898.

After an arduous 6-day wagon trip from Flagstaff, Goodfellow discovered that the route to his uncle's cabin was a steep, narrow 3-mile trail down into the canyon, and the only way to get their possessions to the valley floor was to lower them down 500 feet using ropes and pack burros. In 1933, Lillias Goodfellow wrote about the experience: "I fervently wished that I had never come to Arizona. I honestly believed that I could never reach the cabin alive . . . and I was sure that if I ever did get there, I would never be able to climb out again."

The family did, however, settle in, and they soon found themselves in the tourist business, as more and more people kept showing up asking to see what was becoming a famous natural attraction. They built a road into the valley, built cabins, and in the mid-1920s constructed a then-modern ten-room lodge, complete with running water.

Today's visitors have an easier time than the Goodfellows and can see the bridge from above, via a paved handicapped-accessible walkway, or hike several trails into the canyon.

The best views of the natural bridge are from the moderate-to-difficult 0.5-mile Gowan Loop Trail, which is steep and rough and leads to an observation deck at the base of the bridge. Although you can hike the loop in either direction, it is easiest to go clockwise. Start by turning left at the trailhead, going down into the canyon on the steepest part, which includes quite a few uneven rock steps. Then return to the top on an easier grade on the other side of Pine Creek. Hiking boots with good traction are advised, since rocks at the bridge tend to be wet and slippery. This trail is a bit of work, but it is particularly pretty, with lots of trees and impressive boulders, and the views of the natural bridge are spectacular.

The Pine Creek Trail, which also has some steep sections and is rated moderate, is about 0.5 mile long (one-way). The first 400 feet are maintained and well-marked, but once you get down to the creek bottom, it is undeveloped. The riparian area along the creek, filled with lush vegetation, offers good opportunities to see wildlife.

The 300-foot (one-way) Waterfall Trail is short and steep, with a series of steps leading partway down into the canyon and ending at a picturesque waterfall cave.

Those who want to see the bridge from above can do so via a very easy, paved walkway, which runs from a parking area to the edge of the canyon, with several viewpoints down into the valley and of the bridge. A paved nature trail is also being developed.

The wetlands along the creek, particularly under and near the bridge, have created an unusually moist environment that is ideal for wildlife. Among the more than 100 species of birds you may see are American dippers, ruby-crowned kinglets, ash-throated flycatchers, several types of tanagers, Bell's vireo, and dark-eyed juncos. Swallows and ravens often nest in protected caves, and throughout the park there are great horned owls, Steller's jays, American robins, and mountain bluebirds.

The park is also home to woodrats, rock squirrels, spotted and striped skunks, racoons, cottontail rabbits, javelina, white-tailed deer, and elk. The nocturnal ringtail cat lives in the park but is seldom seen. Occasionally, a mountain lion or black bear are spotted. Several species of rattlesnakes also are found in the park, plus collared lizards, Arizona alligator lizards, short-horned lizards, tiger salamanders, Arizona toads, and northern leopard frogs.

Swimming is prohibited directly under the bridge but allowed elsewhere in the chilly creek, which in summer ranges from 62 degrees F to 67 degrees F. Although the creek is not deep or wide enough for real swimming, you can wade or at least cool your feet. The best spot is just downstream of a footbridge along the Gowan Loop Trail.

The lodge, built in the 1920s, serves as the park's visitor center, with antiques and historic photos on display in the lobby. An adjacent room houses a gift and souvenir shop.

Individualized tours of the rest of the historic lodge are offered, depending on staff availability, and take 20 to 30 minutes. Reservations are recommended. Many of the lodge's ten guest rooms contain original furnishings and are decorated with period wall coverings and historic photos of the area. The bathrooms have claw-foot tubs, and an observation deck on the third floor offers panoramic views of the park.

Spring and fall are the best times to visit. March and April are known for splendid wildflower displays, and fall colors in October can be especially pretty. Temperatures during those times range from highs in the 60s and 70s to lows in the 30s and low 40s. Winters can be cold and snowy, with the steep and winding road into the valley sometimes closed for up to a day by snow. High temperatures in winter usually reach the 50s, while lows drop into the upper teens and 20s. The park is busiest in summer, especially on weekends and holidays. While summer daytime temperatures are usually in the 80s and 90s, the thermometer sometimes exceeds 100 degrees F. Summer nighttime temperatures usually drop into the 50s.

Because the park is located at the bottom of a very steep 14-percent grade, those towing trailers are strongly advised to leave them in a parking area provided at the top of the road, about 1.5 miles from the park. Motorists are also advised to use lower gears, especially with trucks, motor homes, and other large vehicles. Park regulations prohibit taking any glass containers on trails. Dogs are also prohibited on trails into the canyon but may be taken on leashes to the canyon-edge viewpoints.

Although there are no camping facilities in the park, camping and hiking are available in the surrounding Tonto National Forest.

SOUTH-EASTERN ARIZONA

This is what most people think of as pure Arizona—the Sonoran Desert and its trademark giant saguaro cactus, which can sometimes grow to a height of 50 feet. In addition to the stately saguaros, the region is home to numerous species of cactus and other desert plants, some unique in the world. Several parks in this region provide rugged hiking trails and classic Arizona desert beauty, along with exquisite cactus gardens and opportunities for nature study. There are cattle ranches, and because of extensive irrigation and a year-round growing season, this region grows massive amounts of cotton and has also become America's fruit and vegetable basket, producing oranges, grapefruit, tomatoes, melons, lettuce, and carrots, among others. To provide the water, lakes have been created, and some of these have become state parks that offer boating, fishing, and other water-based activities. Over half of the state's population lives in Maricopa County, which encompasses Phoenix, the state's largest city. To the south of Phoenix is Tucson, the state's second largest city. Southern Arizona is also the area first explored by Spanish conquistadores, as well as being home to the wildest towns of the Old West. These aspects of Arizona's history are preserved in several state parks.

BOYCE THOMPSON ARBORETUM STATE PARK

Hours/Season: 8:00 A.M. to 5:00 P.M. daily; closed Christmas
Area: 323 land acres
Elevation: 2,400 feet

Opposite: *Stalagmites, stalactites, and other formations in Kartchner Caverns State Park* (photo by Princely Nesadurai, Arizona State Parks)

Facilities: Visitor center, interpretive center, picnic tables, restrooms, public telephone, gift shop, plant shop, phone: (520) 689-2811
Attractions: Hiking, botanical garden, demonstration gardens, historic buildings, wildlife viewing, bird-watching, interpretive exhibits, interpretive programs
Nearby: Lost Dutchman State Park, McFarland State Historic Park
Access: 3 miles west of Superior on US 60

Desert plants in a scenic, shady, and peaceful environment are the attraction at the Boyce Thompson Arboretum State Park. Visitors here can stroll leisurely along tree-lined paths, hike through a rugged desert canyon, and seriously study more than 3,000 water-stingy plants from around the world, all displayed in a natural setting.

This living museum of plants that can survive in dry conditions was the brainchild of mining magnate William Boyce Thompson. In 1917, Thompson led a Red Cross expedition taking medical supplies to the Russian people after the Russian Revolution. Passing through arid sections of Siberia, Thompson was impressed with all that plants do for humanity and got the idea to create an arboretum devoted to water-efficient plant species and their uses.

The arboretum was built from 1923 to 1929, and Thompson gave it an endowment and a mission to display, study, and preserve the plants of the arid and semiarid regions of the world, helping the public to better appreciate the importance of plants in our lives. Today, the arboretum is managed jointly by the University of Arizona, Arizona State Parks, and The Boyce Thompson Southwestern Arboretum, Inc., a private nonprofit corporation.

A network of interconnecting trails, totaling about 4.5 miles, leads visitors along a bubbling creek, through cactus and herb gardens to historic buildings and greenhouses, and along natural desert trails. Interpretive signs and exhibits are located throughout the arboretum, and those so inclined can learn about the park's numerous species of cacti, the spiny ocotillo, green-stemmed paloverde, as well as the agave, a long-lived desert plant that flowers only once—the year before it dies.

Depending on your interests, a trip to the arboretum can be an easy walk through a delightful desert garden or an opportunity to spend hours or days studying firsthand the world's plants that have best adapted to dry environments.

The 1.5-mile Main Trail offers a close-up view of thousands of species of plants from around the world, traversing various arid and semiarid habitats, from rich riparian to burning desert. Beginning and ending at the arboretum's visitor center, the Main Trail meanders through gardens of cacti, succulents, herbs, shrubs, and trees. It follows Queen Creek through a riparian area and also leads through forests of pine, eucalyptus, pistachio, olive, and palm. Along the trail are river she-oaks from Australia. These look like pines trees but are actually flowering plants, and what appear to be tiny pine cones are the she-oak's seed pods.

Generally flat and mostly wheelchair-accessible, the Main Trail has one

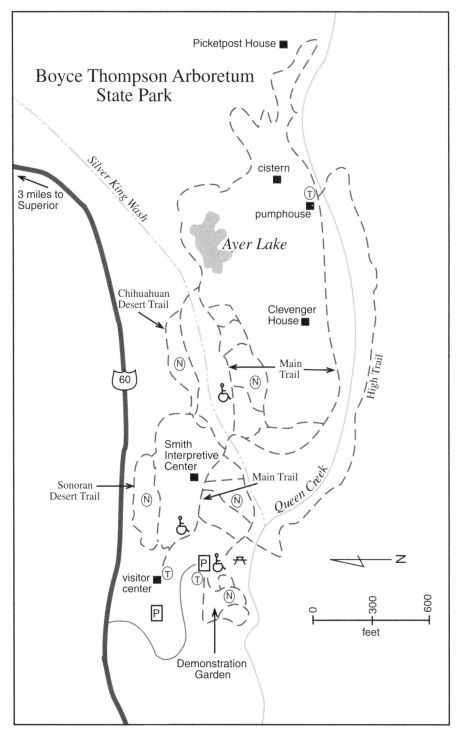

Picketpost House ■

Boyce Thompson Arboretum
State Park

Silver King Wash

3 miles to
Superior

60

cistern ■

Ⓣ

pumphouse

Ayer Lake

Chihuahuan
Desert Trail

Clevenger
House ■

Ⓝ

Main
Trail

Ⓝ

High Trail

Smith
Interpretive
Center ■

Main Trail

Sonoran
Desert Trail

Ⓝ

Ⓝ

Queen Creek

Ⓝ

P

Ⓝ

visitor ■
center

Ⓣ

P

Ⓣ

N

P

Ⓝ

0   300   600

feet

Demonstration
Garden

rather steep section (not handicapped-accessible) that follows a natural desert hillside around a reservoir, Ayer Lake, which is used for irrigation and is home to two endangered species of desert fish—the Gila topminnow and the desert pupfish.

Branching off of the Main Trail are numerous side trails and short loops that lead to additional gardens and groves. These include the Pine Grove, with pine, spruce, cypress, and other conifers; and the Sonoran Desert Trail, with a myriad of desert plants. Southwestern gardeners can learn about how to improve their home landscaping in the Demonstration Garden, which shows examples of how drought-resistant plants can be used for landscaping, plus irrigation and water-harvesting techniques.

The 0.5-mile High Trail starts at the picnic grounds, and then crosses a natural area of Sonoran Desert, offering views of the arboretum's gardens and riparian area, as well as the surrounding mountains. The moderately difficult trail ends at a junction with the Main Trail.

Water draws wildlife, and here Queen Creek and Ayer Lake, along with the variety of plant life, attract more than 300 species of birds, mammals, reptiles, and amphibians. Most of the birds and animals are easiest to see first thing in the morning, just after the arboretum opens. Birders may spot cactus wrens, verdin, white-winged doves, Gambel's quail, hooded orioles, western tanagers, and numerous hummingbirds. From mid- to late March, a migrating flock of turkey vultures returns for their summer stay and can often be glimpsed until September.

Visitors should also keep their eyes open for frogs and toads along the river and for snakes and lizards in the dryer parts of the park. Snakes include four types of rattlesnakes; and lizards that may be seen sunning themselves include Gila monsters, chuckwallas, collared lizards, desert spiny lizards, and Arizona alligator lizards.

The most commonly seen mammals are cliff chipmunks, rock squirrels, and desert cottontail rabbits; but oft-seen tracks or droppings give evidence of the park's nocturnal inhabitants, such as black-tailed and mule deer, bobcats, coyotes, ringtail cats, badgers, and javelina.

At the arboretum's visitor center there are exhibits, a gift shop and bookstore, and a greenhouse. Nearby, the arboretum's original visitor center, the Smith Interpretive Center, has additional displays that include cacti and succulents from around the world. Constructed in 1925, the building is made of rhyolite, a native stone.

In keeping with its role as a research and educational institution, as well as being a fun place to visit, the arboretum provides information, seeds, and plants to government agencies, as well as to the public, and also sells plants and seeds in its gift shop.

During World War II, when it was feared the Germans would monopolize the world's cork supply, the arboretum established a nursery of cork oak trees and distributed the trees throughout the Southwest. More recently, the arboretum's researchers discovered that oil from jojoba seeds contains a type of liquid wax that can be substituted for sperm whale oil,

One of the many cactus gardens at Boyce Thompson Arboretum State Park

and jojoba seeds have been distributed to scientists for experimentation for possible industrial uses.

From January through March, there are afternoon programs Wednesdays through Sundays, featuring such various topics as the arboretum's birds, edible desert plants, wildflowers, and plants that attract hummingbirds and butterflies. Annual events include the Fall Landscaping Festival in late October, the Arid Land Plant Show in early April, and the Herb Festival in early May.

Choosing when to visit depends mostly on your interests. Spring comes early and is beautiful, with new growth and an abundance of flowers. Early spring—February and March—is the busiest time at the park. Then from mid-April through May, it is the cacti's turn to bloom. Colors are also spectacular in fall, and the weather is particularly pleasant then. Summers are the quietest time at the arboretum. The weather is hot—although usually about 5 degrees F to 10 degrees F cooler than downtown Phoenix, where temperatures can reach 120 degrees F—but the arboretum offers plenty of shade. Still, summer visitors are advised to wear hats, sunscreen, and sunglasses and carry drinking water if they plan to spend much time on the trails. Winters are cool but not cold, with highs in the 60s and lows in the 40s. Although there are fewer flowers to see in winter, the scene is brightened by aloe flowers and South African ice plants.

According to arboretum regulations, all children must be accompanied by adults and stay with those adults during their visit. Pets are permitted on the trails and in the gardens if leashed but are prohibited from buildings and bodies of water. Pet owners should be prepared to clean up after their animals.

Among nearby attractions are two other state parks, Lost Dutchman, about 33 miles to the northwest, and McFarland State Historic Park, about 28 miles to the southwest, which are discussed in their own sections of this book.

CATALINA STATE PARK

Hours/Season: Overnight; year-round
Area: 5,811 land acres
Elevation: 2,700 feet
Facilities: Visitor center, historic sites, picnic tables, equestrian center, nature trail, restrooms with showers, group-use areas, public telephone, 48 campsites (23 with electric hookups), RV dump station (open 8:00 A.M. to 5:00 P.M. only), phone: (520) 628-5798
Attractions: Hiking, mountain biking, horseback riding, interpretive exhibits
Nearby: Coronado National Forest
Access: 9 miles north of Tucson on AZ 77

Considered one of Arizona's best parks for hiking and horseback riding, Catalina State Park sits at the foot of the majestic Santa Catalina Mountains, adjacent to the Coronado National Forest. Situated in a mesquite woodlands surrounded by Sonoran Desert terrain, the park offers great scenery, wildlife viewing and bird-watching opportunities, shady campsites, and seven varied trails.

More than one thousand years ago, Hohokam Indians lived in these mountains. They were followed by the Pimas, and then the Apaches. Spanish explorers arrived in the area in the late 1600s, and according to one story, the Jesuit priest Father Eusebio Kino named the mountains the Santa Catarinas, probably in honor of Saint Catherine. Somewhere along the line, however, Catarina became Catalina.

Another story is that the correct name was Santa Catalina from the start but was misspelled by early cartographers and even the U.S. Postal Service, which established the Santa Catarina Post Office in 1882. Just to add a bit more confusion, historians also report that early Spanish settlers called the mountains *La Iglesia,* Spanish for "the church," because they thought the imposing mountains resembled a cathedral.

Most visitors today are less concerned with how the mountains were named than with how to get into them, and Catalina State Park provides an excellent staging area for both short walks and extended backpacking trips into the Coronado National Forest and the Pusch Ridge Wilderness Area. Of the park's seven trails, four are completely within the park, and the remaining three leave the park, opening up numerous opportunities to connect with additional trails for multi-day backpacking trips.

Trails within the park boundaries are generally easy to follow, but those in the national forest and wilderness area are less well-maintained, and it is strongly advised that those taking the longer trails carry detailed topographic maps, which can be purchased at the park visitor center. Compasses and plenty of water are also recommended. Because summers are hot, the best times for hiking are late fall through early spring. At other times of year, it is best to start very early in the day or take a short evening hike.

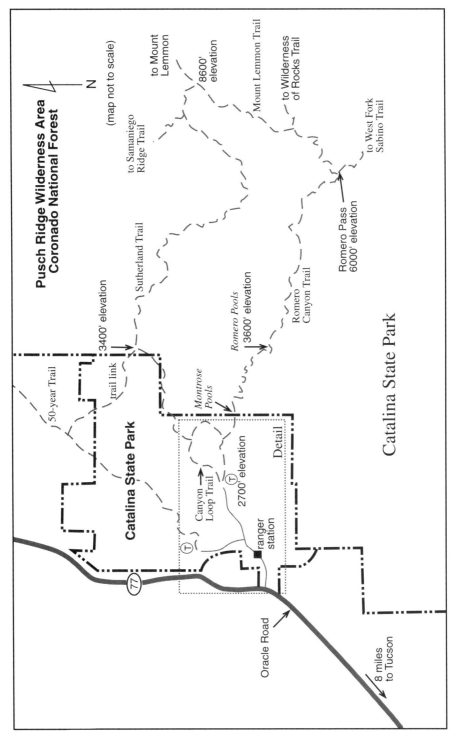

Pusch Ridge Wilderness Area
Coronado National Forest

N

(map not to scale)

to Mount Lemmon

8600' elevation

Mount Lemmon Trail

to Wilderness of Rocks Trail

to Samaniego Ridge Trail

to West Fork Sabino Trail

Sutherland Trail

3400' elevation

Romero Pass 6000' elevation

Romero Pools 3600' elevation

Romero Canyon Trail

50-year Trail

trail link

Catalina State Park

Montrose Pools

Detail

Canyon Loop Trail

2700' elevation

ranger station

77

Oracle Road

8 miles to Tucson

Catalina State Park

The park's easiest hike is the flat, 1.4-mile (one-way) Bridle Trail. It runs from the Equestrian Center past the campground and group-use area, along the south base of a hillside, ending at the park's main trailhead, where you can join most of the park's other trails. Along the way, you will have an opportunity to inspect stands of giant saguaro cactus and enjoy panoramic views of the surrounding mountains.

Those who want a good introduction to the southern Arizona desert environment, as well as those out for an after-dinner stroll, should consider the Nature Trail. This 1-mile loop starts with a steep but short climb, and then becomes quite easy. It meanders among blue and yellow paloverde, pincushion cactus, desert Christmas cactus, chainfruit cholla, staghorn cholla, barrel cactus, saguaro, prickly pear, and mesquite, all described on interpretive signs. Along the trail, there are also colored concrete depictions of footprints that might be seen in the park, including a mountain lion, a roadrunner, and a human's hiking boots.

Another easy loop is the 1-mile Birding Trail. It has a few steep sections but is mostly flat. Located between two washes, it offers a good chance to see a wide variety of bird species.

Those interested in history will enjoy the Romero Ruin Interpretive Trail. Another good after-dinner walk, this easy 0.3-mile loop begins with a stairway to the mesa top, and then is relatively flat. Named for Francisco Romero, a rancher who built a house here in the mid-1880s, the trail meanders among the ruins of Romero's ranch, plus ruins from a Hohokam Indian village that is believed to have been first occupied as early as A.D. 500. The Hohokam village, in its final form around 1150, was a walled community that is believed to have covered almost 1 acre. Romero built his house at the site but stayed for only a short period, probably because he and his cattle were often the target of Apache raids.

The 2.3-mile Canyon Loop Trail connects short sections of two longer trails to create a loop that is easy to moderate in difficulty, covers a variety of terrain, and offers spectacular scenery, both near and far. If you can hike only one trail at Catalina State Park, this should be the one. Starting at the communal trailhead, it follows Romero Canyon Trail east for 0.6 mile, and then heads north for another 0.6 mile before connecting with Sutherland Trail. From there, the trail goes west 0.8 mile back to the trailhead.

The trail is steep at both the beginning and end, and although there are a few rocky stretches, the middle is mostly sandy, relatively flat, and easy-going. What makes this trail so appealing is that you see so much in such a short distance. It wanders through a typical Sonoran Desert environment of mesquite, cholla, prickly pear, and barrel cactus; but it also leads through magnificent stands of giant saguaro, with tall sotol and ocotillo. In one section, there are beautiful rock formations, then there is a picturesque stream, and from its higher elevations the trail offers spellbinding panoramic views of the surrounding mountains and desert. The trail crosses a wash several times, so if you are hiking when it is flowing—usually from late winter into spring—you may end up wading through 6 inches of water or hopping from rock to rock.

The Romero Canyon Trail leads to a turnoff to the Montrose pools just outside of the park boundary (about a mile from the trailhead) in the Pusch Ridge Wilderness Area. You can swim in the pools, although they are usually dry in summer. From the Montrose Pools cutoff, the trail becomes rocky and narrow, climbing steadily, and providing hikers with beautiful views of the mountains. Continuing, the trail leads through fields of boulders with a sprinkling of saguaros. The rocky trail continues to climb, reaching one ridge after another, each with seemingly better views than the last. Then finally Romero Canyon comes into view, with a large waterfall, a picturesque creek, and several groupings of deep pools, which usually contain water year-round. The pools are about 2.8 miles from the trailhead, and there is another 4.4 miles to 6,000-foot Romero Pass. At the pass, hikers can choose among several other wilderness trails, including the Mount Lemmon Trail, which leads to the summit of 9,157-foot Mount Lemmon.

Sutherland Trail is more difficult than Romero Canyon Trail, climbing even higher into the Santa Catalina Mountains. Terrain is similar to Romero Canyon Trail, and like Romero Canyon Trail it connects with several other

Hiking the Canyon Loop Trail in Catalina State Park

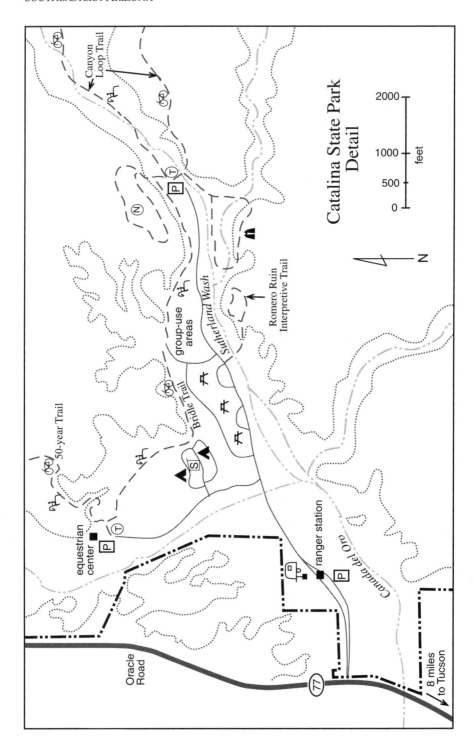

Catalina State Park
Detail

trails, including the Mount Lemmon Trail. The Sutherland Trail treks just under 15 miles to an 8,600-foot pass, and then down the Mount Lemmon Trail to Romero Pass.

The 50-year Trail, which starts at the equestrian center and heads northeast out of the park, provides a link to the Sutherland Trail. Its total length (one-way) is about 8 miles. Although somewhat rough and rocky in spots, it is one of the most popular trails among experienced mountain bikers.

Mountain bikers can ride on all trails within the boundaries of the state park, except the Birding Trail, Nature Trail, and Romero Ruin Interpretive Trail. Mountain bikes are also prohibited in the Pusch Ridge Wilderness Area, although they are allowed in other areas of the Coronado National Forest.

This was a cattle ranch before it became a state park, and horses and horseback riders are still welcome. The park's equestrian center has a barn, corrals, and a dry camping area, and horses are welcome in most parts of the park, except the Birding Trail, Nature Trail, and Romero Ruin Interpretive Trail. Several local stables offer rides into the state park and the wilderness area.

There are excellent opportunities for wildlife viewing and birding, both in the park and on the trails leading into the Pusch Ridge Wilderness Area. Hikers are apt to see mule deer, desert cottontail rabbits, rock squirrels, and plenty of lizards, including the Gila monster. There are also occasional sightings of javelina, coyotes, kit and gray foxes, ringtail cats, badgers, and, in the rugged higher elevations, bighorn sheep. Among the most commonly seen birds are Gambel's quail, red-tailed hawks, common poorwills, roadrunners, mourning doves, northern cardinals, and ladder-backed woodpeckers. The best time to see most of the park's wildlife is during the cooler seasons, from October through April. The exceptions, however, are lizards and snakes, which tend to be more active during the summer.

The campground has nicely spaced sites, well-shaded with mesquite. There is an abundance of rock squirrels, and there are splendid views of the Santa Catalina Mountains to the southeast.

At the visitor center, there are exhibits on what you can expect to see in the park, plus books and maps for sale. Guided hikes and walks are offered periodically from October through May. These often include half- and full-day hikes, birding walks, and wildflower walks from March through May. Annual events include Archeology Day, in March, with guided hikes to archeological sites, and a Solar Energy Potluck, held in May, with demonstrations of solar cooking and power.

The busiest time at the park is from January through May, when the campground fills daily. By summer, it is hot—with highs over 100 degrees F and lows in the 70s—but that is the best time to see cactus in bloom. Those wanting to avoid crowds should consider October, when there are fewer people and temperatures are beginning to cool somewhat. November and December are very pleasant weather-wise, but the winter crowds are beginning to arrive, and the campground is usually full on the weekends.

LOST DUTCHMAN STATE PARK

Hours/Season: Overnight; year-round
Area: 300 land acres
Elevation: 2,000 feet
Facilities: Visitor center, picnic tables, restrooms with showers, 35 camp-sites (no RV hookups) and 1 hike-in or bike-in campsite, nature trail, public telephone, RV dump station, amphitheater, group camping area, group shelters, phone: (602) 982-4485
Attractions: Hiking, mountain biking, picnicking, bird-watching, wild-life viewing, interpretive programs
Nearby: Boyce Thompson Arboretum State Park, Superstition Wilderness Area of the Tonto National Forest
Access: 5 miles north of Apache Junction on AZ 88

▲ The view of the mysterious Superstition Mountains at sunset, when the rugged, rocky landscape turns blood-red, stops you in your tracks. Accented by tall saguaro cactus, their arms reaching to the cloudless sky, these mountains capture the quintessential image of the American West—strong, defiant, and solitary.

Lost Dutchman State Park sits quietly at the foot of the Superstitions, providing not only spectacular views, but a handy base camp for hikers heading out into the mountains, perhaps in search of the Lost Dutchman Gold Mine.

According to legend, a family from northern Mexico named Peralta developed a rich gold mine in the Superstitions in the 1840s, but during one of their treks to haul gold back to Mexico they were ambushed by Apaches, and almost the entire party was killed. Then, in the 1870s, a German immigrant named Jacob Waltz, known as "the Dutchman," is said to have found the abandoned mine, worked it, and stashed piles of gold in the mountains. Waltz's partner, Jacob Weiser, died mysteriously, killed by Apaches or, some say, by Waltz. Waltz died in 1891, claiming that the mine and caches of gold existed, but numerous searches have come up empty-handed.

Although there are still those who spend time scouring the Superstitions for their hidden fortunes, most hike for the pure joy of hiking, for the beautiful scenery, and the opportunity to see a variety of birds, lizards, and other small animals. There are several short trails within the park boundary, but most lead out of the park into the Tonto National Forest's Superstition Wilderness.

Hikers planning treks into the wilderness should consider getting detailed topographic maps, available at the visitor center. Because summers here are very hot, with high temperatures well above 100 degrees F, the best seasons for hiking are from late fall through early spring. Those who want to hike at the hotter times of year will want to go out very early in the day—usually before sunrise—or wait until evening. At all times, hikers should carry plenty of water. Mountain bikes are permitted on trails within the state park and into the national forest but not into the wilderness area.

The park's easiest walk is a 0.25-mile handicapped-accessible loop. The Native Plant Trail is lined with interpretive markers identifying the various plants of the park, including saguaro cactus, mesquite, paloverde, Mormon tea, ocotillo, creosote bush, and teddy bear cholla. There is also a bird-feeding station and a small pond, with a properly aimed bench for those who prefer that their bird-watching be done sitting down.

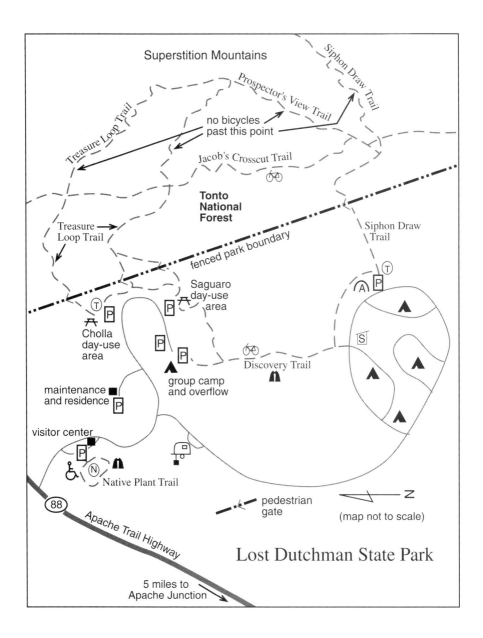

Lost Dutchman State Park

Saguaro cactus at the foot of the Superstition Mountains at Lost Dutchman State Park

Also entirely inside the park is the Discovery Trail, which is an easy walk of about 0.3 mile (one-way), with signs describing the area's geology and physical features. The trail also has a bird-feeding station, with a viewing bench and a small pond, which attracts birds, rabbits, squirrels, and an occasional javelina. Along the trail is one hike-in or bike-in campsite.

Among trails into the Tonto National Forest is the moderate Siphon Draw Trail, a 1.6-mile (one-way) hike from the park campground to the wilderness boundary. The first half is relatively flat, through rocky terrain covered with low shrubs and grasses, while the last section is steeper, providing panoramic views of the surrounding mountains and into the valley below. If weather conditions have been just right, numerous wildflowers bloom along the trail from February through April. Beyond the wilderness boundary, hikers can continue higher into the mountains, although the trail is not maintained, is very steep in spots, and can be difficult to follow. Those considering this longer and much more difficult hike should check on trail conditions first with park rangers.

Branching off of the Siphon Draw Trail is the Prospector's View Trail, 0.7 mile (one-way), which essentially connects Siphon Draw with the Treasure Loop Trail, which must be used to access it. It is generally moderate, although there are a few steep stretches. The trail provides good views toward Phoenix, as well as the mountains, and at its higher elevations passes through stands of saguaro and paloverde.

The 2.4-mile Treasure Loop Trail, which begins and ends within the state park boundaries, can be hiked in its entirety or combined with Prospector's View and Siphon Draw Trails to create a longer loop. The Treasure Loop section by itself is a very popular, moderately difficult trail that is close to the Superstition Wilderness, offering splendid views of the surrounding countryside. It has several steep sections and an overall elevation change of almost 500 feet.

Considered easy, Jacob's Crosscut Trail runs 0.85 mile along the base of the mountains in the Tonto National Forest but just outside the boundary to the wilderness area. It connects Prospector's View and Treasure Loop Trails, producing a scenic loop. Jacob's Crosscut Trail can also be followed away from the park (both north and south) to become a 6.5-mile (one-way) hiking, mountain biking, or equestrian trail through the Sonoran desert and along the base of the mountains. Trailhead directions for this longer version of the trail can be obtained from park rangers.

The park, located in Sonoran Desert upland, contains paloverde, mesquite, jojoba, creosote bush, and ironwood trees, plus saguaro and numerous other species of cactus. Desert wildflowers can be beautiful from February through April, and cactus are usually in bloom from April through June, with May the best time to see blooming saguaro.

Mammals often seen in the park and adjacent national forest include jackrabbits, desert cottontails, and Harris antelope ground squirrels; and there are also coyotes and occasional javelina and mule deer. Summer visitors often see lizards, such as the whiptail and zebra-tailed, and Gila monsters. The park is also home to rattlesnakes and tarantulas. Birds frequently spotted include Gambel's quail, mourning doves, roadrunners, Harris hawks, Gila woodpeckers, cactus wrens, cardinals, and black-throated sparrows.

The visitor center at the park's entrance contains exhibits on the park's wildlife, including its poisonous creatures, plus displays on flower identification and the giant saguaro cactus. From November through mid-April, guided hikes of 2 to 3 miles are offered most Saturdays, and there are usually evening hikes offered each month during that same time period just before the full moon. Also from November through mid-April, campfire programs are offered most Friday evenings, covering various subjects, such as astronomy, desert plants, or the human history of the Superstition Mountains. Annual events include Lost Dutchman Days in February.

The busiest time at the park is winter, particularly January through March when the campground is often filled with residents from Canada and the northern states seeking Arizona's warmth. Temperatures at that time range from highs in the 60s and 70s to lows in the 30s and 40s, occasionally dropping below freezing. A slow time at the park is summer, which can be unbearably hot, with highs in June, July, and August averaging over 100 degrees F, and lows in the upper 60s and 70s. A good time to visit, to avoid both the summer heat and winter crowds, is fall and early winter, when daytime high temperatures range from the upper 60s to upper 80s, and nights drop into the 30s, 40s, and 50s.

In addition to hiking in the Tonto National Forest and its Superstition Wilderness Area, nearby attractions include Boyce Thompson Arboretum State Park, which is discussed in its own section of this book.

MCFARLAND STATE HISTORIC PARK

Hours/Season: 8:00 A.M. to 5:00 P.M. Thursday through Monday; closed
  Christmas
Area: 2.5 land acres
Elevation: 1,500 feet
Facilities: Museum, picnic tables, restrooms, phone: (520) 868-5216
Attractions: Historical exhibits, interpretive programs
Nearby: Lost Dutchman State Park, Picacho Peak State Park, Boyce
  Thompson Arboretum State Park, Pinal County Historical Society
  Museum, Casa Grande Ruins National Monument
Access: In Florence off AZ 287, at the corner of Main Street and Ruggles
  Avenue

Florence is such a refined-sounding name for a town—dignified, perhaps artistic, as in Florence, Italy. But this town of Florence, founded in
1866, was far better known for its stagecoach robberies and gunfights than
for afternoon socials and fine art. And the large building that today comprises McFarland State Historic Park was right in the thick of it.

The Pinal County Courthouse from 1878–91, this structure also served as
the sheriff's office and jail and the county clerk's office. When a new county
courthouse was built in 1891, the building became the county hospital, although patients with tuberculosis and other highly contagious diseases
were kept in an adjacent building, known as the "pest house."

Today, operated as an historical museum, this former courthouse, jail,
and hospital allows visitors to savor the flavor of Florence's Wild West
days, as well as its attempts at civilization. The courtroom has been restored, with rich, dark woods, and you can see the judge's bench, jury box,
lawyers' tables, and rows of spectator seats. Also open for viewing are the
restored county clerk's office, a fully equipped hospital room, examining
room, and sheriff's office and jail. There are displays of historic news clippings and political cartoons, tools and other artifacts from Arizona's
Territorial days, and a "Please Touch" exhibit of 100-year-old artifacts.

History buffs will particularly enjoy the exhibits on local celebrities from
Florence's early days, including Pearl Hart, credited with conducting the
last stagecoach robbery in Arizona. There is also a display on Pauline
Cushman, an actress and Union spy during the Civil War, who was captured by the Confederates and sentenced to hang but rescued in the nick of
time. You can also learn about Mike Rice, another local resident who made
his mark in Florence and almost died right here in the county courthouse,
which at the time also housed the jail. It was August 1887 when Rice, a jailer
at the time, held off a lynch mob of more than forty men, with the help of
Pauline Cushman, a local bartender, and the four prisoners the lynch mob
had its sights on. Rice had given the prisoners guns, on the condition that
they surrender them after the mob had been dispersed. Surprisingly, even
to Rice, they did.

Among the museum's newest permanent exhibits is a room devoted to the Florence Prisoner of War Camp, with displays and a 7-minute video. The camp, built in 1942, was first used as a training facility and then housed German, Italian, and Austrian prisoners of war, at one point holding 5,600 prisoners. The camp no longer exists, but the state park's exhibit shows what life was like for both the prisoners and the American troops stationed there, with displays of photographs and personal items.

The old courthouse is a good example of Arizona Territorial architecture, combining features of Mexican and Anglo-American styles, with traditional adobe mud-brick walls laid on a foundation of river rocks and topped with a wood-shingled pitched roof. The park is named for Ernest W. "Mac" McFarland, who bought the property in 1974 and donated it to the Arizona State Parks System. McFarland is believed to be the only American to serve his state as United States senator, state governor, and chief justice of the state Supreme Court.

Annual events include the Tours of Historic Florence, held the first Saturday in February, and a series of tours, lectures, and other activities during the Arizona State Park System's observation of historic preservation, held each spring.

Visitors to McFarland State Historic Park will want to schedule additional time to see some of the other historic buildings in Florence—some 135 are listed on the National Historic Register—and to stop at the Pinal County Historical Society Museum at 715 South Main Street. The historical society's museum includes displays of pottery, baskets, arrowheads, and other Indian artifacts from Mexico and the Southwest, farm and mining machinery, medical equipment from the 1920s, a barbed wire collection, old woodworking tools, and numerous pioneer items from early Florence.

Another worthwhile side trip is Casa Grande Ruins National Monument, located about 10 miles west of Florence, via AZ 287, in Coolidge. The monument contains the ruins of a Hohokam village built about 650 years ago, including its namesake "Great House," which stands four stories high, with walls that are 4 feet thick at the base. Self-guided trails lead through the ruins. There is also a visitor center with exhibits on life in a Hohokam village, and an observation deck in the picnic area provides views of additional archeological sites, as well as panoramic vistas of the surrounding countryside.

Nearby state parks include Picacho Peak and Lost Dutchman (both with camping) and Boyce Thompson Arboretum, which are all discussed in their own sections of this book.

PATAGONIA LAKE STATE PARK

Hours/Season: Overnight; year-round
Area: 640 land acres, 265 lake surface acres
Elevation: 3,750 feet

Facilities: Visitor center, marina, store, picnic tables, restrooms with showers, 106 campsites (34 with electric and water hookups) and 12 boat-in campsites, boat ramps, public telephone, group shelter, RV dump station, phone: (520) 287-6965

Attractions: Boating, swimming, water-skiing, fishing, hiking, bird-watching, wildlife viewing, interpretive programs

Nearby: Tubac Presidio State Historic Park, Patagonia–Sonoita Creek Preserve, Tumacacori National Monument

Access: 12 miles northeast of Nogales on AZ 82 and then 4 miles north on the park access road

This popular multipurpose park not only offers practically every type of water sport, but it also has a shady hiking trail, good fishing, a campground with views of the lake, and so many birds you may think you have stumbled into an aviary. It will also be the gateway to the Sonoita Creek State Natural Area, a rich riparian and watershed area that is being developed by the Arizona State Park System and is expected to be open for hiking and horseback riding in the future.

Created in 1968 by the damming of Sonoita Creek, the 265-acre lake is 2.5 miles long and 90 feet deep at the dam. Located amid rolling hills of mesquite, cactus, and desert grasses, it has a designated swimming area with a sandy beach and a high, arched pedestrian bridge that offers wonderful views across the lake.

Powerboaters have no horsepower restrictions, although the eastern half of the lake is designated a no-wake area, and skiers are asked to ski counterclockwise in the western section. Although canoes, paddle boats, sailboats, and sailboards are permitted anywhere on the lake, rangers strongly recommend they remain in the eastern section. The park store and marina has fishing and boating supplies, and it rents boats, including rowboats, canoes, and paddle boats. Because the lake gets crowded on summer weekends, water-skiing and the use of personal watercraft are banned on Saturdays, Sundays, and holidays from May through September.

This is considered one of southern Arizona's premier fishing lakes, and anglers have been known to catch flathead catfish weighing up to fifty pounds. There are also channel catfish, largemouth and smallmouth bass, crappie, bluegill, and sunfish; and in winter the lake is stocked with rainbow trout. There are several handicapped-accessible fishing piers.

The Sonoita Creek Trail, open to both hikers and mountain bikers, runs along the shoreline, traversing changing scenery. From desert terrain of cactus, ocotillo, mesquite, and junipers, it wanders through grassy fields into a wetlands of marsh grasses and cattails, ending at a particularly scenic spot where Sonoita Creek enters the lake. About 0.5 mile (one-way), the trail is mostly easy to follow, although low sections can be a bit mucky after a rain or when the lake level is high. There are interpretive signs describing the plants and wildlife that might be seen along the trail. Because of the trail's proximity to grazing land, you might also encounter a cow or two.

The trail is an excellent place to see numerous species of birds, but the entire park is actually a bird-watcher's paradise. Great blue herons walk the shoreline in search of dinner, and a wide variety of birds can be observed chirping, singing, and having a grand old time throughout the park. Among birds you might spot are eared grebes, green-winged teals, Gambel's quail, American coots, mourning doves, Gila woodpeckers, rock wrens, black-tailed gnatcatchers, mountain bluebirds, northern mocking-birds, black-throated sparrows, white-crowned sparrows, and Lawrence's goldfinches. Bird-watching is particularly good in March, April, and early May.

Park residents also include white-tailed deer, javelina, coyotes, bobcats, racoons, striped and spotted skunks, black-tailed jackrabbits, desert cotton-tails, cliff chipmunks, rock squirrels, and the white-nosed coati, a gregarious and curious member of the racoon family. Among reptiles and amphibians are Gila monsters, banded geckos, collared lizards, Arizona alligator lizards, several species of rattlesnakes, red-spotted toads, and canyon treefrogs.

The park has several camping areas. Sites are well-spaced, with some evergreens and desert plants, such as mesquite and cactus. Many offer views of the lake. Unlike many of the RV-oriented parks, there are numerous sites here that are well-suited for tent camping. The park's entry gate is locked at 10:00 P.M.

Sailing at Patagonia Lake State Park

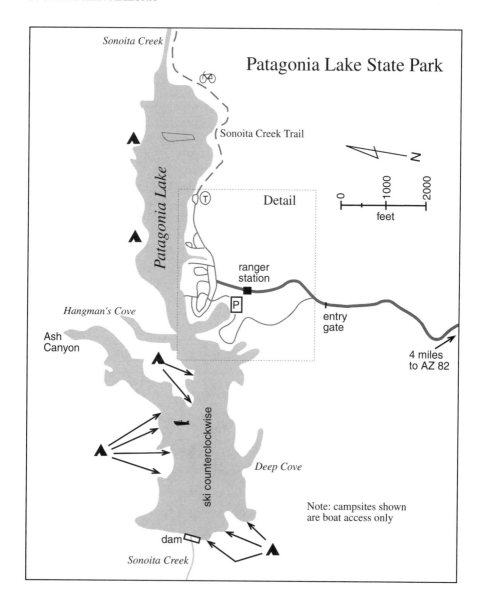

The visitor center/ranger station has exhibits and information on park activities, which may include occasional evening talks on various subjects, such as the plants and animals of the park. Annual events include the Mariachi Celebration in late March, with regional mariachi bands, food, and other activities.

Under development is the Sonoita Creek State Natural Area, adjacent to the state park. Covering some 5,000 acres, it is considered a very sensitive watershed. When fully open, it will be accessible only by foot, horseback, and possibly mountain bike. Plans call for trails with interpretive signs describing the area's natural features, as well as historic sites that include a 1908 railroad bridge and an American Indian petroglyph site. Endangered species in the natural area include the Gila topminnow, which is a small fish, and the tillandsia, which is a plant similar to Spanish moss that grows on trees in protected side canyons. An interpretive center providing information on the natural area is open in the park, but there are no access points into the natural area and no opening date had been determined at this writing. However, this will be an exciting addition to the state park system and is well worth asking about.

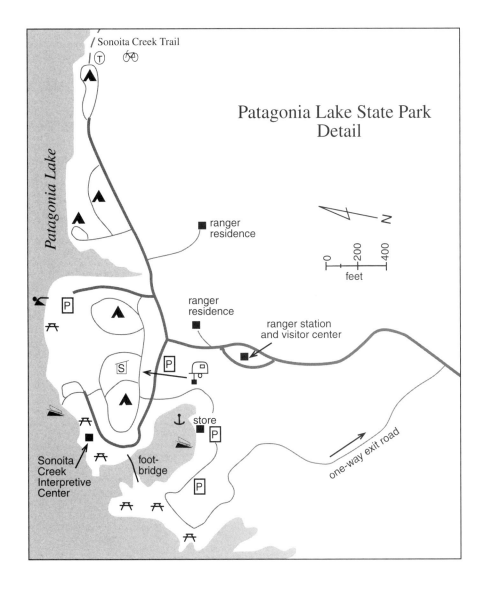

Patagonia Lake State Park is busiest during summer; so busy, in fact, that park campgrounds are completely full almost every weekend from May through October, and even day-users are often turned away Sunday afternoons. Those who want to visit in summer should try to arrive Sunday night through Thursday. Winters are much quieter, and although campers generally have no trouble finding a site, those with hookups are usually claimed early in the day. Spring and fall are also busy but not as crowded as summer.

The weather here is pleasant year-round. Summer highs are usually in the 80s and 90s, with lows in the 50s and 60s. Winter low temperatures seldom drop below the 20s, and winter days can be delightful, with temperatures rising into the 60s.

Those interested in birding should make a point of visiting the Patagonia–Sonoita Creek Preserve, about 5 miles east of the state park. This 750-acre wildlife sanctuary, managed by the nonprofit Nature Conservancy, is open to the public Wednesdays through Sundays, with guided tours Saturday mornings.

Located in a cottonwood-willow riparian forest, the preserve contains the world's tallest and oldest Fremont cottonwoods, plus Arizona black walnut, velvet mesquite, and a variety of willows along Sonoita Creek. More than 275 bird species have been spotted, including rare species, such as the gray hawk, green kingfisher, and rose-throated becard. Great blue herons can sometimes be seen nesting in the cottonwoods along the preserve's eastern boundary. Among other species seen in the preserve are black-bellied whistling ducks, black vultures, bald eagles, peregrine falcons, Inca doves, vermilion flycatchers, great horned owls, Gila woodpeckers, northern mockingbirds, and hooded orioles. Mammals that frequent the preserve include white-tailed deer, javelina, bobcats, and an occasional mountain lion.

To get to the preserve, take AZ 82 to Patagonia, turn west onto Fourth Avenue, and then south onto Pennsylvania Avenue. Cross the creek and go about a mile to the preserve entrance.

Also nearby, and especially interesting for history buffs, are Tubac Presidio State Historic Park and Tumacacori National Monument, which are both discussed in the Tubac Presidio State Historic Park section of this book.

PICACHO PEAK STATE PARK

Hours/Season: Overnight; year-round
Area: 3,640 land acres
Elevation: 2,000 feet
Facilities: Ranger station, picnic tables, restrooms with showers, playground, nature trail, 95 campsites (12 with electric and water hookups), RV dump station, phone: (520) 466-3183

Attractions: Hiking, bird-watching, wildlife viewing, photography, historical exhibits

Nearby: Catalina State Park, McFarland State Historic Park, Casa Grande Ruins National Monument

Access: 40 miles north of Tucson off I-10 exit 219

Spectacular desert scenery, spring wildflowers, bird-watching, and several serious hiking trails are among the attractions at Picacho Peak State Park, which was also the site of a Civil War battle.

The park's namesake, Picacho Peak, has been used as a landmark by travelers for hundreds of years, from the prehistoric Hohokam and later Spanish missionaries, to Anglo pioneers and gold-seekers. Towering 1,500 feet above the desert floor, this imposing peak began its existence as a series of lava flows, which were then molded by the forces of erosion into the saddle-shaped peak that today dominates much of the landscape between Tucson and Phoenix.

A wagon road was built through Picacho Pass in the late 1840s by the Mormon Battalion, members of the Church of Jesus Christ of Latter-day Saints that had been recruited to fight in the Mexican War and marched 2,000 miles from Iowa to California. Forty-niners then used this trail to get to the California gold fields, and by the late 1850s the road was being used by the Jackass Mail and Butterfield Overland Stage, which had a depot in the pass.

This was also the site of Arizona's largest battle of the Civil War. A detachment of Union forces from California encountered a Confederate scouting party at Picacho Pass in April, 1862, and attacked. The 1.5-hour battle claimed the lives of three Union soldiers, who were buried on the battlefield. Monuments dedicated to both the Mormon Battalion and the Civil War battle are located in the park, and each year, on the second weekend in March, the battle is reenacted, with authentic Civil War encampments and about 150 authentically costumed reenactors firing black powder rifles and pistols.

Today, Picacho Peak attracts numerous hikers, who take one of two trails to the top to enjoy breathtaking panoramic views. On a clear day, you can see both Tucson and Phoenix.

Historical marker at Picacho Peak State Park

The park's most difficult hiking trail is Hunter Trail, which climbs some 1,400 feet through the rugged Sonoran desert to the top of Picacho Peak. The 2-mile (one-way) route is steep and rocky, with steel cables attached to the rock in particularly steep areas to provide needed stability. This is more mountain climbing than hiking, and only experienced hikers should attempt it.

Sunset Vista Trail, the other route to the top of Picacho Peak, is 3.1 miles (one-way), with the first 2 miles (rated moderate) gradually climbing a desert path through hillsides of saguaro and other cacti. However, then it joins Hunter Trail for the final ascent and becomes extremely steep and difficult.

Those planning to follow either trail to Picacho Peak's summit should allow at least 4 hours round trip, carry no less than half a gallon of water per person, wear good hiking shoes, and take gloves for hand protection when using the cables. Park rangers also strongly recommend that dogs not be taken on these trails, because the sharp rocks will cut through the pads on the animals' feet.

Other park trails are easier, but, except for the Nature Trail, all are rocky and have relatively steep sections. Calloway Trail goes 0.7 mile (one-way) to a scenic vista. The Children's Cave Trail, 0.2 mile (one-way), has interpretive signs describing the park's natural features and climbs to a small cave. The Nature Trail, a 0.5-mile loop, is relatively flat, with interpretive signs discussing the desert environment.

From almost all points in the park, you get terrific views of Picacho Peak, and throughout the park are magnificent forests of giant saguaro. If rains are sufficient in November and December, by March the entire mountain turns bright yellow with the blooms of Mexican gold poppies. You are quite likely to also find an abundance of larkspur, broomrape, brittlebush, ocotillo, and numerous varieties of cacti, such as Christmas cholla, fishhook barrel, teddy bear cholla, and strawberry hedgehog. The bulk of the wildflowers bloom in late February and March. Cacti, however, usually display their red, purple, and yellow flowers from March through June, although the saguaro usually puts out its white blooms in May.

Among the wildlife to be found in this desert are numerous species of lizards, including the desert iguana, chuckwalla, zebra-tailed lizard, and Gila monster. Snakes, including rattlesnakes, and several species of bats, spend time in the park. Other animals frequently seen include white-throated wood rats, rock squirrels, Harris antelope squirrels, desert cottontail rabbits, black-tailed jackrabbits, and coyotes. Usually present but only occasionally seen are mule deer, javelina, kit foxes, and bobcats.

Birds you are likely to spot are cactus wrens, blue-gray gnatcatchers, Gila woodpeckers, western kingbirds, gilded flickers, mourning doves, white-winged doves, Gambel's quail, red-tailed hawks, turkey vultures, Wilson's warblers, sparrows, and roadrunners.

The park has two campgrounds. One, essentially just a parking lot, has recreational vehicle hookups and nearby showers. The other, larger campground has well-spaced sites, low desert vegetation, and is quite a bit nicer

Giant saguaro cactus at Picacho Peak State Park

except that it does not have any RV hookups or showers. Backcountry camping is not permitted in the park.

Because summers here are hot, with daytime temperatures often exceeding 100 degrees F, and lows in the 70s, the best months, especially for hikers, are from November through March. Winters are pleasant, with daytime highs usually in the 60s and 70s, and lows seldom dipping below freezing. Spring can be windy, with daytime temperatures in the 80s during April, and fall does not last long, with daytime temperatures averaging 90 degrees F

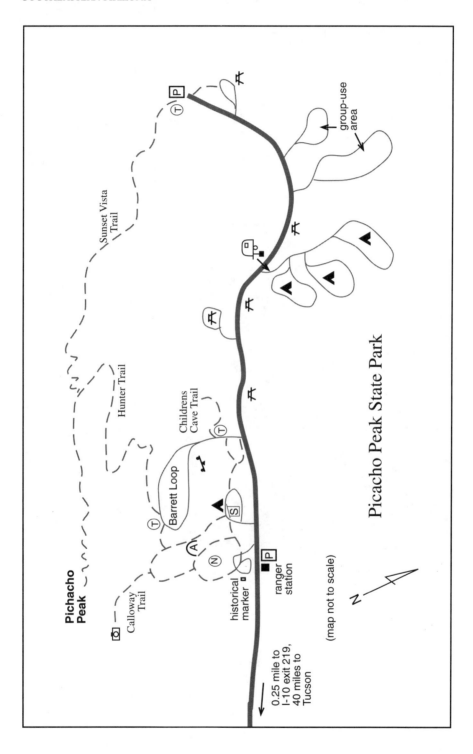

Pichacho Peak

Calloway Trail

Sunset Vista Trail

Hunter Trail

Childrens Cave Trail

Barrett Loop

group-use area

historical marker

ranger station

Picacho Peak State Park

0.25 mile to I-10 exit 219, 40 miles to Tucson

N

(map not to scale)

in October but only 76 degrees F in November. The slowest visitation time is June through August.

Those interested in ancient cultures will want to consider a visit to Casa Grande Ruins National Monument, which is located about 18 miles north of the park, via AZ 87, in Coolidge. The monument contains the ruins of a Hohokam village built about 650 years ago, including its namesake "Great House," which stands four stories high, with walls that are 4 feet thick at the base. Self-guided trails lead through the ruins. There is also a visitor center with exhibits on life in a Hohokam village, and an observation deck in the picnic area provides views of additional archeological sites, as well as panoramic vistas of the surrounding countryside.

Also nearby are Catalina State Park and McFarland State Historic Park, which are discussed in their own sections of this book.

ROPER LAKE STATE PARK

Hours/Season: Overnight; year-round
Area: Main section—319 land acres, 32 lake surface acres; Dankworth Ponds Unit—80 land acres, 15 lake surface acres
Elevation: 3,130 feet
Facilities: Ranger station, picnic tables, restrooms with showers, outdoor hot tub, 75 campsites (20 with electric hookups), nature trails, public telephone, boat ramp, amphitheater, group campground, group shelter, RV dump station, phone: (520) 428-6760
Attractions: Hiking, hot springs, swimming, fishing, boating, birdwatching, wildlife viewing, archeological sites, interpretive programs
Access: From Safford take US 191 south for 6 miles, turn east onto access road for 0.5 mile to the Roper Lake main unit; the park's Dankworth Ponds Unit is 2.5 miles south via US 191

This multiuse park offers lakes for fishing and swimming, several trails, and the only natural mineral springs hot tub in the Arizona State Park System. With a combination of desert and wetlands, the park is a good wildlife viewing and birding location and also has interpretive nature trails and a "village" of early American Indian dwellings.

The park has two sections—the main unit, with a 32-acre lake, and the Dankworth Ponds day-use area about 2.5 miles away, with a 15-acre lake.

The main Roper Lake section includes the campgrounds, swimming beach, and hot tub. The campgrounds, with good views and easy lake access, are mostly paved, with a limited amount of trees and other vegetation.

Most boaters here are anglers, using aluminum boats powered by electric trolling motors—gasoline motors are prohibited both in Roper Lake and Dankworth Pond. Occasionally, one sees a canoe or sailboat on Roper Lake, and a small number of sailboarders have discovered that winds are

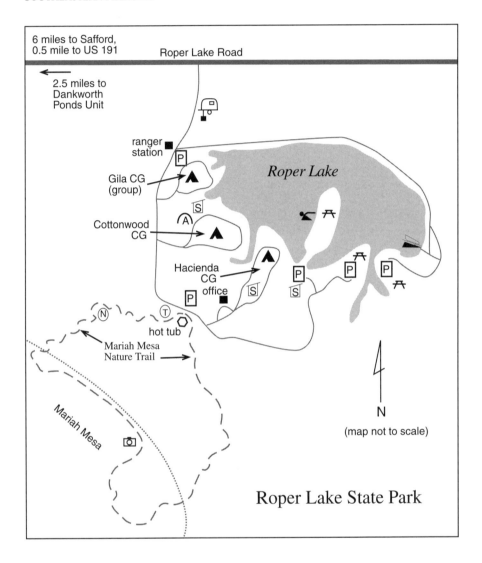

6 miles to Safford,
0.5 mile to US 191

Roper Lake Road

2.5 miles to
Dankworth
Ponds Unit

ranger
station

Gila CG
(group)

Cottonwood
CG

Roper Lake

Hacienda
CG

office

hot tub

Mariah Mesa
Nature Trail

Mariah Mesa

N

(map not to scale)

Roper Lake State Park

generally good from late March through May. Dankworth Pond does not have a boat ramp and is a bit small for boating, but you can carry a canoe down to the shore and paddle around.

Roper Lake is stocked with rainbow trout from November through March. Largemouth bass, crappie, sunfish, and channel catfish are also caught in both Roper Lake and Dankworth Pond. Next to Roper Lake are two small ponds, sometimes dry, which in recent years have been used for raising catfish and two endangered species—the Gila topminnow and the desert pupfish. Jutting into Roper Lake is an attractive day-use island, with picnic tables, tall palm trees, and a sandy swimming beach.

The stone and concrete outdoor hot tub, fed by a natural artesian spring, is large enough for six to eight people. Its year-round temperature is about 102 degrees F, and some users claim the waters are medicinal. The hot tub is drained each night. There is a 15-minute per person time limit when someone is waiting, and bathing suits are required.

The Mariah Mesa Nature Trail at the park's main unit is an easy to moderate 0.5-mile loop that climbs onto a mesa, providing wonderful panoramic views of the lake and surrounding mountains. A brochure, keyed to numbers along the trail, describes the salt cedar, soaptree yucca, sotol, creosote bush, ocotillo, mesquite, cholla, and other desert plants common to this area. Although well-maintained, the trail can be muddy immediately after a rainstorm.

In the Dankworth Ponds Unit, the 1.75-mile Dos Arroyos Trail tells a different environmental story, meandering through a lush riparian area, with a side trail onto a low desert mesa where several reconstructed Indian

Reconstructed Indian dwellings at Roper Lake State Park

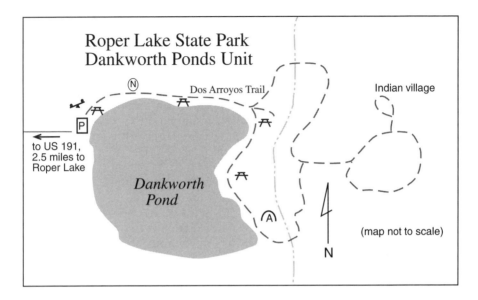

Roper Lake State Park
Dankworth Ponds Unit

Dos Arroyos Trail

Indian village

to US 191,
2.5 miles to
Roper Lake

Dankworth
Pond

(map not to scale)

N

dwellings can be seen. Mostly flat and easy, the wetlands section is particularly scenic.

Birds are abundant in both sections of the park, although you will likely see more birds in the Dankworth Ponds Unit because there are wetlands and less human activity there. Among bird species to watch for are great blue herons, night herons, egrets, American coots, killdeer, Gambel's quail, mourning doves, boat-tailed grackles, yellow-headed blackbirds, house finches, and red-tailed hawks. There are often ducks and geese on both Roper Lake and Dankworth Pond.

Be on the lookout for beaver and turtles at Dankworth Pond. Both park units have jackrabbits, skunks, badgers, coyotes, bobcats, javelina, rattlesnakes, and Gila monsters; and tarantulas are sometimes seen just after summer rains.

During the winter, a Saturday evening lecture series at the amphitheater presents programs on wildlife, ecology, archeology, plants, geology, and other subjects. Annual events include an antique auto show in early October and the Battle of the Bands, with regional groups competing, in early March.

The busiest time at the park is from February through April, when daytime temperatures range from the upper 60s to low 80s, with nighttime lows in the 30s and 40s. Summers here are hot, with highs often over 100 degrees F, but with lows dropping into the 60s and 70s. Fall, which is particularly pretty when the cottonwoods have turned bright gold, is also a busy time. High temperatures are usually in the 70s and 80s, with lows mostly in the 40s. The park's quietest months are December and January. Daytime temperatures often get into the upper 50s and 60s, while nights drop into the 20s and 30s.

TOMBSTONE COURTHOUSE STATE HISTORIC PARK

Hours/Season: 8:00 A.M. to 5:00 P.M. daily; closed Christmas
Area: 12,000 square feet
Elevation: 4,539 feet
Facilities: Visitor center/museum, picnic tables, restrooms, phone: (520) 457-3311
Attractions: Historic exhibits, interpretive programs
Nearby: Historic Tombstone
Access: In Tombstone, off US 80, at the corner of Toughnut and Third Streets

Tombstone, Arizona, is probably the best-known Wild West town that ever existed. The subject of legends, songs, books, and more than two dozen movies, its history has been so confused that it is virtually impossible to separate the reality from the myth. Tombstone Courthouse State Historic Park is the anchor for the reality.

This state park consists of just one building—a handsome 12,000-square-foot two-story brick Victorian that served as the Cochise County Courthouse from 1882 until 1929, when the county seat was moved to Bisbee. Built at a cost of almost $50,000, it housed the jail and offices of county officials, including the sheriff, treasurer, and board of supervisors, in addition to a large courtroom.

Tombstone owes its existence, and its name, to Ed Schieffelin, a prospector who was warned by his Army buddies that all he would ever find in those hills would be his tombstone. But Schieffelin managed to avoid the Apaches his friends thought would do him in, and when he finally found the silver that would make him a millionaire he gave the name *Tombstone* to the town that quickly sprang up.

Considered one of the roughest towns in the Old West, Tombstone at one time had more than 100 saloons operating around the clock, serving a population of about 10,000 miners, gamblers, cowboys, shopkeepers, and prostitutes. Gunfights were a way of life, and trips to Boothill Graveyard were frequent.

Today, the town is devoted 100 percent to reliving its Wild West heritage, particularly the "Gunfight at the OK Corral," which Hollywood has romanticized almost beyond recognition. Tourism is the name of the game, and to support it, the town has made a great effort to glamorize its wicked past, maintaining its frontier buildings, staging shootouts in the streets, and doing a good job of combining authentic Old West history with today's slick entertainment. This is a fun place, but sometimes it becomes difficult to distinguish truth from fiction.

That is where the Tombstone Courthouse State Historic Park comes in. This is the real thing, well-documented and authentically presented. The best part is that the truth is fun, too.

Gallows at Tombstone Courthouse State Historic Park

The courthouse is now a museum, dedicated to Tombstone and the surrounding areas as they existed in the late nineteenth century. The courtroom has been meticulously restored, and other rooms are devoted to various aspects of life at that time, such as cattle ranching, mining, the military, saloons, gambling, and the Apache Wars. Of course, there is also an exhibit on that famous gunfight at the OK Corral, where Wyatt Earp, his brothers Virgil and Morgan, and Doc Holliday shot and killed Frank and Tom McLaury and Billy Clanton in a gun battle that is believed to have lasted no more than thirty seconds.

In the courtroom, a 15-minute video dramatizes another deadly moment in Tombstone's past, but one that has not been so widely publicized. In the Tombstone courtroom, a man was tried for murder after his revenge killing of a man who had caused the drowning deaths of two children. Another of the park's most popular exhibits is not even inside the courthouse: Outside in the courtyard is a reconstruction of the gallows used to hang seven convicted criminals, the only people to be legally executed in Tombstone.

For the more refined, displays inside the courthouse include fine antiques that were brought into the Arizona Territory by horse-drawn wagons and steam locomotives in the late 1800s, glass cases holding antique dolls and toys, musical instruments, a complete attorney's office of the era, a post office, an assay office, and a fine collection of historic photos. Nearby is an exhibit on photo restoration.

Tombstone's social life is recalled in exhibits that include a corner saloon, a faro table and other gambling paraphernalia, whiskey jugs, and a formal invitation to a hanging. Other documents include a town government license to operate a brothel, and a section from a diary written by Tombstone resident George Parsons in September of 1880: "A man will go to the devil pretty fast in Tombstone. . . . Faro, whiskey, and bad women will beat anyone."

The museum's gift shop offers the usual souvenirs, plus a fine selection of books on the Old West, particularly Tombstone. The park/museum also participates in the town's various activities throughout the year, including Helldorado Days in late October. During this celebration, the state park sponsors the Antique Power Show, which includes restored engines, tractors, washing machines, and just about any other type of old-time powered machine.

There are numerous attractions throughout the town of Tombstone, including dozens of historic buildings, such as the Bird Cage Theatre, built in 1881 and known in its time as the wildest saloon between New Orleans and San Francisco. There are several other museums and historic sites, including the OK Corral and Boothill Graveyard, with the marked graves of about 250 of Tombstone's early, but now late, citizens.

TUBAC PRESIDIO STATE HISTORIC PARK

Hours/Season: 8:00 A.M. to 5:00 P.M. daily; closed Christmas
Area: 10 land acres
Elevation: 3,500 feet
Facilities: Visitor center, museum, picnic tables, restrooms, phone: (520) 398-2252
Attractions: Historical exhibits, interpretive programs, hiking, horseback riding
Nearby: Patagonia Lake State Park, Tumacacori National Historical Park
Access: In Tubac off I-19 exit 34

Considered Arizona's oldest European community, Tubac, originally a small Pima Indian village, was settled by the Spanish in 1691 as a mission farm and ranch after a Spanish mission was established at nearby Tumacacori by Jesuit priest Eusebio Francisco Kino. Spanish colonists began settling in the area in the 1730s, in what was then the northern frontier of New Spain.

After a Pima revolt against Spanish domination in 1751, the Presidio San Ignacio de Tubac was established the following year. The purpose of the fifty-soldier military post—the main focus of Tubac Presidio State Historic Park—was to protect Spanish colonists and the Tumacacori Mission, and to keep the Indians under control.

Tubac and its presidio had its ups and downs over the years, being abandoned and recommissioned several times. In the late 1850s, under the flag of the United States, entrepreneur Charles Poston moved into the abandoned house of the presidio commandant and established the Sonora Exploring and Mining Company. But that was not all. He hauled in a printing press and, in 1859, printed Arizona's first newspaper. He also printed his own money, performed marriage ceremonies, and baptized children. By 1860, Tubac was the largest town in Arizona, but due at least in part to Apache raids, that could not last, and by 1863 one visitor wrote that Tubac "is now a city of ruins and desolation."

Visitors to Tubac today will find a small community of artists, writers, retirees, and, right in the middle of town, the state park, on the site of the original 1752 presidio.

Arizona's first state park, established in 1957, Tubac Presidio includes a museum and a visitor center with a small theater where you can watch a 7-minute video on the history of Tubac. Exhibits include detailed models of the original presidio, displays on the local Pima and Apache Indians, the Spanish missions and military, and daily life here in the 1700s. A "Please Touch" exhibit invites visitors to handle a variety of historic artifacts. There is also a small cannon and a print shop with Poston's original 1859 press.

Outdoor exhibits include an *arrastra*, a primitive mule-powered rock crusher used in mining. Eroded adobe ruins of the early fort can be viewed, and probably the park's most impressive feature is an underground exhibit that shows the foundation, lower walls, and floor that were discovered during a 1976 excavation, along with artifacts from various periods.

Also on the grounds is a restored 1885 schoolhouse. The one-room school is built of adobe, with a high ceiling and windows that help keep it cool in summer. It contains original and reconstructed desks and about half a dozen blackboards—one for each grade. Living history programs for area schools bring students in to experience a typical school day in 1880s Arizona.

The Anza Trail, a 4.5-mile hiking and horseback riding trail, goes from the state park to Tumacacori National Historical Park. The trail follows the beginning of the route taken by Spanish explorer Juan Bautista de Anza in 1775 from Tumacacori to California, in an expedition that culminated with the founding of San Francisco. Part of the trail also follows an historic acequia, or irrigation ditch, that dates from at least the 1700s. Informational displays are set up along the flat, easy trail, which involves fording the Santa Cruz River twice. There are numerous riparian and desert plants along the trail, including stands of elderberry, mesquite, desert willow, and

Living history demonstration shows off an 1859 printing press at Tubac Presidio State Historic Park. (photo by Princely Nesadurai, Arizona State Parks)

An early nineteenth-century Spanish mission at Tumacacori National Historical Park, near Tubac Presidio State Historic Park

cottonwood, plus desert grasses and cactus. Hikers will likely see lizards, as well as roadrunners, turkey vultures, and neo-tropical birds, such as the trogon. Hikers should carry drinking water, as river water is not considered safe to drink.

Hikers will find that it can be very hot during the summer, when temperatures regularly soar to over 100 degrees F and lows rarely drop below 60 degrees F. Winter days are mild, however, with highs in the 60s, but lows drop below freezing. Both fall and spring see highs in the 70s and 80s and lows in the 30s and 40s.

Guided tours of the state park's historic attractions are offered by reservation, depending on staff availability, and living history demonstrations are presented Sunday afternoons from October through March. Annual events include Anza Days, in mid- to late October, with historical reenactments, music, storytelling, and other activities. Special events are also scheduled during Archeology Awareness Month in March and during the Arizona State Park System's observation of historic preservation, held each spring.

Tumacacori National Historical Park is just 4.5 miles south of the state park via I-19, the I-19 frontage road, or the Anza Hiking Trail. The park includes the massive ruins of the mission San José de Tumacácori, built by

Spanish missionaries in the early 1800s, plus ruins of two earlier missions that had existed on the site. Also displayed in the park's museum are artifacts dating back to 1691, when the first mission was established by Jesuit priest Eusebio Francisco Kino.

About 40 miles to the southeast, via I-19 and AZ 82, is Patagonia Lake State Park, which is discussed in its own section of this book.

KARTCHNER CAVERNS STATE PARK
(UNDER DEVELOPMENT)

▲ A massive limestone cave, Kartchner Caverns has multicolored walls of flowstone draperies, long pencil-thin stalactites and stalagmites, and numerous fanciful formations created over thousands of years. There are two rooms, each 100 feet tall and the length of a football field, connected by 2.5 miles of passageways. While it is one of the most beautiful caves in the country, what makes Kartchner Caverns truly unique is its pristine condition, virtually unchanged since it was first seen by human eyes.

All evidence indicates that humans had not entered the cave until its discovery by two avid cavers in 1974, and they were so awed by its beauty and purity that to protect the cave they swore themselves to secrecy. Amazingly, they kept the secret—telling only three trusted friends—and eventually tracked down the land's owner, J. A. Kartchner. Upon seeing the cave, Kartchner was also awed, and he agreed that everything possible must be done to protect it. Eventually, it was decided that the best course would be to place the cave in the hands of federal or state governments, and in 1988 the State of Arizona purchased the cave. It was then carefully secured, and its existence was finally announced to the public.

Arizona's largest known cave, Kartchner Caverns is a spectacular landscape of natural beauty, a secret, surreal world below the earth's surface. But this is a fragile living ecosystem, with water dripping and formations continuing to evolve, so a state-of-the-art preservation system is being created to protect the cave while allowing people to tour it, to see the caverns in an almost perfectly natural condition, so everyone who ventures inside experiences the cave as if they were very first to see its wonders. Part of this cave protection includes the use of multiple air locks that will help keep the cave at its natural year-round humidity level of almost 100 percent and constant temperature of 68 degrees F, in contrast to the extreme heat and dryness of the desert above. Efforts will also be made to protect the small colony of bats that spends summers in the cave.

When Kartchner Caverns opens, visitors will see the cave on guided tours only. The 550-acre park will have a 16,000-square-foot visitor center with a "cavatorium" to help visitors learn what it is like to explore a cave. There will also be an outdoor amphitheater, a small campground, and a series of surface hiking trails with panoramic views of the San Pedro River Valley and the nearby Whetstone Mountains.

Kartchner Caverns State Park is located 8 miles south of I-10, off AZ 90 near Benson. For current information, contact the Arizona State Parks office in Phoenix at (602) 542-4174.

ORACLE STATE PARK (UNDER DEVELOPMENT)

A wildlife refuge and environmental learning center, Oracle State Park has been open to schools and other organized groups for several years but closed to the general public. That is about to change. Located about 40 miles northeast of Tucson in the foothills of the Santa Catalina Mountains, the 3,948-acre park has more than 15 miles of hiking trails, including about 7 miles of the Arizona Trail. The property was owned by a ranching family for about seventy-five years before being given to the Defenders of Wildlife,

Ranger leading a children's hike at Oracle State Park (photo by Princely Nesadurai, Arizona State Parks)

which managed it as a wildlife refuge for ten years before donating it to the state of Arizona for use as a park and preserve.

On the edge of the Sonoran Desert at an elevation of 4,400 feet, there is only one known giant saguaro cactus on the property, but there is an abundance of other desert plants, such as prickly pear and cholla cactus, mesquite, scrub oak, some piñon and juniper, and numerous wildflowers. There are also cypress trees that were planted outside the original ranch house, which is now the park headquarters.

Wildlife is plentiful here. Among the mammals that have been seen within the park's boundaries are javelina, ringtails, porcupines, mountain lions, rock squirrels, desert cottontails, black-tailed jackrabbits, mule deer, and white-tailed deer. There is also a variety of reptiles and amphibians, including Colorado river toads, western box turtles, Arizona alligator lizards, bullsnakes, and western diamondback rattlesnakes. Birds spotted in the park include black-throated sparrows, Gambel's quail, cactus wrens, northern cardinals, pyrrhuloxia, northern flickers, northern mockingbirds, common poorwills, great horned owls, red-tailed hawks, prairie falcons, and golden eagles.

When the park is opened to the general public, there will be hiking, guided nature walks, picnicking, ranger talks, and tours of the historic Kanally Ranch House, an early 1930s adobe building in Mediterranean Revival style. A 1-mile wildlife viewing interpretive loop trail is also planned. The park will continue to give group tours and environmental education programs.

Oracle State Park is located in the town of Oracle off Mount Lemmon Road. For current information, call the park office at (520) 896-2425.

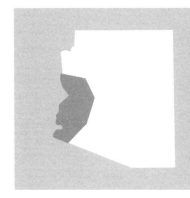

WESTERN ARIZONA

▲ Known locally as "Arizona's West Coast," this land of sun, sand, and sparkling blue water is Arizona's version of oceanfront property. Here, the Colorado River and its various reservoirs follow the state's western boundary for almost its entire length, offering an abundance of opportunities for boating, sailing, swimming, and snoozing on sandy beaches of several state parks. But this is also a land of extremes, from the driest and hottest desert to lush (but still hot) wetlands. Because the Colorado River and its assorted tributaries and lakes provide practically the only water in this harsh desert, these river valleys and lakeshores are particularly good spots for wildlife viewing, especially birding. Yuma, western Arizona's largest town, has been an important river crossing point since before the arrival of Spanish conquistadores in the 1500s and is also the site of Arizona's first prison. Two state parks in Yuma bring this history to life.

ALAMO LAKE STATE PARK

Hours/Season: Overnight; year-round
Area: 5,642 land acres, 3,000 lake surface acres
Elevation: 1,235 feet
Facilities: Visitor center, picnic tables, restrooms with showers, playground, public telephone, 133 developed campsites (41 with electric and water hookups, 17 with electric, water, and sewer), 117 undeveloped campsites, group camping area with group shelter, RV dump station, boat ramps, boat rentals, convenience store, auto and boat fuel, fish-cleaning station, phone: (520) 669-2088

Boating at Buckskin Mountain State Park

Attractions: Boating, fishing, hiking, horseback riding, bird-watching, wildlife viewing, stargazing
Access: Turn north off US 60 in Wenden and go 38 miles on Alamo Lake Road

Among Arizona's best parks in which to get away from it all, Alamo Lake also offers abundant opportunities for bird-watching and what is considered the best largemouth bass fishing in the state. Created in the 1960s by the damming of the Bill Williams River, this desert lake's primary reason for being is flood control, and heavy runoff can cause the lake to rise

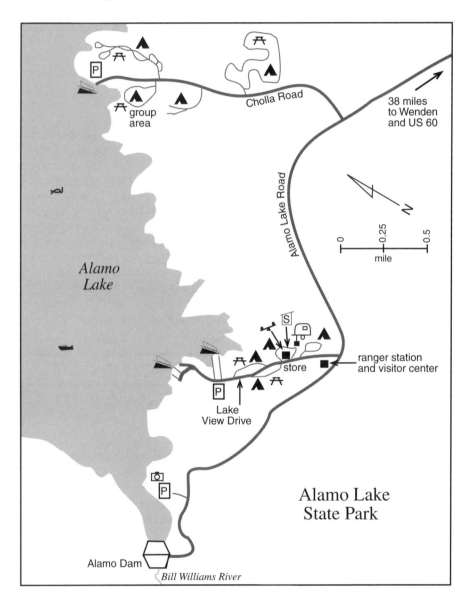

as much as 100 feet—sometimes up to 11 feet in just a day.

Almost 40 miles from the nearest community, the park is a quiet escape, offering a rugged desert landscape, with splendid views of the lake and the nearby Buckskin, Artillery, and Rawhide Mountains. Although there are no designated hiking or horseback riding trails, there are a number of paths created by animals and early human inhabitants of the area both in and

Hiking cross-country at Alamo Lake State Park

around the park. There are also numerous old mining roads, and hikers and horseback riders can go cross-country trekking anywhere in the park. Although this is not a big biking area, bikes are welcome on established park roads, and mountain bikers occasionally explore the old mining roads.

Alamo Lake State Park is surrounded by property, including two wilderness areas, managed by the Bureau of Land Management, and visitors can use the park as a staging area for backpacking and day hikes. Particularly scenic is the 6 miles of river valley below the dam, with a steep-walled canyon and rich riparian habitat.

The park, in a transition between Upper Sonoran and Mohave Desert terrain, is home to numerous desert plants, including teddy bear cholla, desert Christmas cactus, catclaw acacia, hedgehog cactus, brittlebush, tamarisk, paloverde, creosote bush, mesquite, and an abundance of ocotillo. It is also one of the few areas in the Southwest where you can see both saguaro cactus and large tree-like yucca called Joshua trees.

Along the banks are willows and cottonwood trees, and after a rainy

Fishing at Alamo Lake State Park (photo by Princely Nesadurai, Arizona State Parks)

winter the park bursts into color with numerous species of wildflowers, including evening primrose, California poppy, sacred datura, and desert trumpet.

Although the lake is open to any and all types of boats, powerboats are the overwhelming majority, though you will see an occasional sailboat or canoe. There are no boat-in campsites; boaters can sleep on their boats anywhere on the lake. Because this is primarily a fishing lake, most boats here are used for fishing, and the park has a recharging station for trolling motor batteries.

Occasionally, but only when water is being released from the lake, adventurous paddlers can canoe from the dam down the Bill Williams River to Lake Havasu, a distance of about 35 miles. Water-skiing and swimming are permitted but not encouraged, because of underwater hazards such as tree branches. Swimming or wading along the shoreline can be particularly dangerous because of sudden steep drop-offs, which change with the lake's fluctuating water level, and abandoned fishing line and hooks hidden in the brush.

Extremely popular for both bank and boat fishing, the park hosts dozens of fishing tournaments each year, mostly in the spring and fall. Famous for its largemouth bass, the park also offers anglers a chance at catfish, bluegill, crappie, and tilapia.

Bird-watchers here have a fairly good chance of seeing bald and golden eagles, and a bald eagle nesting site is located near the upper end of the lake. Other species frequently spotted include a variety of ducks and geese, great blue herons, snowy egrets, white pelicans, cormorants, western grebes, American coots, osprey, quail, owls, falcons, red-tailed hawks, and numerous species of hummingbirds and songbirds.

Other park wildlife includes mule deer, kit fox, coyote, javelina, black-tailed jackrabbit, ringtailed cat, rock squirrel, and an occasional bobcat or mountain lion. Desert bighorn sheep are sometimes spotted in the rocky canyon below the dam. Beaver can be seen along the Bill Williams River below the dam and occasionally in the lake. During summer, the wild descendants of burros brought to the area in the 1800s by copper, gold, and silver miners can sometimes be seen. The park is also home to a variety of bats, plus numerous lizards and snakes, including three species of rattlesnake.

Because of its isolation, and therefore lack of light pollution, Alamo Lake is becoming increasingly popular with stargazers, who set up their telescopes year-round.

The busiest time of year is spring, when the weather is mild, bringing anglers out in full force. Fall can also be busy, although not usually as much as spring. Both spring and fall weekends are usually packed, so mid-week is the best time for a visit. Summers are typically very hot, with temperatures soaring to over 120 degrees F, and the park gets little use then. Winters are relatively mild, with afternoon temperatures in the 40s and 50s. Although the park is still fairly quiet in winter, the season is growing in popularity.

BUCKSKIN MOUNTAIN STATE PARK

Hours/Season: Overnight; year-round
Area: 1,677 land acres
Elevation: 420 feet
Facilities: Buckskin Unit—89 campsites (8 with electric, water, and sewer; 60 with electric and water; 21 with cabana and electric), interpretive center, cactus garden, restaurant, convenience store, auto and boat fuel, boutique, arcade, picnic tables, restrooms with showers, playground, playing field, boat ramp, swimming beach, public telephone, RV dump station, phone: (520) 667-3231; River Island Unit—37 campsites (22 with water hookups), nature trail, amphitheater, group shelter, boat ramp, swimming beach, restrooms with showers, playing field, public telephone, RV dump station, phone: (520) 667-3386
Attractions: Boating, swimming, fishing, hiking, bird-watching, interpretive programs, historical exhibits
Nearby: Cattail Cove State Park, Lake Havasu State Park, Bill Williams River National Wildlife Refuge
Access: 11 miles north of Parker or 27 miles south of Lake Havasu City on AZ 95

Water sports, scenic beauty, mild winters, and lots to do make Buckskin Mountain State Park a popular year-round destination. On the banks of the Colorado River below Lake Havasu, this park offers a somewhat wider range of attractions and activities than other state parks along what is known as "Arizona's West Coast."

Here you will find several well-maintained hiking trails, attractive campgrounds with trees and grass lawns, cactus gardens, displays of historic mining equipment, plenty of wildlife, good fishing, and beautiful scenery. The park is in two sections: the main Buckskin Unit and the smaller and less developed River Island Unit about 1.5 miles to the north.

The Buckskin Unit has the main park office, an interpretive center, a cactus garden with identifying signs, campsites with RV hookups, a boat ramp, a playground, and a playing field with a basketball court. Particularly popular are the cabana camping units—shade shelters with electricity and a place to set up a tent facing the river. A concessionaire operates a restaurant, a store with various supplies and sporting goods rentals, and an auto and boat fuel station. Buckskin Mountain has the distinction of being the only state park in Arizona that has an arcade (also operated by the concessionaire), complete with old-fashioned arcade games, modern video games, and pool tables.

The 0.5-mile round trip Lightning Bolt Trail is easy to moderate. It climbs through desert terrain of cholla, paloverde, creosote bush, mesquite, beavertail cactus, cholla, and even a few saguaro, leading to an overlook that provides a panoramic view of the river valley.

The moderately difficult Buckskin Trail, 2 miles round trip, takes off from the Lightning Bolt Trail and has similar terrain. It leads to an area of old copper mines and along the way offers excellent views of the Colorado River and surrounding mountains. The trail is rocky, with a few steep sections. Drinking water and sturdy hiking boots are recommended.

In the River Island Unit, there are RV campsites with water, tent sites, and a small beach. There is also the 1-mile round trip Wedge Hill Trail, an easy to moderate hiking trail offering good views of the river and nearby Parker Dam. A trail guide describing the flora and fauna is available.

Both sections of the park are popular with boaters, and there are no horsepower restrictions. During the summer, most craft here are of the high-power variety, and water-skiing and the use of personal watercraft are big activities. Although boats are not available for rent in the park, businesses in the nearby communities of Parker and Lake Havasu will deliver rental boats directly to the park's boat ramps.

Fishing is a major attraction here, especially from fall through spring, when largemouth and smallmouth bass, catfish, sunfish, and crappie are caught.

Camping along the beach at Buckskin Mountain State Park (photo by Princely Nesadurai, Arizona State Parks)

Also popular in both sections of the park are wildlife viewing and bird-watching. Among park residents are cottontail rabbits, Harris antelope squirrels, and plenty of lizards, including the chuckwalla, a potbellied lizard that sometimes grows to over a foot long. Coyotes are occasionally seen and often heard at night; and there are infrequent sightings of gray fox, bighorn sheep, and bobcats, particularly in the higher elevations.

Among birds that frequent the park are numerous waterfowl, including mallards, ring-necked ducks, Canada geese, and tundra swans, plus woodpeckers, wrens, swifts, western screech owls, golden eagles, hawks, hummingbirds, great blue herons, and a variety of sparrows.

In spring, assuming there has been sufficient winter rain, the park bursts into bloom with a display of desert wildflowers, including gold and orange

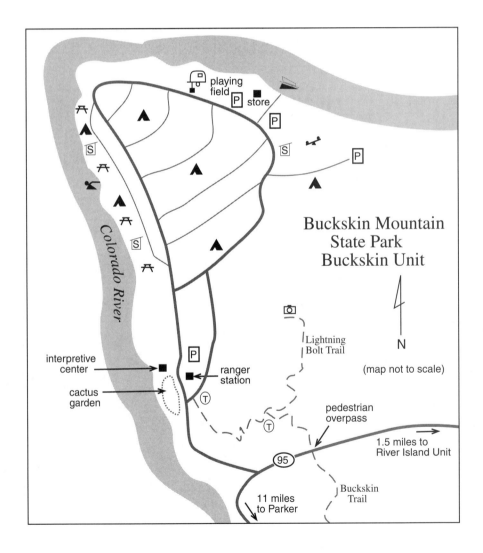

poppies, monkeyflowers, wild larkspur, desert buckwheat, owl clover, and evening primrose. Also in bloom are numerous cactus, such as hedgehog, with its large purple flowers, and cholla, sporting its red or purple flowers. Saguaro usually bloom in late spring, with large white flowers appearing on the tips of the branches.

Park rangers offer a wide variety of interpretive programs almost daily in winter and occasionally in summer, including guided hikes, lectures, video presentations, and field trips to nearby attractions, such as the Swansea ghost town, a mining town that prospered in the late nineteenth and early twentieth centuries.

The quietest months at the park are November and December; it is fairly busy the rest of the year, with retirees from Canada and northern U.S.

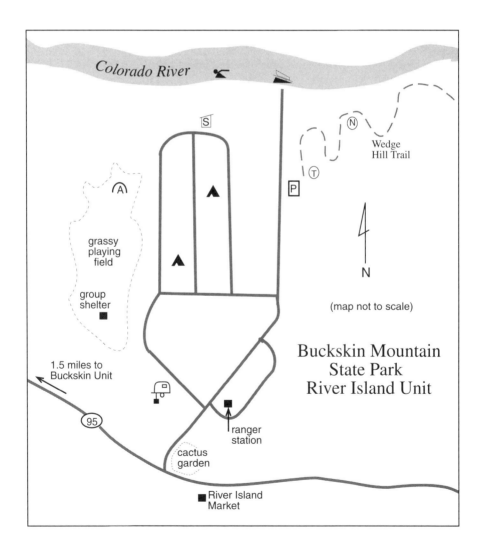

states in the cooler seasons, and boaters—many from southern California—during the hot summers, when temperatures can reach 120 degrees F. Winters are pleasant, and although nighttime temperatures may dip into the 30s, days often warm into the 60s.

Those with a particular interest in seeing wildlife should consider a trip to the Bill Williams River National Wildlife Refuge, with headquarters about 6 miles north of the park along AZ 95. Named for a colorful nineteenth-century mountain man, the wildlife refuge covers over 6,000 acres of desert riparian and upland habitat along the Bill Williams River and its confluence with the Colorado River. The refuge provides an excellent opportunity to see a wide variety of birds and animals, with over 275 species of birds. Migrating species, such as western tanagers and black-throated gray warblers, are often spotted in spring and fall, and the vermilion flycatcher is a frequent summer resident. Fall through spring is best for seeing mammals, such as mule deer, javelina, bobcats, beavers, foxes, and muskrats. Bighorn sheep are occasionally spotted, and at least one mountain lion is known to live in the refuge. Camping is not permitted in the wildlife refuge; there are no maintained trails; and vehicles must remain on the designated county road.

Also nearby are two other state parks, Cattail Cove and Lake Havasu, which are discussed in their own sections of this book.

CATTAIL COVE STATE PARK

Hours/Season: Overnight; year-round
Area: 4,500 land acres
Elevation: 455 feet
Facilities: Visitor center, picnic tables, restrooms with showers, public telephone, 39 campsites with electric and water RV hookups and 125 boat-in campsites, cactus garden, amphitheater, fish-cleaning station, boat ramp, RV dump station, phone: (520) 855-1223
Attractions: Boating, swimming, fishing, hiking, interpretive programs
Nearby: Lake Havasu and Buckskin Mountain State Parks, Lake Havasu City, London Bridge, Bill Williams River National Wildlife Refuge
Access: 15 miles south of Lake Havasu City on AZ 95

▲ This family-oriented park has a pretty beach, palm trees swaying in the breeze, and good hiking trails. Sitting along the shore of Lake Havasu, in an area of eucalyptus and palm trees, cottonwoods, mesquite, Indian laurel, and its namesake cattails, the park offers spectacular scenery.

Primary activities here are water sports, with no speed or horsepower limitations, which results in an abundance of powerboats, including a growing number of personal watercraft. A few sailboat enthusiasts use the park as well. Local boat-rental companies will deliver boats to the park's boat ramp.

The park's main camping area has closely spaced but well-maintained sites. It is near the lake, with easy access to the water, trailheads, and boat ramp. Boat-in-only campsites are spread up and down the lakeshore about 6 miles in each direction from park headquarters. Most have picnic tables, trash cans, and a shelter, plus access to a nearby composting toilet.

Sand Point Marina, a concession area just north of the main park facilities, has a full-service marina, boat docks and slips, boat rentals, a restaurant, and a full-hookup RV park.

The 3-mile round trip Whytes Trail follows the shoreline, mostly along a bluff some 30 to 50 feet above the water's edge, offering dramatic views of rocky coves and the mountains across Lake Havasu. It also provides good close-up views of cactus, paloverde, brittlebush, and other desert plants, as well as the Parker Dam and a pumping station, before ending at one of

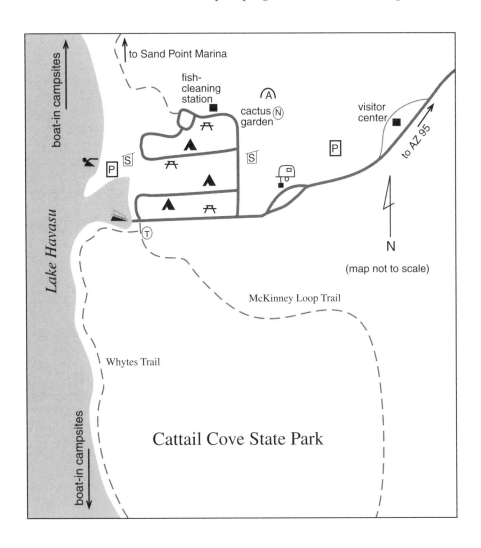

the park's boat-in campsites. Sandy, with a few steep spots, the trail is easy to moderate.

The easy 1-mile McKinney Loop trail, which connects with Whytes Trail, wanders through low desert hills, among brush and trees, including cottonwoods, eucalyptus, and Russian olives, and is a particularly good spot for birding.

A small, well-marked cactus garden provides instant identification of dozens of species of cactus and other desert plants.

Among the bird species that frequent the park are a variety of waterfowl, including the Canada goose, snow goose, white pelican, blue-winged teal, pintail, ring-necked duck, mallard, common loon, and western grebe. Throughout the park are numerous boat-tail grackles—sleek, shiny black birds with tails that dip down in the shape of the hull of a boat. There are also a variety of gulls and terns, doves, hummingbirds, wrens, larks, starlings, and warblers.

Among animals that visitors may encounter are rabbits, beavers,

Playing ball at a campsite at Cattail Cove State Park

racoons, and skunks. Present but not often seen are foxes and coyotes, and those with sharp eyes might be lucky enough to spot a bighorn sheep along the steep hillsides. The park is also home to plenty of lizards and snakes, including rattlesnakes, king snakes, bull snakes, coachwhips, and racers.

Anglers try for largemouth and striped bass, bluegill, and crappie.

During winter months, programs are held several evenings each week in the park's amphitheater, with subjects such as the area's wildlife or fish, its military history, prehistoric peoples, and construction of the nearby Parker Dam. Each year, in late November, a Harvest Fair features live entertainment, demonstrations, homemade arts and crafts, and food.

A new visitor center includes exhibits on the flora and fauna of the area. Facilities also include a horseshoe pit and other outdoor games, with equipment available.

The best times to visit are spring and fall, when the weather is usually perfect for hiking, and the park is at its quietest. For those who plan to get in the water, October can be ideal, since water and daytime air temperatures remain warm, and nights are pleasantly cool. Winter is often busy in the park, and although temperatures here almost never get really cold, with average December and January lows in the mid- to upper 30s, water temperatures drop to below 50 degrees F, making water sports suitable only for polar bears. Summer brings out the boating and swimming crowd, with air temperatures often above 110 degrees F, and water temperatures approaching 90 degrees F. Park rangers discourage hiking during June, July, and August, because of the extreme heat.

Nearby is Lake Havasu City with its famous London Bridge. See the section on Lake Havasu State Park for details. Also nearby is the Bill Williams River National Wildlife Refuge, which is discussed in the section on Buckskin Mountain State Park.

LAKE HAVASU STATE PARK

Hours/Season: Overnight; year-round
Area: 10,859 land acres
Elevation: 480 feet
Facilities: Visitor center, picnic tables, group shelter, cactus garden, restrooms with showers, public telephone, 74 campsites (no RV hookups) and 50 boat-in-only campsites, RV dump station, boat ramps, fish-cleaning station, phone: (520) 855-2784
Attractions: Boating, swimming, fishing, hiking, interpretive programs
Nearby: Cattail Cove State Park, Buckskin Mountain State Park, Lake Havasu City, London Bridge, Havasu National Wildlife Refuge, Bill Williams River National Wildlife Refuge
Access: Located on the north side of Lake Havasu City on London Bridge Road, off AZ 95 via Industrial Boulevard

Arizona may not have an ocean, but here, along what Arizonans refer to as their "west coast," you will find clear blue water, sandy beaches, speedboats, plenty of sunshine, spectacular sunsets, and even sea shells. In fact, Lake Havasu has practically everything one expects at the ocean, except salt water and salty air. Created by damming the Colorado River, Lake Havasu, about 27 miles long and 5 miles wide, is the state's favorite beach resort.

The park is located in rolling, sandy hills along the banks of the lake. A riparian zone along the water's edge is forested with cottonwoods, willows,

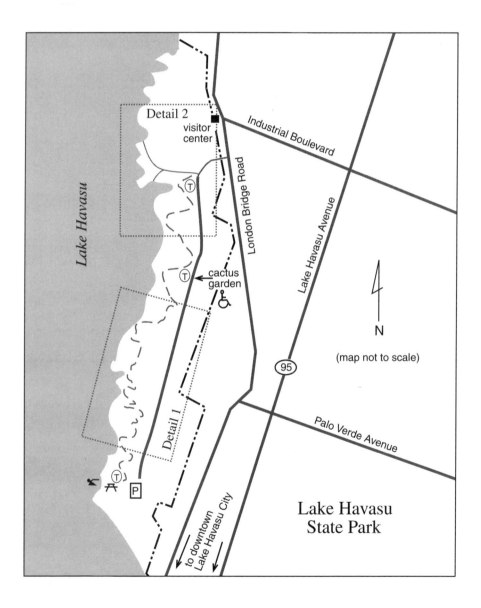

Boating at Lake Havasu State Park

salt cedars, and cattails; and just a few feet inland lies a desert zone of creosote bush, honey mesquite, and a variety of cactus and other desert plants. The abundant shells, which give the shoreline a decidedly ocean feel, are from fresh-water mollusks, a favorite food of the resident seagulls, who spread the shells throughout the park.

Mild winters and hot summers make boating pleasurable year-round, although the best months are April through October. In most parts of the lake, there are no speed or horsepower restrictions, and most boats here are the high-powered type, with water-skiing a popular pastime. A few sail-boarders and canoeists also use the park, especially in spring and fall when there are not quite as many powerboats on the water. The best spot for canoe-ing is just north of the main section of the park. Although there are no boat rental companies operating in the park, companies in Lake Havasu City do a booming business delivering boats directly to the park's boat ramps.

The attractive campsites are spacious, with a variety of shrubs and trees offering privacy, and close to the lake, swim beaches, and hiking trails. There are no RV hookups, but generator use is permitted. One section of thirty-two sites can be reserved for groups. Most of the boat-in-only camp-sites have shade shelters, picnic tables, grills, and nearby composting toilets, but no drinking water.

The Mohave Sunset Hiking Trail runs almost the entire length of the developed section of the park, some 1.5 miles (one-way). From the day-use area at the south end of the park, the sandy trail wanders among a stand of young cottonwoods before entering the dense brush that separates the campground from the lake. Here it meanders to and from the water's edge, providing access to quiet little coves and sandy beaches. North of the campground, the trail alternately climbs sandy hills to overlooks, offering beautiful panoramic vistas across the lake, and enters a paved, wheelchair-accessible cactus garden, with signs identifying various cactus and other desert plants. (The cactus garden can also be reached from the park road.) The trail ends at the parking area for the boat ramps, near the park entrance. The trail is mostly easy, although walking through sand on a hot day can be tiring.

Throughout the park, there are numerous birds, such as Gambel's quail, mourning doves, boat-tail grackles, seemingly countless ducks and geese, pelicans, hummingbirds, wrens, larks, starlings, and warblers. Park visitors are also likely to see red-winged and Brewer's blackbirds. Some of the birds stay year-round, and some winter in the park, but many are migratory, passing through each spring and fall. The best time to see the most birds is from November through January. The chorus of songbirds in the campground can be delightful, especially when they are not being drowned out by RV generators.

Other park inhabitants include desert cottontails, ground squirrels, racoons, skunks, an occasional snake, and plenty of lizards, including the desert iguana, Great Basin whiptail, and Yarrow's spiny lizard. During the winter, coyotes are often heard and sometimes spotted in the early evening. Kit foxes and gray foxes also live in the park but are seldom seen; and, in recent years, a bobcat has taken up winter residence in the park and is occasionally observed.

The best fishing is for largemouth and striped bass, bluegill, crappie, catfish, and carp. There are opportunities for both bank and boat fishing, and the park has a railed, wheelchair-accessible fishing dock near the south boat ramp.

Park facilities include horseshoe pits and a volleyball court, with equipment available from park offices.

Interpretive programs are presented about three evenings each week in winter, with subjects such as the plants and wildlife of the area, local attractions, American Indians of the Southwest, and mountain man Bill Williams, who lived in the area in the nineteenth century. During winter, there are also guided hikes usually twice a week and informal ranger talks several mornings each week. Annual events include the Hava-Salsa Challenge in April, with salsa tasting and judging, plus live entertainment, children's games, and arts and crafts booths. Each February, there is a chili cook-off, again with tasting and judging, plus live music and other activities.

Choosing the best time to visit the park depends mostly on what you want to do. On June, July, and August weekends the park is packed with boaters—many from southern California—who spend their days on the water.

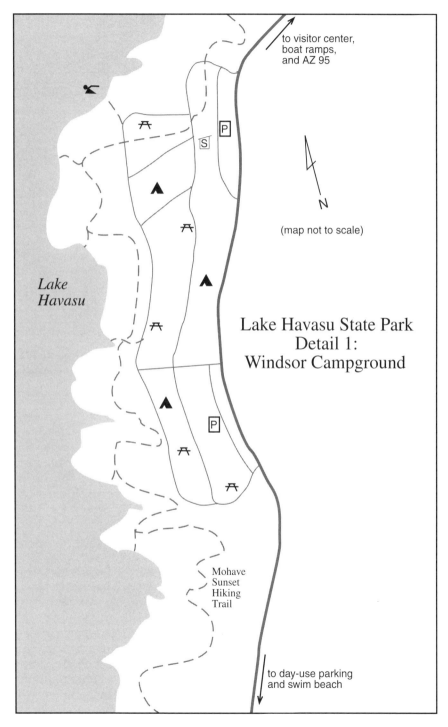

to visitor center,
boat ramps,
and AZ 95

N

(map not to scale)

Lake Havasu

Lake Havasu State Park
Detail 1:
Windsor Campground

Mohave
Sunset
Hiking
Trail

to day-use parking
and swim beach

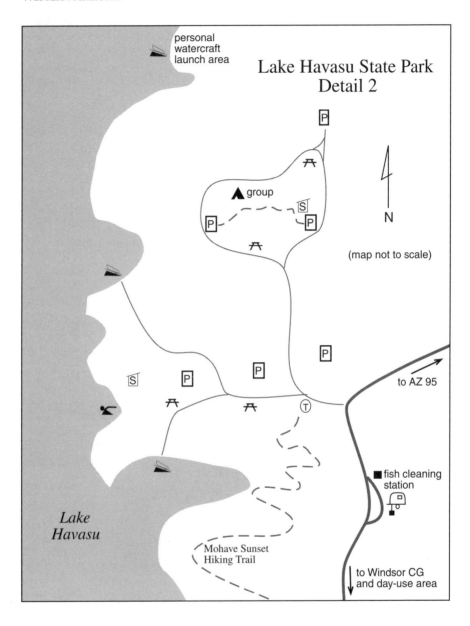

personal watercraft launch area

Lake Havasu State Park Detail 2

group

N

(map not to scale)

to AZ 95

fish cleaning station

Lake Havasu

Mohave Sunset Hiking Trail

to Windsor CG and day-use area

But summers are hot: Daytime temperatures soar to over 120 degrees F—the record of 128 degrees F was set in 1995—and nights often remain in the upper 80s or low 90s. Summer hiking is not recommended because of the heat, and those who insist on walking the trails at that time definitely need to wear hats and carry water. Winters are particularly popular with "snowbirds," those residents of Canada and the northern parts of the

United States who often fill the campground from January through March. Temperatures are mild, with highs in the 60s, and lows usually in the 30s and 40s. A particularly good time to visit is October, when nights are cool enough to require a light jacket or sweater, but days are in the upper 80s or low 90s, and the water is still warm enough for swimming.

Within a few miles of the park entrance—go south on London Bridge Road—is downtown Lake Havasu City and its famed London Bridge. Built in 1831, the stone bridge over London's Thames River survived time, terrorists, and German bombs. But, in the early 1960s, it was discovered that the bridge was sinking into the banks of the Thames from the weight of modern-day traffic.

Bought by an Arizona developer for just under $2.5 million, the bridge was dismantled stone by stone, shipped to America, and reconstructed at the edge of Lake Havasu, across an inlet on the Colorado River. Shops, restaurants, and various attractions occupy an "English village" at the foot of the bridge, and boat tours leave from beneath it.

Ten miles north of Lake Havasu City, via AZ 95, is the Havasu National Wildlife Refuge, a prime wetlands area that each winter attracts numerous migratory birds, plus raptors, including bald eagles and peregrine falcons. The refuge also contains a substantial amount of desert and is home to coyotes, bobcats, and bighorn sheep.

Also nearby is the Bill Williams River National Wildlife Refuge to the south of Lake Havasu City. See the section on Cattail Cove State Park for details. Another nearby state park for water sports enthusiasts is Buckskin Mountain, also described in its own section of this book.

YUMA CROSSING STATE HISTORIC PARK

Hours/Season: 8:00 A.M. to 5:00 P.M. daily; closed Christmas
Area: 25 land acres
Elevation: 140 feet
Facilities: Visitor center, museum, picnic tables, restrooms, phone: (520) 329-0471
Attractions: Historical exhibits, interpretive programs
Nearby: Yuma Territorial Prison State Historic Park, historic Yuma
Access: In Yuma; from I-8, exit onto Fourth Avenue south, cross the Colorado River, and turn left (east) into the park

Everybody came to Yuma. From prehistoric times through the early twentieth century, especially during the development of the American West, the Colorado River crossing at Yuma was the region's chief transportation hub, from foot travel to horseback, then to river boats and the railroad, and finally to the automobile. Today, Yuma Crossing State Historic Park commemorates the importance this crossing has played in the history of the West, particularly the role of various forms of transportation.

Indian tribes, including the Quechan and Cocopah, had farmed in the area for hundreds of years before Spanish explorers passed through in the sixteenth century searching for the fabled Seven Cities of Gold. The Spanish established two missions near the crossing in 1779, but these were later destroyed in an Indian rebellion. Then in the nineteenth century, famed explorer and scout Kit Carson and other American mountain men arrived, and thousands of gold-seekers used the river crossing on their treks to California.

Yuma became a major river port in the 1860s. Goods were brought from California, first by ocean-going ships around Baja California through the Sea of Cortez (now called the Gulf of California), and then up the Colorado River on shallow-draft steamboats. From Yuma, supplies were distributed throughout the Arizona Territory, heading north on river steamers and cross-country on large wooden freight wagons pulled by teams of mules.

Fort Yuma was established in 1849, but it was not until the 1860s that the fort's quartermaster's depot became a military supply hub, routing goods to American forts throughout Arizona, New Mexico, western Texas, southern Nevada, and southern Utah. The depot was especially busy in the 1870s during the height of the Apache wars, maintaining a six-month supply of food, clothing, ammunition, and other goods. It also kept up to 900 mules at

Restored nineteenth-century buildings at Yuma Crossing State Historic Park (photo by Princely Nesadurai, Arizona State Parks)

a time and housed the men needed to drive the freight wagons. The depot declined in importance with the arrival of the railroad in 1877 and officially ceased operations in 1883.

Today, with four restored original buildings and another two being restored, the park offers a look into this unique period in the American West, when settlers were swarming into this vast, untamed land. Among original buildings is the commanding officer's quarters, built in 1859 and believed to be Arizona's oldest surviving Anglo-built adobe structure. Other original buildings include the adobe office of the quartermaster, storehouse, kitchen, corral house, and the stone water reservoir.

The transportation museum contains numerous exhibits on the various modes of travel that have been used here, explaining how Yuma developed as a transportation center and why this was important to the settlement of the West. Pathways wind through tree-shaded and neatly landscaped grounds among the historic buildings and outdoor exhibits. Historic wagons and related artifacts are displayed, plus there is a functioning Southern Pacific steam locomotive and coach car. Visitors can watch an informative video that describes the history of the crossing and its role in the settlement of the West. Guided tours, historical reenactments, demonstrations, and other special events are regularly scheduled. There is also a grassy picnic area, and the cooling waters of the Colorado River are close at hand.

Visitors to Yuma will find it hot—often the hottest spot in the nation—with daytime highs from June through September well above 100 degrees F. Winters, on the other hand, are very pleasant, with daytime temperatures usually in the upper 60s and 70s, and lows rarely dropping below freezing.

For an entirely different perspective on life in the Old West, stop at Yuma Territorial Prison State Historic Park, about a mile to the east, which is discussed in its own section of this book. There are also several other museums in the Yuma area that provide views of the region's past, including the Arizona Historical Society Century House Museum and Gardens, at 240 Madison Avenue. The preserved home of a late nineteenth-century merchant, the museum has period rooms, exhibits on Yuma history, gardens, and aviaries filled with exotic birds.

YUMA TERRITORIAL PRISON STATE HISTORIC PARK

Hours/Season: 8:00 A.M. to 5:00 P.M. daily; closed Christmas
Area: 9 land acres
Elevation: 141 feet
Facilities: Visitor center/museum, picnic tables, restrooms, phone: (520) 783-4771
Attractions: Historical exhibits, walking trail
Nearby: Yuma Crossing State Historic Park
Access: In Yuma; take I-8 exit 1 onto Giss Parkway heading east and turn north onto Prison Hill Road, which leads to the park

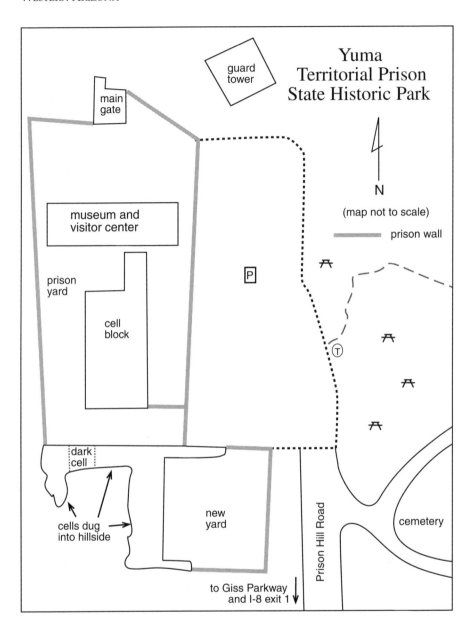

Yuma
Territorial Prison
State Historic Park

N

(map not to scale)

prison wall

guard tower

main gate

museum and visitor center

prison yard

cell block

P

dark cell

cells dug into hillside

new yard

Prison Hill Road

cemetery

to Giss Parkway
and I-8 exit 1

▲ This was hell on earth, a den of horror where lawbreakers, their heads
shaved and their legs shackled with heavy chains, were confined in
small, gloomy caves infested with bedbugs, black widow spiders, and
desert scorpions. Or so the dime novels of the day and later western movies
would have us believe. And although most of these aspects of Yuma Territorial Prison are accurate to at least some degree, this was also considered a

model and enlightened prison for its day and was even criticized by some for coddling its population of murderers, rapists, and thieves.

Today, the cells, main gate, and guard tower are all that remain of the original prison, but a museum has been added, and the facility is operated as a state park, providing visitors with an unusual, sometimes disturbing, and certainly eye-opening look into an era of American history that is long gone.

The first seven inmates took up residence at the prison on July 1, 1876, but these were hardly new surroundings for them, since they had arrived in Yuma earlier that year to help build it. The Arizona Territory's first prison, territorial legislators had wanted to build it near Phoenix, but political chicanery won the day when representatives from Yuma County quietly replaced the word Phoenix with the word Yuma in the bill, which was passed and signed before anyone caught on.

Surrounded by adobe walls, some 8 feet thick at the base and 18 feet high, the prison included punishment cells and a main cell block, bathing room, kitchen, dining hall, massive guard tower, and superintendent's residence. By 1885, it also had its own electric generator, which provided power for the prison, with some left over for the town of Yuma. Electricity also made possible the installation of large fans, which helped cool the cell block during the stifling hot summers and led to accusations from town residents that the prisoners lived in better conditions than those on the outside.

The prison also had one of the first public libraries in the Arizona Territory, which was used by community residents as well as prisoners and guards and was financed in part by a twenty-five cent fee for visitors to tour the prison.

During its thirty-three years in operation, the prison housed 3,069 inmates, including twenty-nine women. Upon arriving, prisoners were issued striped uniforms—either black and gray or black and yellow—and the men's heads were shaved (women convicts were spared this indignity).

Crimes ranged from murder to prize fighting, with robbery being the most common. Three men were imprisoned for seduction, which essentially meant that they had promised marriage to a woman, had sexual relations with her, and then abandoned her. There were also 164 inmates incarcerated for selling liquor to Indians, a fairly serious crime in that day; and twenty-seven convicts, including some of the women, were being punished for adultery. Eleven Mormons served time at Yuma for polygamy.

Among the prison's more infamous inmates was Buckskin Frank Leslie, a hard-drinking gunslinger who was well-known in the Tombstone area as a ladies' man. After he shot dead a jealous husband—the jury ruled it was self-defense—Leslie married the new widow. But she soon divorced him, reportedly telling friends that his peculiarities got to be too much when he insisted she stand against a wall so he could shoot an outline of her body.

Soon it was Leslie's turn to be jealous, when his girlfriend began seeing another man, a young ranch hand. Leslie shot them both—the ranch hand survived, but his girlfriend died—and Leslie was sentenced to life in prison.

At Yuma, he was considered a model prisoner, spending much of his time in the prison infirmary helping doctors during several epidemics. He was pardoned and released after serving only seven years of his life sentence.

In 1909, the prison closed, and prisoners were transferred to a new territorial prison in the town of Florence, southeast of Phoenix. Then, from 1910 to 1914, it was home to Yuma Union High School, whose students adopted the nickname "the criminals." The superintendent's residence became the county hospital, which it remained until it and several other prison buildings were demolished to make room for the relocated tracks of the Southern Pacific Railroad.

The homeless moved into some of the cells during the depression; several films were made there during the 1930s and 1940s; and, during World War II, the main guard tower was used as an observation site by Civil Defense workers.

Visitors to the prison today enter through the same iron sally port, or main gate, where both prisoners and visitors entered over one hundred years ago. They then proceed to the museum. Built in 1940 on part of the dining hall foundation, the museum has extensive displays on prison life, including the sordid details of the lives of many of the convicts, as well as artifacts, such as guns used by the guards, uniforms, and a ball-and-chain used on prisoners who didn't play by the rules.

There are exhibits on the women who served time in Yuma, including the infamous Pearl Hart, who committed the last stagecoach robbery in Arizona. What is ironic is that she never served time for the actual stage robbery. Hart and her lover Joe Boot had no trouble robbing the Globe stage, near Florence, Arizona, but had not planned an escape route and were soon captured. The two were tried together: Boot was convicted and sentenced to thirty years in prison, but, because she was pretty and flirted with the all-male jury, Pearl Hart was acquitted.

The judge reportedly was outraged, believing that justice had not been served. He insisted that Hart be tried on a charge of possession of a stolen gun, which she had taken from the stage driver during the robbery. This time she was convicted and sentenced to five years in the territorial prison. Again using her feminine charms, Hart became a celebrity at the prison and was often written about in the national press. After her release, she had a brief acting career and then married, settled down, and apparently led a respectable life. Joe Boot, meanwhile, escaped from Yuma Territorial Prison and was never seen again.

There is also an exhibit containing photos and diary excerpts from the Mormons who were imprisoned here after the federal government decreed that polygamy was a crime, plus displays depicting life in the late 1800s and early 1900s, both within and outside the prison walls. An entertaining 35-minute video on the territorial prison's history can be seen in the museum, and living history programs and guided tours are scheduled occasionally.

From the museum, visitors enter the prison yard, where they can step inside the cramped cells and try to imagine what life here was like. The infamous dark cell, a 15-by-15-foot cave with a strap-iron cage in the middle, was reserved for the most incorrigible prisoners. One of the tiny "new cells," built in 1900 to relieve overcrowding, is authentically furnished with two cots, an iron ring set in concrete in case a prisoner needed to be chained in, and a bucket, which served as the prisoners' toilet.

Outside the prison yard are picnic tables and a shelter, a 2,100-foot walking trail, and the prison cemetery, which contains the remains of many of the convicts who died at the prison, most from tuberculosis.

Yuma summers are hot, with average daytime high temperatures above 100 degrees F. Wintertime is usually shirtsleeve weather, with daytime temperatures in the upper 60s and 70s, and nights dropping into the upper 30s and 40s.

Those interested in seeing more of Arizona's early days can stop at Yuma Crossing State Historic Park, about a mile west, which is discussed in its own section of this book.

Examining the cells at Yuma Territorial Prison State Historic Park

APPENDIX

NEW MEXICO ADDRESSES AND TELEPHONE NUMBERS

New Mexico State Parks, P.O. Box 1147, Santa Fe, NM 87504-1147;
(505) 827-7173 or toll-free (888) 667-2757, fax (505) 827-1376;
http://www.emnrd.state.nm.us/nmprks/
Bluewater Lake State Park, P.O. Box 3419, Prewitt, NM 87045;
(505) 876-2391, fax (505) 876-2307
Bottomless Lakes State Park, HC 12, Box 1200, Roswell, NM 88201;
(505) 624-6058, fax (505) 624-6029
Brantley Lake State Park, P.O. Box 2288, Carlsbad, NM 88221;
(505) 457-2384, fax (505) 457-2385
Caballo Lake State Park, P.O. Box 32, Caballo, NM 87931; (505) 743-3942
Cimarron Canyon State Park, P.O. Box 147, Ute Park, NM 87749;
(505) 377-6271
City of Rocks State Park, P.O. Box 50, Faywood, NM 88034; (505) 536-2800
Clayton Lake State Park, Rural Route, Box 20, Seneca, NM 88437;
(505) 374-8808
Conchas Lake State Park, P.O. Box 976, Conchas Dam, NM 88416;
(505) 868-2270
Coronado State Park, P.O. Box 853, Bernalillo, NM 87004; (505) 867-5589,
fax (505) 867-2225
Coyote Creek State Park, P.O. Box 477, Guadalupita, NM 87722;
(505) 387-2328
Elephant Butte Lake State Park, P.O. Box 13, Elephant Butte, NM 87935;
office (505) 744-5923, visitor center (505) 744-5421, fax (505) 744-9144
El Vado Lake State Park, P.O. Box 29, Tierra Amarilla, NM 87575;
(505) 588-7247
Fenton Lake State Park, 455 Fenton Lake Road, Jemez Springs, NM 87025;
(505) 829-3630
Heron Lake State Park, P.O. Box 159, Los Ojos, NM 87551; (505) 588-7470,
fax (505) 588-7482
Hyde Memorial State Park, P.O. Box 1147, Santa Fe, NM 87504;
(505) 983-7175, fax (505) 983-2783
Leasburg Dam State Park, P.O. Box 6, Radium Springs, NM 88054;
(505) 524-4068, fax (505) 526-5420
Living Desert Zoo and Gardens State Park, P.O. Box 100, Carlsbad, NM
88220;
(505) 887-5516, fax (505) 885-4478
Manzano Mountains State Park, Route 2, Box 52, Mountainair, NM 87036;
(505) 847-2820

Morphy Lake State Park, P.O. Box 477, Guadalupita, NM 87722; (505) 387-2328

Navajo Lake State Park, 1448 NM 511 #1, Navajo Dam, NM 87419; (505) 632-2278, fax (505) 632-8159

Oasis State Park, 1882 Oasis Road, Portales, NM 88130; (505) 356-5331

Oliver Lee Memorial State Park, 409 Dog Canyon Road, Alamogordo, NM 88310; (505) 437-8284

Pancho Villa State Park, P.O. Box 450, Columbus, NM 88029; (505) 531-2711

Percha Dam State Park, P.O. Box 32, Caballo, NM 87931; (505) 743-3942

Rio Grande Nature Center, 2901 Candelaria Road NW, Albuquerque, NM 87107; (505) 344-7240, fax (505) 344-4505

Rockhound State Park, P.O. Box 1064, Deming, NM 88030; (505) 546-6182

Santa Rosa Lake State Park, P.O. Box 384, Santa Rosa, NM 88435; (505) 472-3110, fax (505) 472-5956

Storrie Lake State Park, P.O. Box 3167, Las Vegas, NM 87701; (505) 425-7278, fax (505) 425-0446

Sugarite Canyon State Park, HCR 63, Box 386, Raton, NM 87740; (505) 445-5607, fax (505) 445-8828

Sumner Lake State Park, HC 64, Box 125, Fort Sumner, NM 88316; (505) 355-2541

Ute Lake State Park, P.O. Box 52, Logan, NM 88426; (505) 487-2284, fax (505) 487-2497

Villanueva State Park, P.O. Box 40, Villanueva, NM 87583; (505) 421-2957, fax (505) 421-3231

OTHER NEW MEXICO INFORMATION

New Mexico Department of Tourism, Room 751, Lamy Building, 491 Old Santa Fe Trail, Santa Fe, NM 87503; (800) 545-2040, fax (505) 827-7402; http://www.newmexico.org/

New Mexico Public Lands Information Center, 1474 Rodeo Road, Santa Fe, NM 87505; (505) 438-7542, fax (505) 438-7582

New Mexico Department of Game and Fish, P.O. Box 25112, Santa Fe, NM 87504; (505) 827-7911 or (800) 862-9310, fax (505) 827-7915

National Forest Service, Southwestern Region, 517 Gold Avenue SW, Albuquerque, NM 87102; (505) 842-3292, fax (505) 842-3800

National Park Service, Southwest Regional Office, 1100 Old Santa Fe Trail, Santa Fe, NM 87501; (505) 988-6100, fax (505) 988-6099

Road Conditions; (800) 432-4269

ARIZONA ADDRESSES AND TELEPHONE NUMBERS

Arizona State Parks, 1300 West Washington, Phoenix, AZ 85007; (602) 542-4174 or (800) 285-3703 from 520 area code within Arizona, fax (602) 542-4180; http://www.pr.state.az.us/

Alamo Lake State Park, P.O. Box 38, Wenden, AZ 85357; (520) 669-2088

Boyce Thompson Arboretum State Park, 37615 Highway 60, Superior, AZ 85273-5100; (520) 689-2811, fax (520) 689-5858

Buckskin Mountain State Park, 5476 Highway 95, Parker, AZ 85344;
(520) 667-3231; River Island Unit; (520) 667-3386, fax (520) 667-3387
Catalina State Park, P.O. Box 36986, Tucson, AZ 85740; (520) 628-5798,
fax (520) 628-5797
Cattail Cove State Park, P.O. Box 1990, Lake Havasu City, AZ 86405-1990;
(520) 855-1223, fax (520) 855-1730
Dead Horse Ranch State Park, 675 Dead Horse Ranch Road, Cottonwood,
AZ 86326; (520) 634-5283, fax (520) 639-0417
Fool Hollow Lake Recreation Area, P.O. Box 2588, Show Low, AZ 85901;
(520) 537-3680, fax (520) 537-4349
Fort Verde State Historic Park, P.O. Box 397, Camp Verde, AZ 86322;
(520) 567-3275, fax (520) 567-4036
Homolovi Ruins State Park, HCR 63, Box 5, Winslow, AZ 86047;
(520) 289-4106, fax (520) 289-2021
Jerome State Historic Park, P.O. Box D, Jerome, AZ 86331; (520) 634-5381,
fax (520) 639-3132
Kartchner Caverns State Park, c/o Arizona State Parks address above
Lake Havasu State Park, 699 London Bridge Road, Lake Havasu City, AZ
86403; (520) 855-2784, fax (520) 855-7423
Lost Dutchman State Park, 6109 N. Apache Trail, Apache Junction, AZ
85219; (602) 982-4485
Lyman Lake State Park, P.O. Box 1428, St. Johns, AZ 85936; (520) 337-4441,
fax (520) 337-4649
McFarland State Historic Park, P.O. Box 109, Florence, AZ 85232;
(520) 868-5216
Oracle State Park, P.O. Box 700, Oracle, AZ 85623; (520) 896-2425,
fax (520) 896-3215
Patagonia Lake State Park, P.O. Box 274, Patagonia, AZ 85624;
(520) 287-6965, fax (520) 287-5618
Picacho Peak State Park, P.O. Box 275, Picacho, AZ 85241-0275;
(520) 466-3183
Red Rock State Park, 4050 Red Rock Loop Road, Sedona, AZ 86336;
(520) 282-6907, fax (520) 282-5972
Riordan Mansion State Historic Park, 1300 Riordan Ranch Street, Flagstaff,
AZ 86001; (520) 779-4395
Roper Lake State Park, Route 2, Box 712, Safford, AZ 85546; (520) 428-6760
Slide Rock State Park, P.O. Box 10358, Sedona, AZ 86339-8358;
(520) 282-3034
Tombstone Courthouse State Historic Park, P.O. Box 216, Tombstone, AZ
85638; (520) 457-3311, fax (520) 457-2565
Tonto Natural Bridge State Park, P.O. Box 1245, Payson, AZ 85547;
(520) 476-4202, fax (520) 476-2264
Tubac Presidio State Historic Park, P.O.Box 1296, Tubac, AZ 85646;
(520) 398-2252
Yuma Crossing State Historic Park, 201 N. Fourth Avenue, Yuma, AZ
85364; (520) 329-0471

Yuma Territorial Prison State Historic Park, 1 Prison Hill Road, Yuma, AZ 85364; (520) 783-4771, fax (520) 783-7442

OTHER ARIZONA INFORMATION

Arizona Office of Tourism, 2702 N. Third Street, Suite 4015, Phoenix, AZ 85004; (602) 230-7733 or (888) 520-3434, fax (602) 240-5475; http://www.arizonaguide.com/

Arizona Public Lands Information Center, 222 Central Avenue, Phoenix, AZ 85004; (602) 417-9300, fax (602) 417-9556

Arizona Game and Fish Department, 2221 W. Greenway Road, Phoenix, AZ 85023; (602) 942-3000, fax (602) 789-3924

Bureau of Land Management (BLM), Arizona State Office, 222 N. Central Avenue, Phoenix, AZ 85004; (602) 417-9200, fax (602) 417-9424

National Forest Service, Apache Sitgreaves (520) 333-4301; Coconino (520) 527-3600; Coronado (520) 670-4552; Kaibab (520) 635-8200; Prescott (520) 771-4700; Tonto (602) 225-5200

National Park Service USDI, Southern Arizona Group, Park Central Mall, 3121 N. Third Avenue, Phoenix, AZ 85013; (602) 640-5250, fax (602) 640-5265

Casa Grande Ruins National Monument, 1100 Ruins Drive, Coolidge, AZ 85228; (520) 723-3172, fax (520) 723-7209

Grand Canyon National Park, P.O. Box 129, Grand Canyon, AZ 86023; (520) 638-7888, fax (520) 638-7815

Montezuma Castle National Monument, P.O. Box 219, Camp Verde, AZ 86322; (520) 567-3322, fax (520) 567-3597

Petrified Forest National Park, P.O.Box 2217, Petrified Forest, AZ 86028; (520) 524-6228, fax (520) 524-3567

Tumacacori National Historical Park, P.O. Box 67, Tumacacori, AZ 85640; (520) 398-2341, fax (520) 398-9271

Tuzigoot National Monument, P.O. Box 68, Clarkdale, AZ 86324; (520) 634-5564

Road Conditions; (602) 241-3100 extension 7623

INDEX

Alamo Lake State Park 239–243
Anza Trail 232, 234
Apache/Sitgreaves National Forest
    166
archeological digs 172
Arizona Historical Society Century
    House Museum and Gardens 259
Arizona state map 156
Arizona Trail 236
Aztec Ruins National Monument 48

Balloon Regatta 138
Bill Williams River National Wildlife
    Refuge 248
Billy the Kid 123
bison 180
Bitter Lake National Wildlife Refuge
    98–99
Blackwater Draw Museum and Site
    110
Bluewater Lake State Park 19–22
Bottomless Lakes State Park 93–99
Boyce Thompson Arboretum State
    Park 199–203
Brantley Lake State Park 99–104
Buckskin Mountain State Park 244–248

Caballo Lake State Park 125–129
Carlsbad Caverns National Park 103–
    104, 107
Casa Grande Ruins National Monu-
    ment 215, 225
Casa Malpais Archeological Park 181
Catalina State Park 204–209
Cattail Cove State Park 248–251
Cibola National Forest 143–144
Cimarron Canyon State Park 55–60
Cimarron River 57
City of Rocks State Park 130–133
Civil War 221
Clayton Lake State Park 60–64
Coconino National Forest 160, 192
Colin Neblett Wildlife Area 57
Colorado River 244, 252, 257
Colorado State Wildlife Area 83
Columbus Historical Museum 149

Columbus, N.M. 146, 149
Conchas Lake State Park 64–68
Coronado National Forest 204, 207, 209
Coronado State Monument 23
Coronado State Park 22–24
Coyote Creek State Park 69–71
Craftsman furniture 186
cross–country skiing 31, 36, 80–81
Cumbres and Toltec Scenic Railroad 37

Dead Horse Ranch State Park 159–163
dinosaur tracks 61–62
Dog Canyon National Recreation Trail
    113–114

Eagle Nest Lake 60
El Vado Lake State Park 24–28
Elephant Butte Lake State Park 133–
    139
endangered species 32, 52, 99, 105, 162,
    202, 219, 226
environmental education 49, 183, 236–
    237

facilities 9
fees 9–10
Fenton Lake State Park 29–32
fish hatcheries 32, 99
Florence, Ariz. 214, 215
Fool Hollow Lake Recreation Area
    164–167
Fort Selden State Monument 142–143
Fort Sumner State Monument 123
Fort Union National Monument 77
Fort Verde State Historic Park 167–170
Fort Yuma 258–259

golfing 67
Gowan, David 195
gunfight at the OK Corral 230

Hart, Pearl 214, 262
Havasu National Wildlife Refuge 257
Helldorado Days 231
Heron Lake State Park 32–37
hiking 8

Homolovi Ruins State Park 170–174
horseback riding 58, 160, 209, 232, 241–242
hot tub 227
hours 10
Hyde Memorial State Park 37–41

Jerome State Historic Park 174–176
Jerome, town of 174–176
Kartchner Caverns State Park 235–236

Lake Havasu City, Ariz. 257
Lake Havasu State Park 251–257
Las Palomas, Mexico 149
Las Vegas, N.M. 77
Leasburg Dam State Park 139–143
Leslie, Buckskin Frank 261–262
Lincoln National Forest 114
Living Desert Zoo and Gardens State
    Park 104–107
London Bridge 257
Lost Dutchman Gold Mine 210
Lost Dutchman State Park 210–213
Lyman Lake State Park 177–181

Manzano Mountains State Park 143–145
McFarland State Historic Park 214–215
McFarland, Ernest W. "Mac" 215
mining 78, 80, 174–175
Montezuma Castle National Monument 170
Mormon Battalion 221
Morphy Lake State Park 72–74

Navajo Lake State Park 41–48
New Mexico Sailing Club 34
New Mexico state map 16

Oak Creek Canyon 189, 192
Oasis State Park 107–110
off-road vehicle use 85
Oliver Lee Memorial State Park 110–116
Oracle State Park 236–237

Pancho Villa State Park 146–149
Patagonia Lake State Park 215–220
Patagonia-Sonoita Creek Preserve 220
Pecos Diamonds 95–96
Pendley, Frank 189
Percha Dam State Park 150–153

Pershing, General John "Black Jack" 146, 148
Petrified Forest National Park 167, 174, 181
petroglyphs 171, 178
Picacho Peak State Park 220–225
Pinal County Courthouse 214–215
Pinal County Historical Society
    Museum 215
Poor Man's Yacht Race 80
Poston, Charles 232
prehistoric Indians 23, 24, 48, 110, 111, 130, 163, 170–174, 178, 180, 206, 215, 225
Pusch Ridge Wilderness Area 204, 207, 209

Red Rock State Park 181–185
regulations 11
reservations 10–11
Rio Chama Trail 25, 34
Rio Grande 23, 128, 137, 141
Rio Grande Nature Center State Park 49–53
Rio Grande Raft Race 23
Riordan Mansion State Historic Park 186–188
rock climbing 59, 80
rock hounding 153–155
Rockhound State Park 153–155
Roper Lake State Park 225–228

safety 12–15
Salinas Pueblo Missions National
    Monument 145
Sangre de Cristo Mountains 69
San Juan River 46
Santa Catalina Mountains 204
Santa Fe, city of 41
Santa Fe National Forest 31–32, 41
Santa Fe Ski Area 41
Santa Rosa Lake State Park 116–120
Schieffelin, Ed 229
scuba diving 20, 45, 67, 95, 120
Sedona, Ariz. 192
Simon Canyon Recreation Area 48
sky diving 68
Slide Rock State Park 189–192
Sonoita Creek State Natural Area 218–219
Space Center, Alamogordo 115
state parks, history of 7–8

Storrie Lake State Park 74–77
Sugarite Canyon State Park 78–83
Sugarite Coal Camp 78, 80
Sumner Lake State Park 120–123
Superstition Mountains 210

Thompson, William Boyce 200
Tombstone Courthouse State Historic
    Park 229–231
Tombstone, Ariz. 229, 231
Tonto National Forest 197, 210, 212–
    213
Tonto Natural Bridge State Park 192–
    197
Truth or Consequences, N.M. 139
Tubac Presidio State Historic Park 231–
    235
Tubac, Ariz. 231–232
Tumacacori National Historical Park
    234
Tuzigoot National Monument 163

Ute Lake State Park 83–87
Villa, Francisco "Pancho" 146
Villanueva State Park 88–91
volunteering 11

western history 59–60, 77, 78, 80, 88–
    89, 99, 101–102, 111–114, 123, 146,
    148–149, 167–170, 172, 174–176,
    186, 189, 195, 206, 210, 214–215,
    221, 229–235, 257–263
White Mountain Archeological Center
    181
White Mountains Trail System 166
White Sands National Monument 116,
    143
windsurfing 66, 75, 85, 102, 177
World War I 148
World War II 202, 215

Yuma Crossing State Historic Park
    257–259
Yuma Territorial Prison State Historic
    Park 259–263

ABOUT THE MOUNTAINEERS

Founded in 1906, The Mountaineers is a Seattle-based non-profit outdoor activity and conservation club with 15,000 members, whose mission is "to explore, study, preserve, and enjoy the natural beauty of the outdoors. . . . " The club sponsors many classes and year-round outdoor activities in the Pacific Northwest, and supports environmental causes by sponsoring legislation and presenting educational programs. The Mountaineers Books supports the club's mission by publishing travel and natural history guides, instructional texts, and works on conservation and history. For information, call or write The Mountaineers, Club Headquarters, 300 Third Avenue West, Seattle, Washington, 98119; (206) 284-6310.

Send or call for our catalog of more than 300 outdoor titles:

The Mountaineers Books
1001 SW Klickitat Way, Suite 201
Seattle, WA 98134
1-800-553-4453
e-mail: mbooks@mountaineers.org
website: www.mountaineers.org

ABOUT THE AUTHORS

Residents of northern New Mexico since 1970, Don and Barbara Laine have spent countless hours exploring the Southwest's mountains, deserts, lakes, rivers, and plains. Their interests include hiking, rafting, photography, and wildlife viewing, as well as loafing in a shady campground. Don spent more than twenty years in radio and newspaper journalism before turning to travel writing and photography full-time in the early 1990s, and his articles and photographs have been published in regional and national newspapers and magazines. Before turning to travel writing and freelance mapping, Barb worked as a draftsman in a land surveying office, and in administration at a nonprofit arts organization and a small private school. Together Don and Barb have authored several travel guides, including *Frommer's Colorado* and *Frommer's Utah*.

Their selfish goal in researching and writing this book was to spend time in the delightful parks that are dotted across New Mexico and Arizona, but their more altruistic motivation was to share their knowledge and appreciation of these parks so that more people can discover the wonders of these very special places.

Other titles you may enjoy from The Mountaineers:

HIKING THE SOUTHWEST'S CANYON COUNTRY, Second Edition,
Sandra Hinchman
A completely updated guide featuring the high desert's most enjoyable trails and the awe-inspiring scenic attractions of the Four Corners, including nearly a hundred hikes and six new trip itineraries, with day-by-day suggestions for dayhikes, backpacks, scenic drives, raft trips, visits to archaeological sites, and more.

GRAND CANYON PLACE NAMES, Gregory McNamee
An entertaining, anecdotal history of more than 325 place names in Grand Canyon National Park and adjacent areas.

A FIELD GUIDE TO THE GRAND CANYON, Second Edition,
Stephen Whitney
The only comprehensive field guide to the natural history of the Grand Canyon, illustrated with 71 plates and containing complete information on more than 480 plants and animals, plus the geologic history of the Canyon.

EXPLORING ARIZONA'S WILD AREAS: A Guide for Hikers, Backpackers, Climbers, X-C Skiers, & Paddlers, Scott S. Warren
A comprehensive guide to 87 areas and the year-round activities available, including U.S. Fish and Wildlife Service–administered lands, Wilderness Areas, and seldom-visited sections of Grand Canyon National Park.

75 HIKES IN™ NEW MEXICO, Craig Martin
The definitive guide to 75 hikes throughout New Mexico, including 48 hikes published for the first time.

100 HIKES IN™ ARIZONA and 100 HIKES IN™ NEW MEXICO,
Scott S. Warren
Fully-detailed hiking guides from the best-selling series.

OUTDOOR FAMILY GUIDE TO THE SOUTHWEST'S FOUR CORNERS, Tom & Gayen Wharton
Part of a series of comprehensive guides to family-friendly outings, offering special tips on family safety and ways to help protect the environment of parks. Includes complete trail descriptions, plus information on flora, fauna, history, safety, and more.

MOUNTAIN BIKE ADVENTURES™ IN THE FOUR CORNERS REGION,
Michael McCoy
One in a series of guides to off-road cycling.

Outdoor Books by the Experts

Whatever the season, whatever your sport, The Mountaineers Books has the resources for you. Our FREE CATALOG includes over 350 titles on climbing, hiking, mountain biking, paddling, backcountry skiing, snowshoeing, adventure travel, natural history, mountaineering history, and conservation, plus dozens of how-to books to sharpen your outdoor skills.

All of our titles can be found at or ordered through your local bookstore or outdoor store. Just mail in this card or call us at 800·553·4453 for your free catalog. Or send us an e-mail at mbooks@mountaineers.org.

Name_____

Address_____

City_____ State _____ Zip+4 _____ - _____

E-mail_____

559-X

Outdoor Books by the Experts

Whatever the season, whatever your sport, The Mountaineers Books has the resources for you. Our FREE CATALOG includes over 350 titles on climbing, hiking, mountain biking, paddling, backcountry skiing, snowshoeing, adventure travel, natural history, mountaineering history, and conservation, plus dozens of how-to books to sharpen your outdoor skills.

All of our titles can be found at or ordered through your local bookstore or outdoor store. Just mail in this card or call us at 800·553·4453 for your free catalog. Or send us an e-mail at mbooks@mountaineers.org.

Please send a catalog to my friend at:

Name_____

Address_____

City_____ State _____ Zip+4 _____ - _____

E-mail_____

559-X

BUSINESS REPLY MAIL

FIRST-CLASS MAIL   PERMIT NO. 85063   SEATTLE, WA

POSTAGE WILL BE PAID BY ADDRESSEE

THE MOUNTAINEERS BOOKS
1001 SW KLICKITAT WAY STE 201
SEATTLE WA 98134-9975

BUSINESS REPLY MAIL

FIRST-CLASS MAIL   PERMIT NO. 85063   SEATTLE, WA

POSTAGE WILL BE PAID BY ADDRESSEE

THE MOUNTAINEERS BOOKS
1001 SW KLICKITAT WAY STE 201
SEATTLE WA 98134-9975